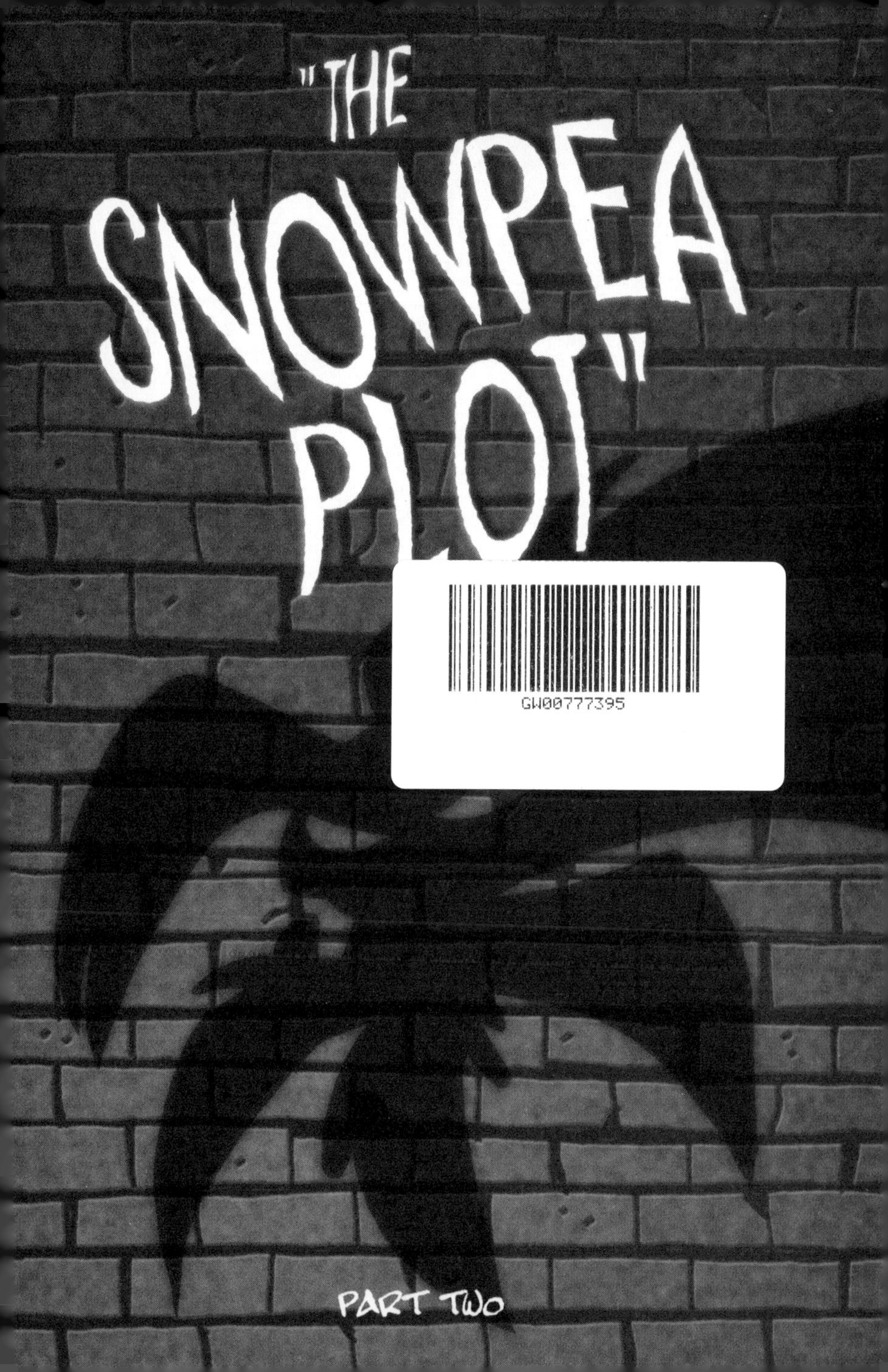
"THE
SNOWPEA
PLOT"
PART TWO

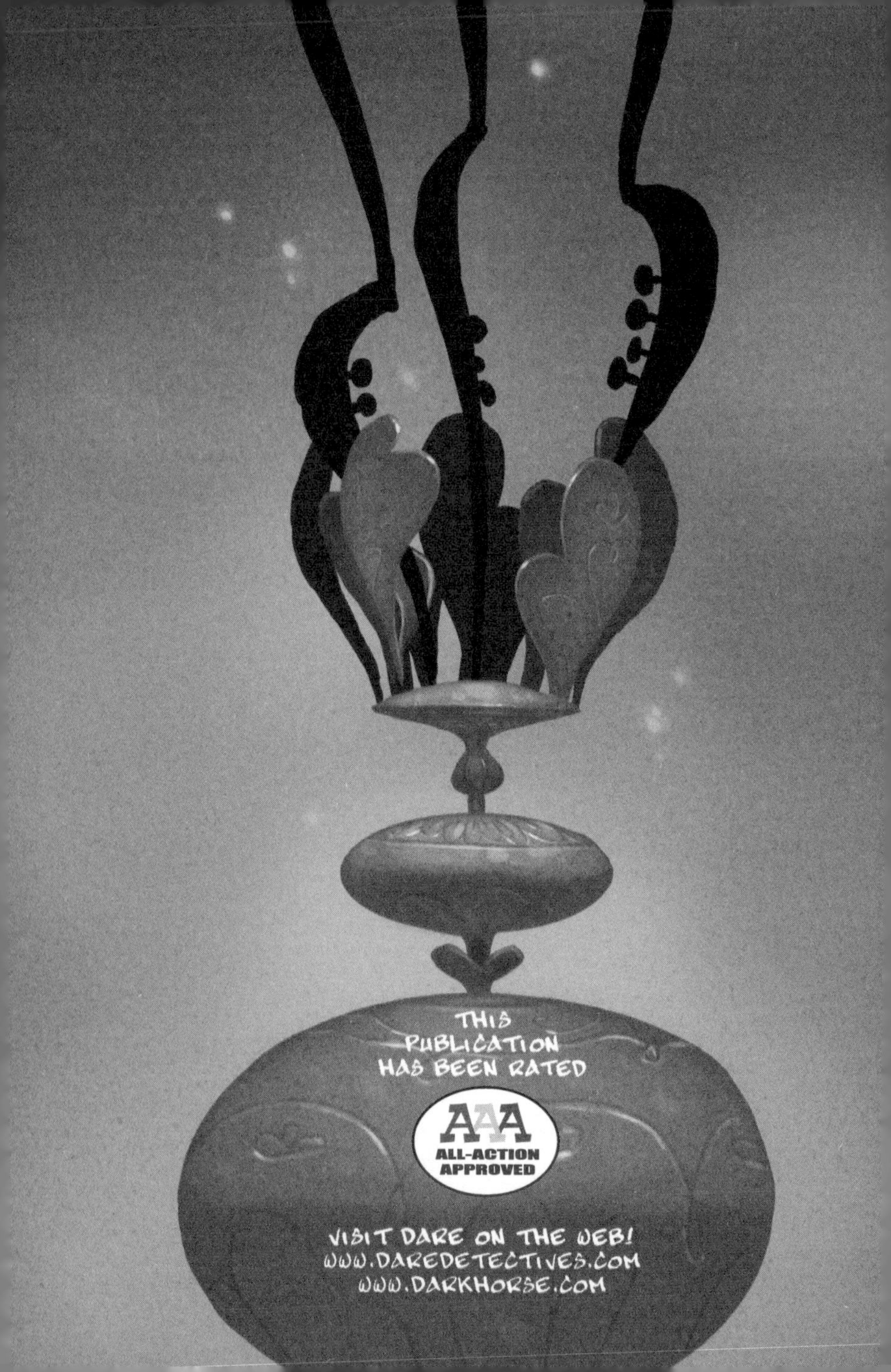

THIS PUBLICATION HAS BEEN RATED
AAA
ALL-ACTION APPROVED
VISIT DARE ON THE WEB!
WWW.DAREDETECTIVES.COM
WWW.DARKHORSE.COM

THE DARE! DETECTIVES™

VOLUME TWO
"THE SNOWPEA PLOT"

STORY AND ART BY
BEN CALDWELL

ADDITIONAL INKS AND COLORS BY

BILL
HALLIAR

MICHAEL
MUCCI

DARK HORSE BOOKS™

PUBLISHER
MIKE RICHARDSON

EDITOR
CHRIS WARNER

THE FONT USED FOR THIS BOOK IS "ARIS"
"ARIS" ©2004 GILLES ARIS
HTTP://FOUDEBD.FREE.FR/

THE DARE DETECTIVES! VOL. 1.2:
"THE SNOW PEA PLOT, PART TWO"

PUBLISHED BY
DARK HORSE BOOKS
A DIVISION OF DARK HORSE COMICS, INC.
10956 S.E. MAIN STREET
MILWAUKIE, OR 97222

DARKHORSE.COM
DAREDETECTIVES.COM

TALK ABOUT THIS BOOK ONLINE!
DARKHORSE.COM/COMMUNITY/BOARDS

TO FIND A COMICS SHOP IN YOUR AREA,
CALL THE COMIC SHOP LOCATOR SERVICE
TOLL-FREE AT 1-888-266-4226

DECEMBER 2005
ISBN: 1-59307-340-2

1 3 5 7 9 10 8 6 4 2
PRINTED IN CANADA

"NEVER TRY TO OUTSMART A WOMAN,
UNLESS YOU ARE ANOTHER WOMAN"

- W. L. PHELPS

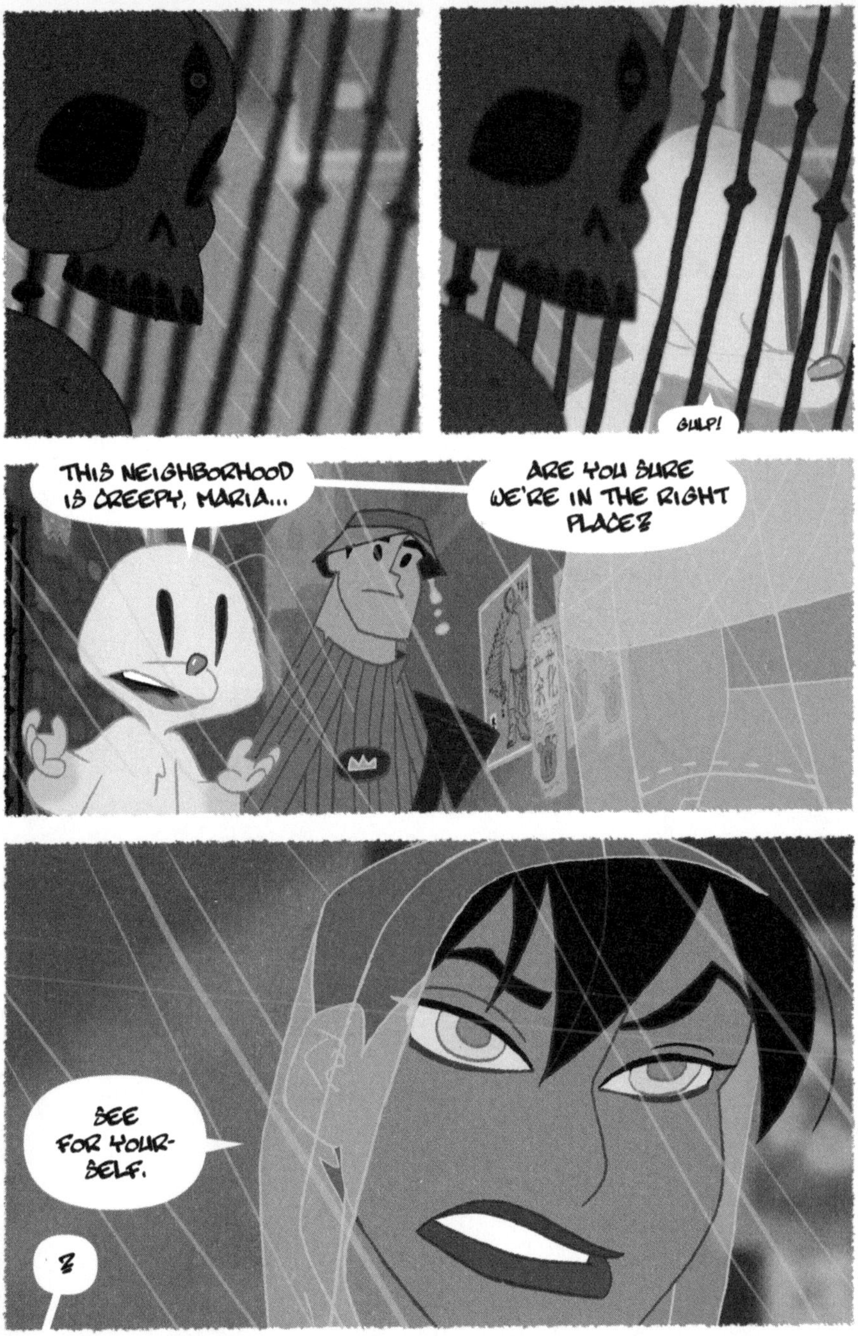
GULP!
THIS NEIGHBORHOOD IS CREEPY, MARIA...
ARE YOU SURE WE'RE IN THE RIGHT PLACE?
SEE FOR YOUR-SELF.
?

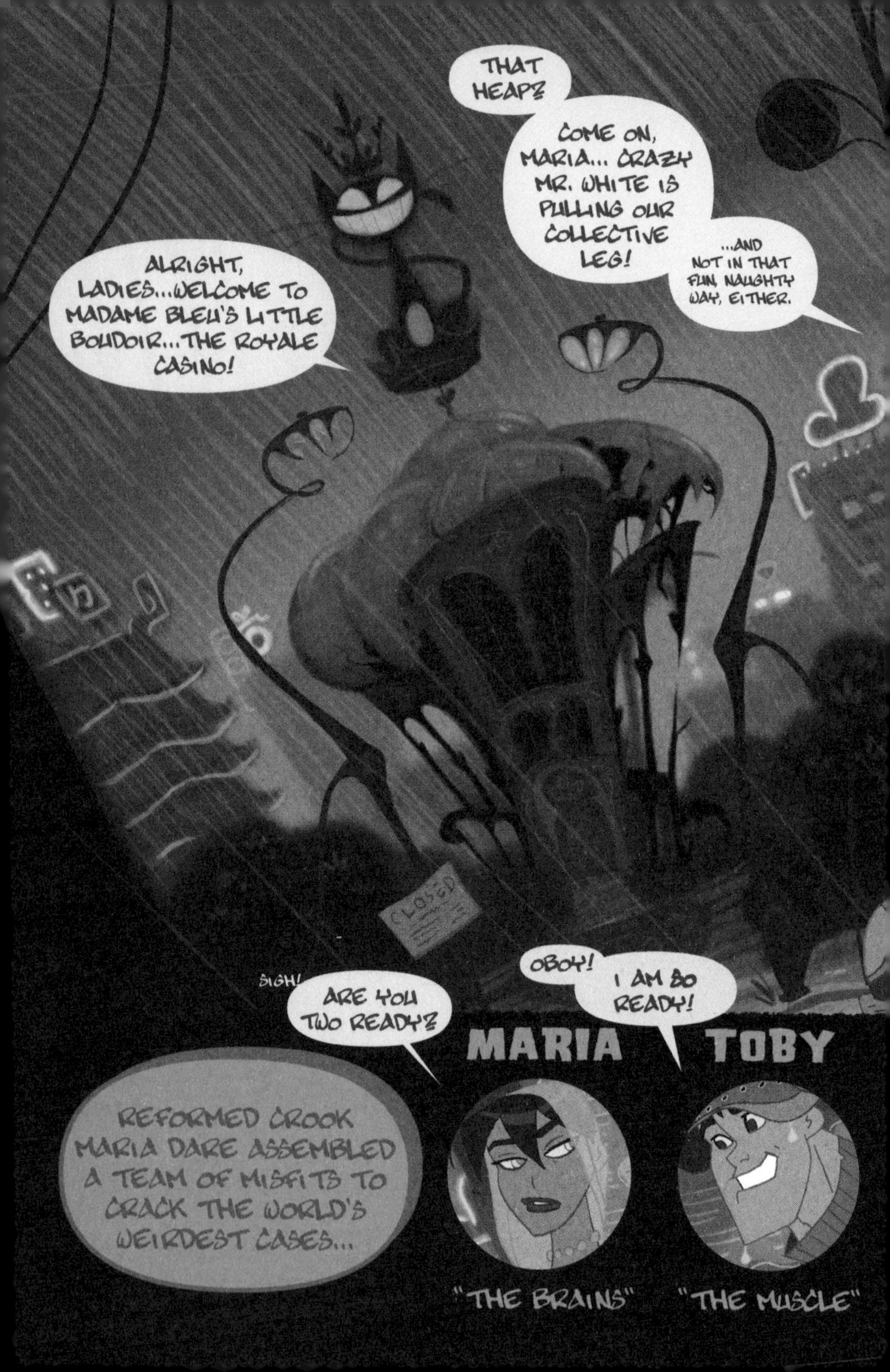
THAT HEAP?
COME ON, MARIA... CRAZY MR. WHITE IS PULLING OUR COLLECTIVE LEG!
...AND NOT IN THAT FUN, NAUGHTY WAY, EITHER.
ALRIGHT, LADIES...WELCOME TO MADAME BLEU'S LITTLE BOUDOIR...THE ROYALE CASINO!
CLOSED
SIGH!
ARE YOU TWO READY?
OBOY!
I AM SO READY!
MARIA
TOBY
REFORMED CROOK MARIA DARE ASSEMBLED A TEAM OF MISFITS TO CRACK THE WORLD'S WEIRDEST CASES...
"THE BRAINS"
"THE MUSCLE"

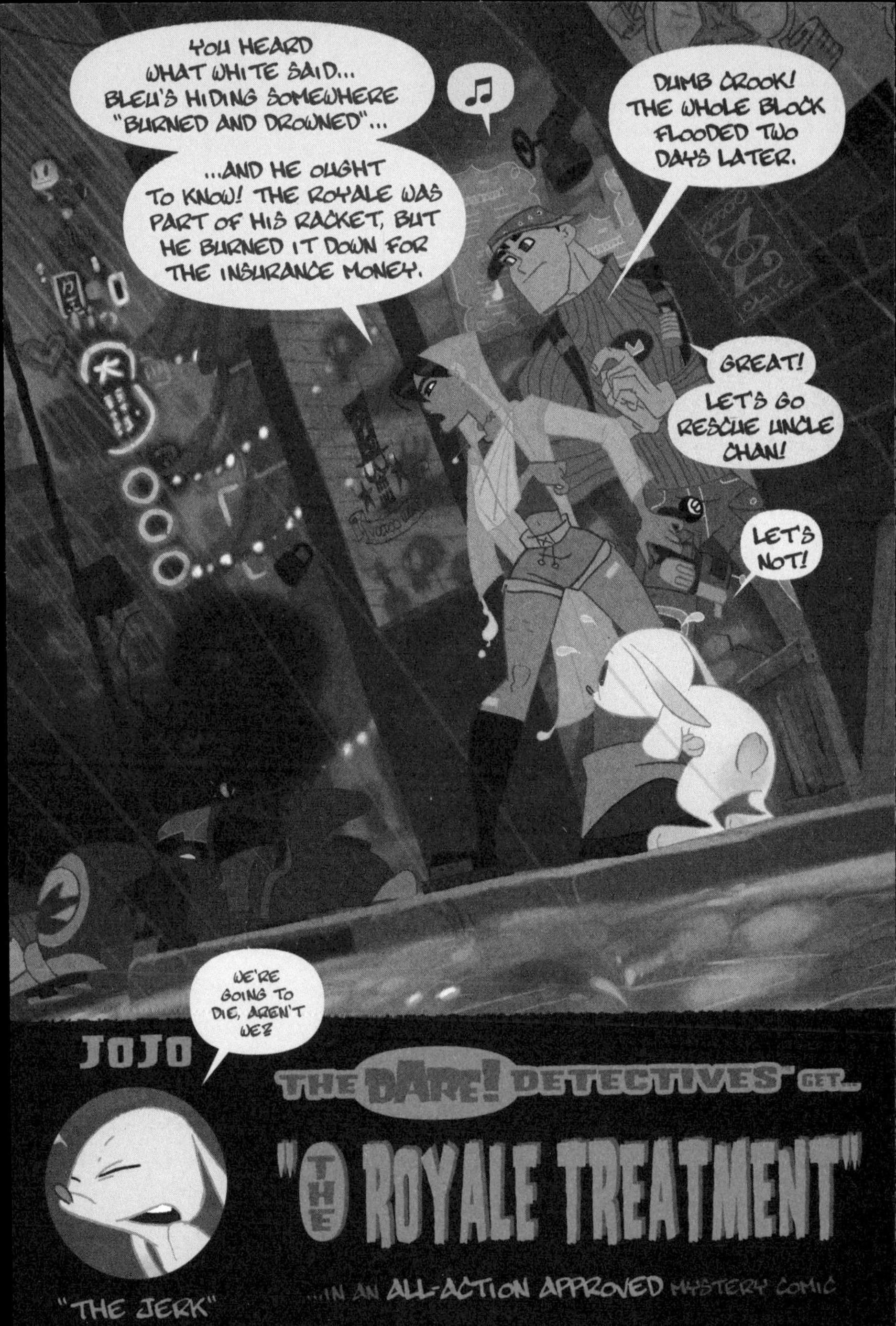
YOU HEARD WHAT WHITE SAID... BLEU'S HIDING SOMEWHERE "BURNED AND DROWNED"...
...AND HE OUGHT TO KNOW! THE ROYALE WAS PART OF HIS RACKET, BUT HE BURNED IT DOWN FOR THE INSURANCE MONEY.
♫
DUMB CROOK! THE WHOLE BLOCK FLOODED TWO DAYS LATER.
GREAT! LET'S GO RESCUE UNCLE CHAN!
LET'S NOT!
WE'RE GOING TO DIE, AREN'T WE?
JOJO
"THE JERK"
THE DARE! DETECTIVES GET...
"THE ROYALE TREATMENT"
...IN AN ALL-ACTION APPROVED MYSTERY COMIC

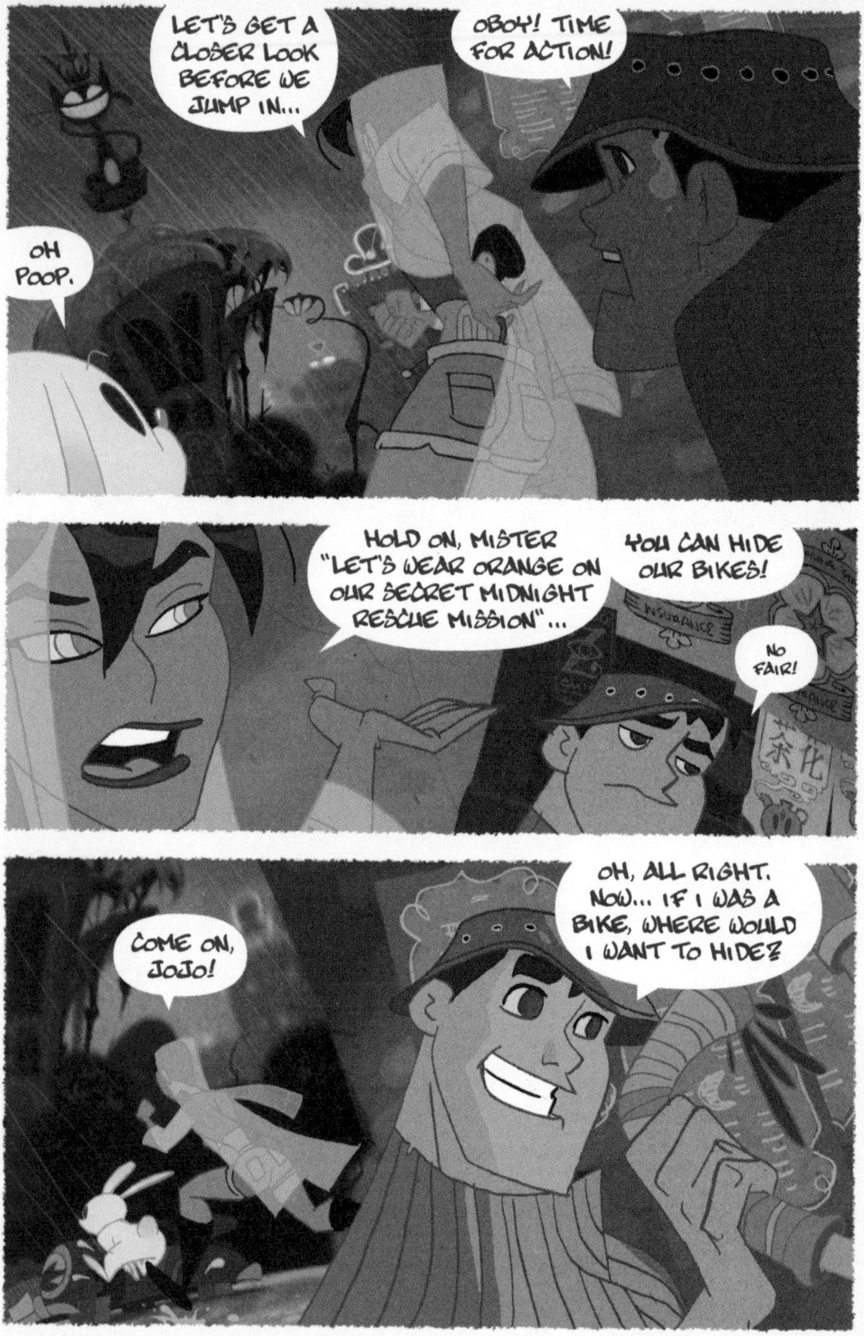
LET'S GET A CLOSER LOOK BEFORE WE JUMP IN...
OBOY! TIME FOR ACTION!
OH POOP.
HOLD ON, MISTER "LET'S WEAR ORANGE ON OUR SECRET MIDNIGHT RESCUE MISSION"...
YOU CAN HIDE OUR BIKES!
NO FAIR!
COME ON, JOJO!
OH, ALL RIGHT. NOW... IF I WAS A BIKE, WHERE WOULD I WANT TO HIDE?

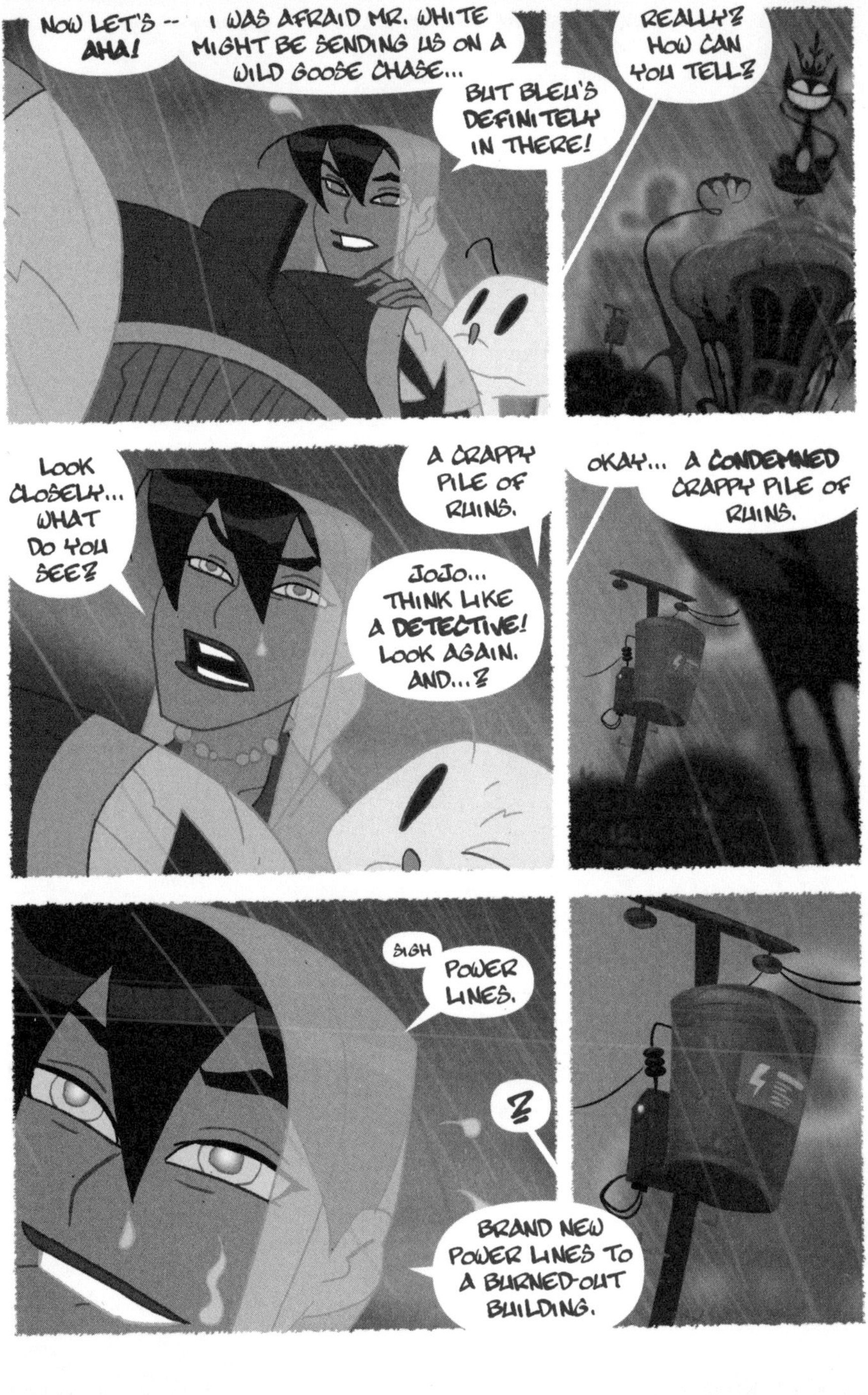
NOW LET'S -- AHA!
I WAS AFRAID MR. WHITE MIGHT BE SENDING US ON A WILD GOOSE CHASE...
BUT BLEU'S DEFINITELY IN THERE!
REALLY? HOW CAN YOU TELL?
LOOK CLOSELY... WHAT DO YOU SEE?
A CRAPPY PILE OF RUINS.
JOJO... THINK LIKE A DETECTIVE! LOOK AGAIN. AND...?
OKAY... A CONDEMNED CRAPPY PILE OF RUINS.
SIGH
POWER LINES.
?
BRAND NEW POWER LINES TO A BURNED-OUT BUILDING.

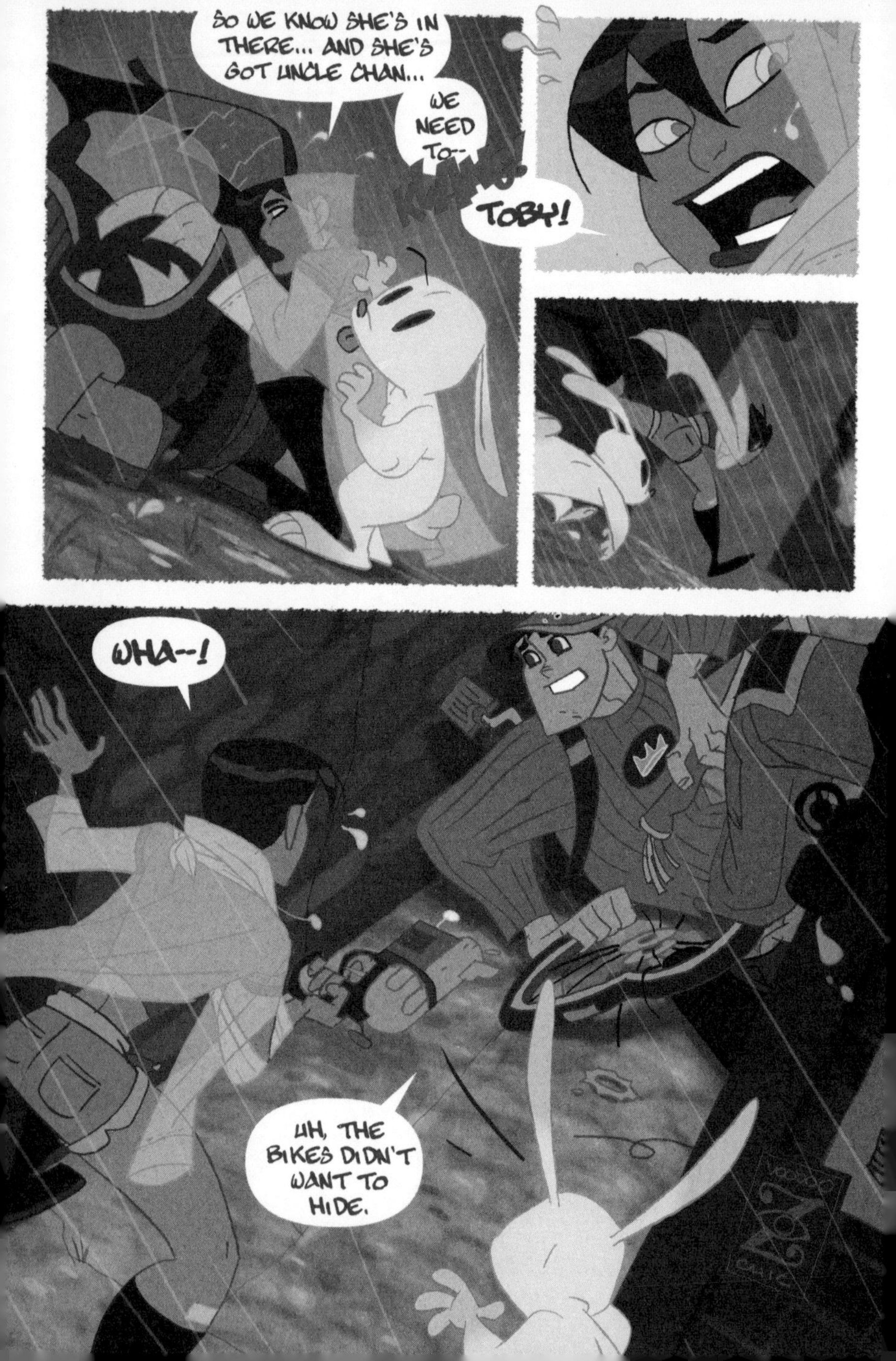
SO WE KNOW SHE'S IN THERE... AND SHE'S GOT UNCLE CHAN...
WE NEED TO--
TOBY!
WHA--!
UH, THE BIKES DIDN'T WANT TO HIDE.

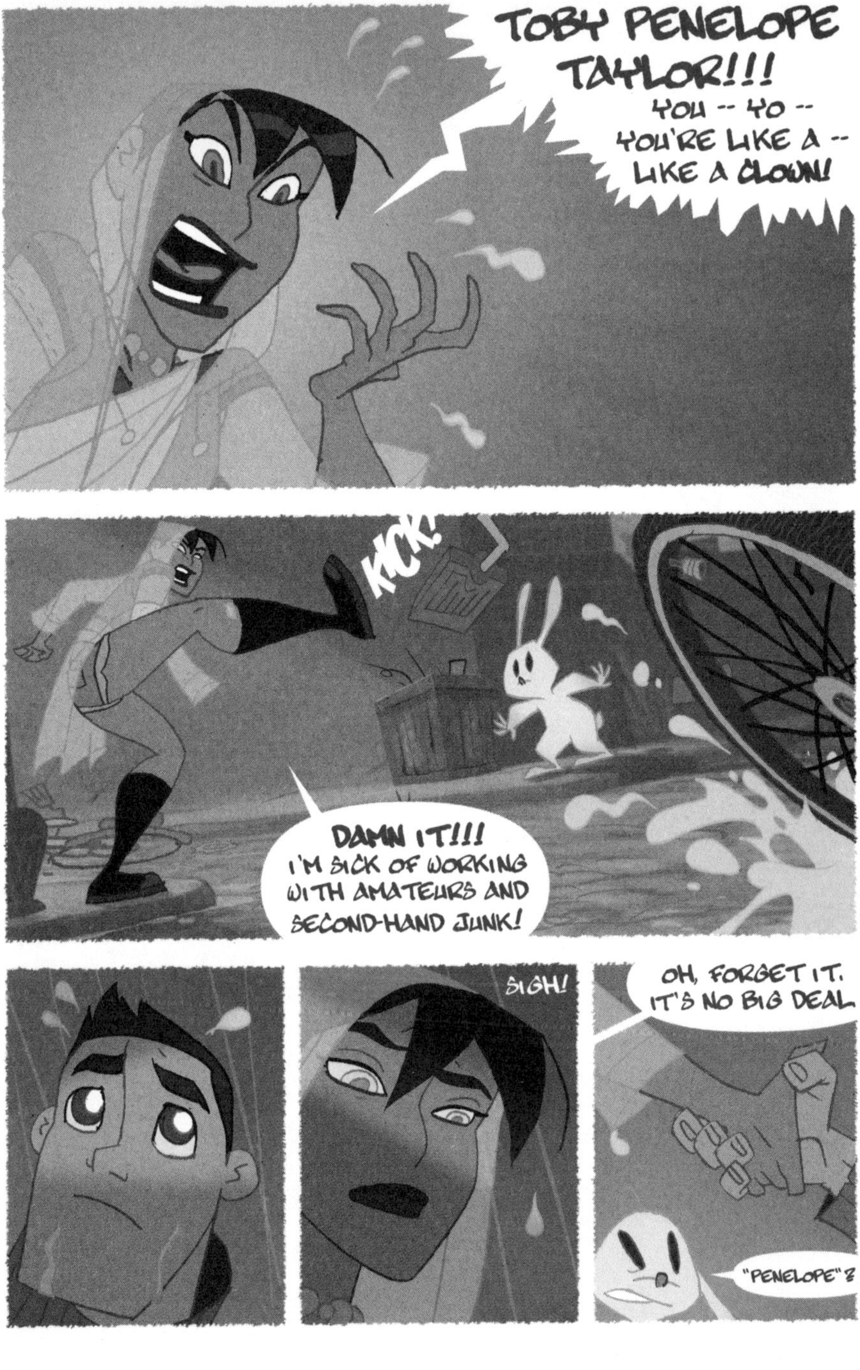
TOBY PENELOPE TAYLOR!!!
YOU -- YO -- YOU'RE LIKE A -- LIKE A CLOWN!
KICK!
DAMN IT!!! I'M SICK OF WORKING WITH AMATEURS AND SECOND-HAND JUNK!
SIGH!
OH, FORGET IT. IT'S NO BIG DEAL.
"PENELOPE"?

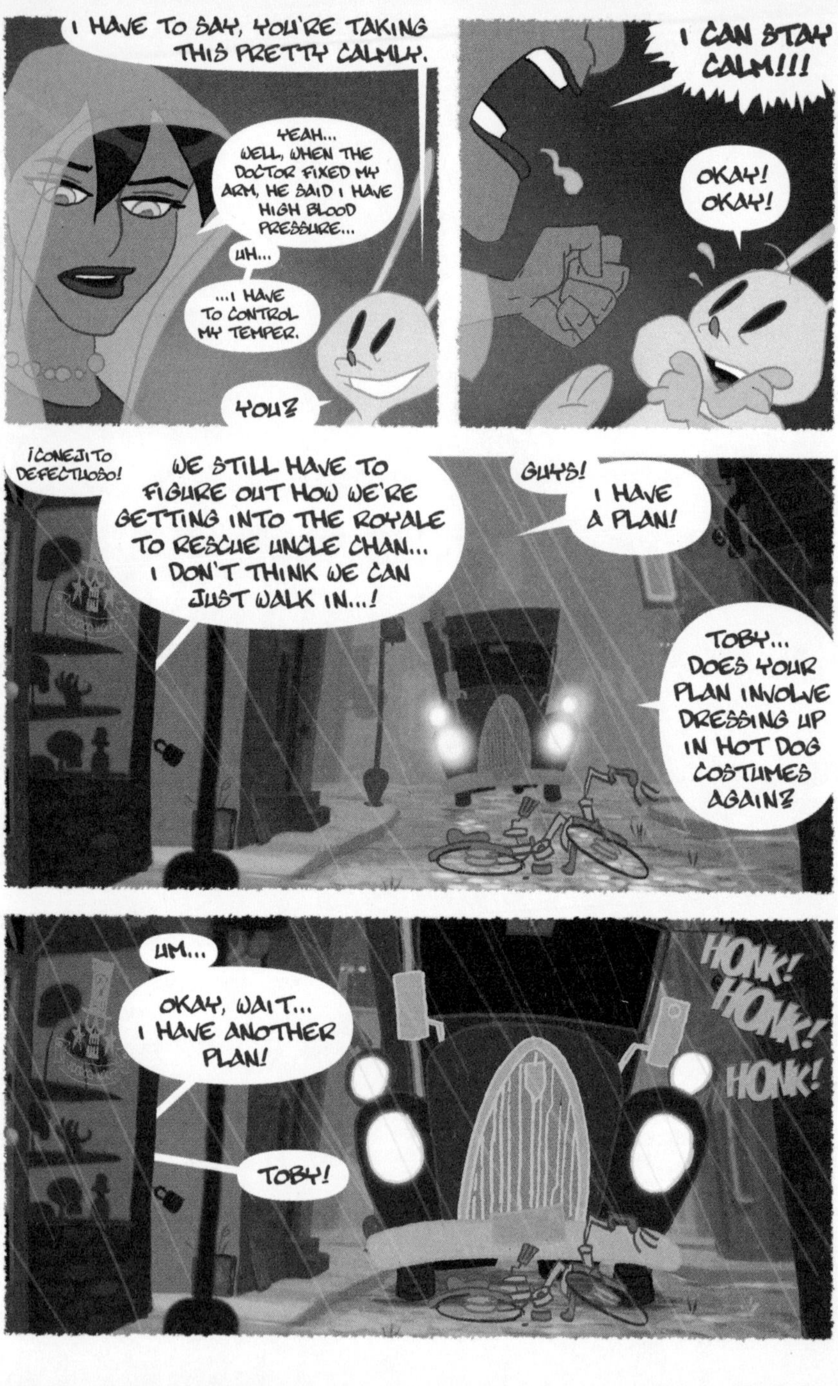
I HAVE TO SAY, YOU'RE TAKING THIS PRETTY CALMLY.
YEAH... WELL, WHEN THE DOCTOR FIXED MY ARM, HE SAID I HAVE HIGH BLOOD PRESSURE...
UH...
...I HAVE TO CONTROL MY TEMPER.
YOU?
I CAN STAY CALM!!!
OKAY! OKAY!
¡CONEJITO DEFECTUOSO!
WE STILL HAVE TO FIGURE OUT HOW WE'RE GETTING INTO THE ROYALE TO RESCUE UNCLE CHAN... I DON'T THINK WE CAN JUST WALK IN...!
GUYS!
I HAVE A PLAN!
TOBY... DOES YOUR PLAN INVOLVE DRESSING UP IN HOT DOG COSTUMES AGAIN?
UM...
OKAY, WAIT... I HAVE ANOTHER PLAN!
TOBY!
HONK! HONK! HONK!

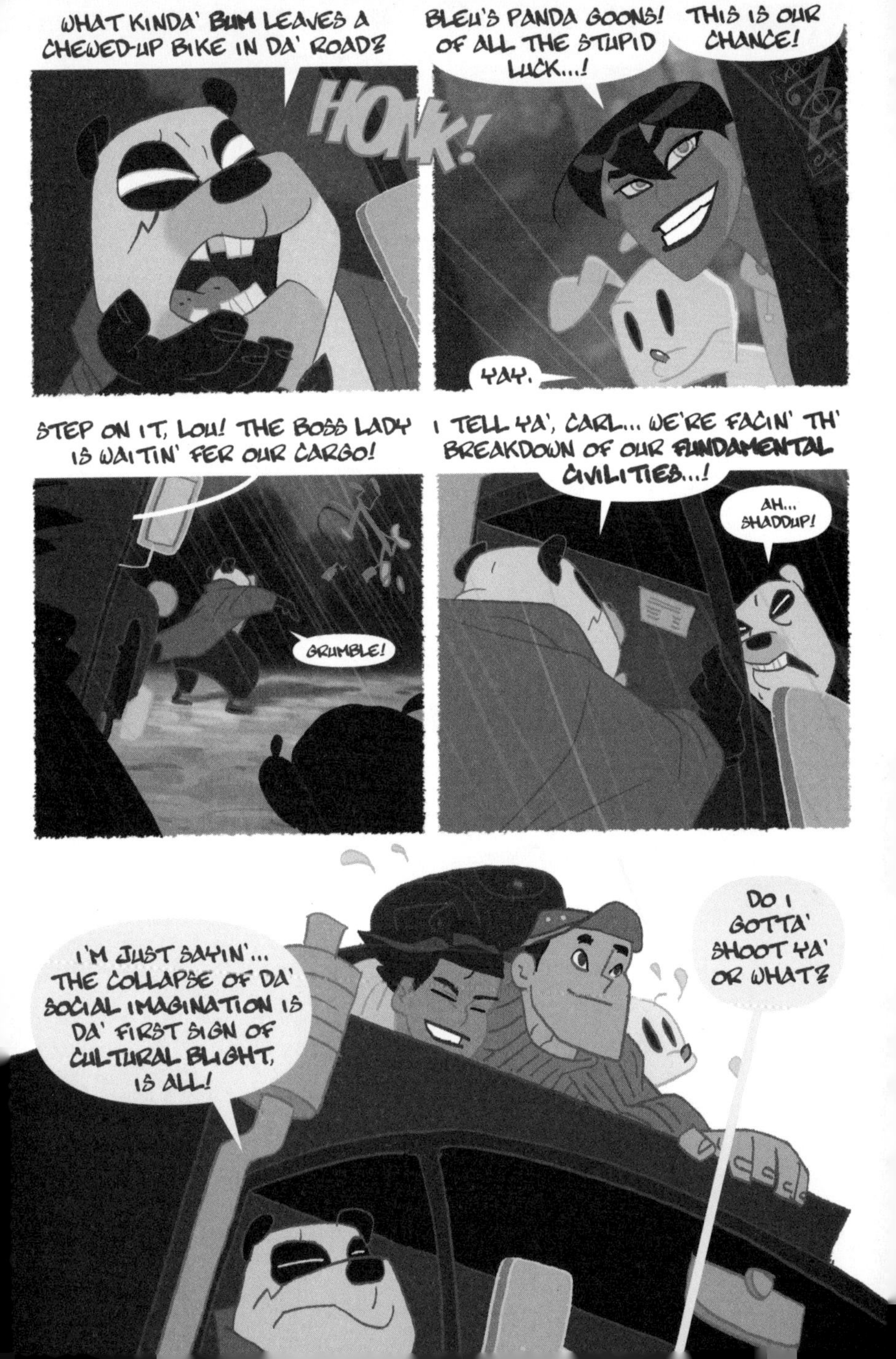
WHAT KINDA' BUM LEAVES A CHEWED-UP BIKE IN DA' ROAD?
HONK!
BLEU'S PANDA GOONS! OF ALL THE STUPID LUCK...!
THIS IS OUR CHANCE!
YAY.
STEP ON IT, LOU! THE BOSS LADY IS WAITIN' FER OUR CARGO!
GRUMBLE!
I TELL YA', CARL... WE'RE FACIN' TH' BREAKDOWN OF OUR FUNDAMENTAL CIVILITIES...!
AH... SHADDUP!
I'M JUST SAYIN'... THE COLLAPSE OF DA' SOCIAL IMAGINATION IS DA' FIRST SIGN OF CULTURAL BLIGHT, IS ALL!
DO I GOTTA' SHOOT YA' OR WHAT?

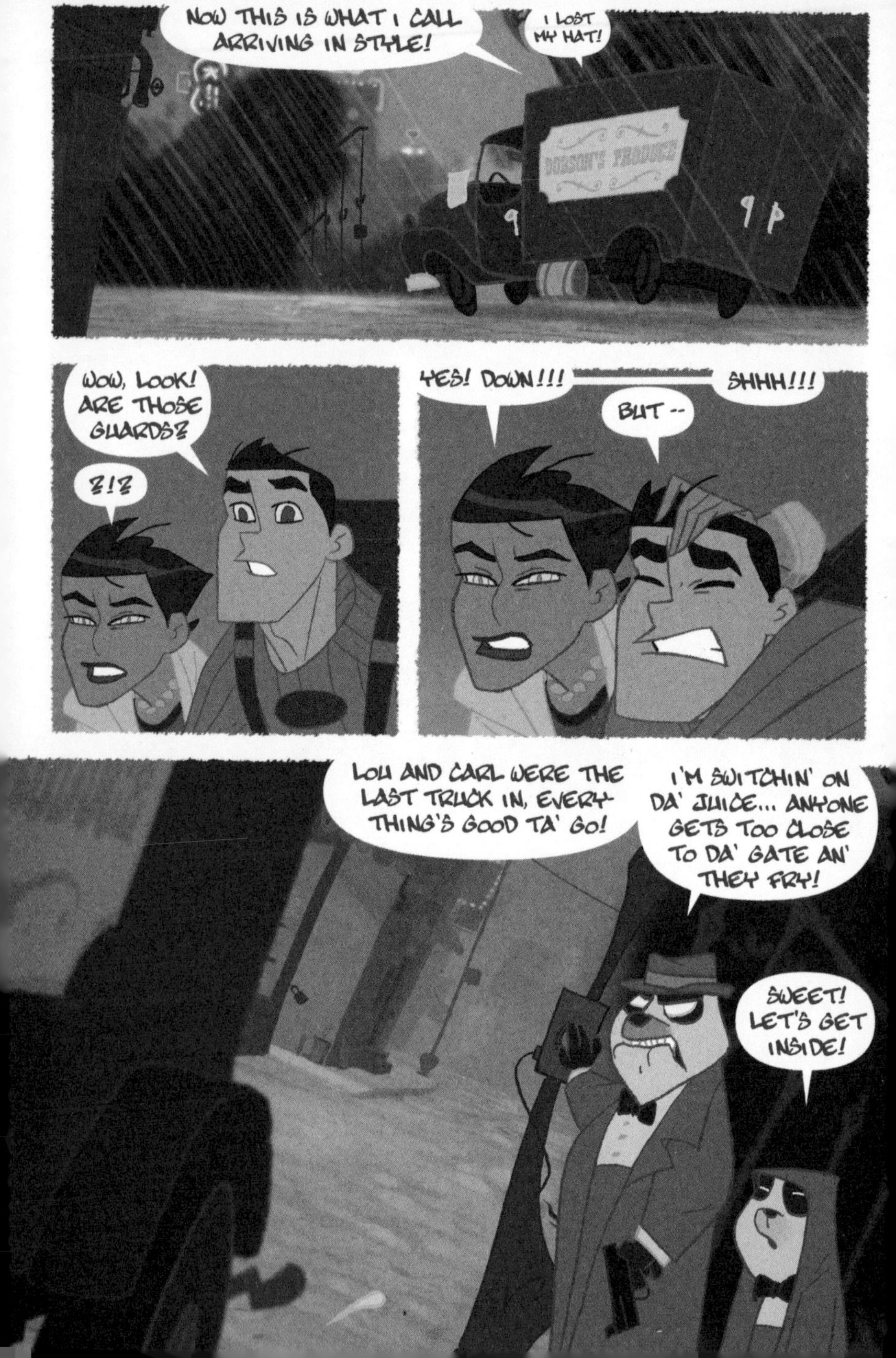
NOW THIS IS WHAT I CALL ARRIVING IN STYLE!
I LOST MY HAT!
WOW, LOOK! ARE THOSE GUARDS?
?!?
YES! DOWN!!!
BUT --
SHHH!!!
LOU AND CARL WERE THE LAST TRUCK IN, EVERY-THING'S GOOD TA' GO!
I'M SWITCHIN' ON DA' JUICE... ANYONE GETS TOO CLOSE TO DA' GATE AN' THEY FRY!
SWEET! LET'S GET INSIDE!

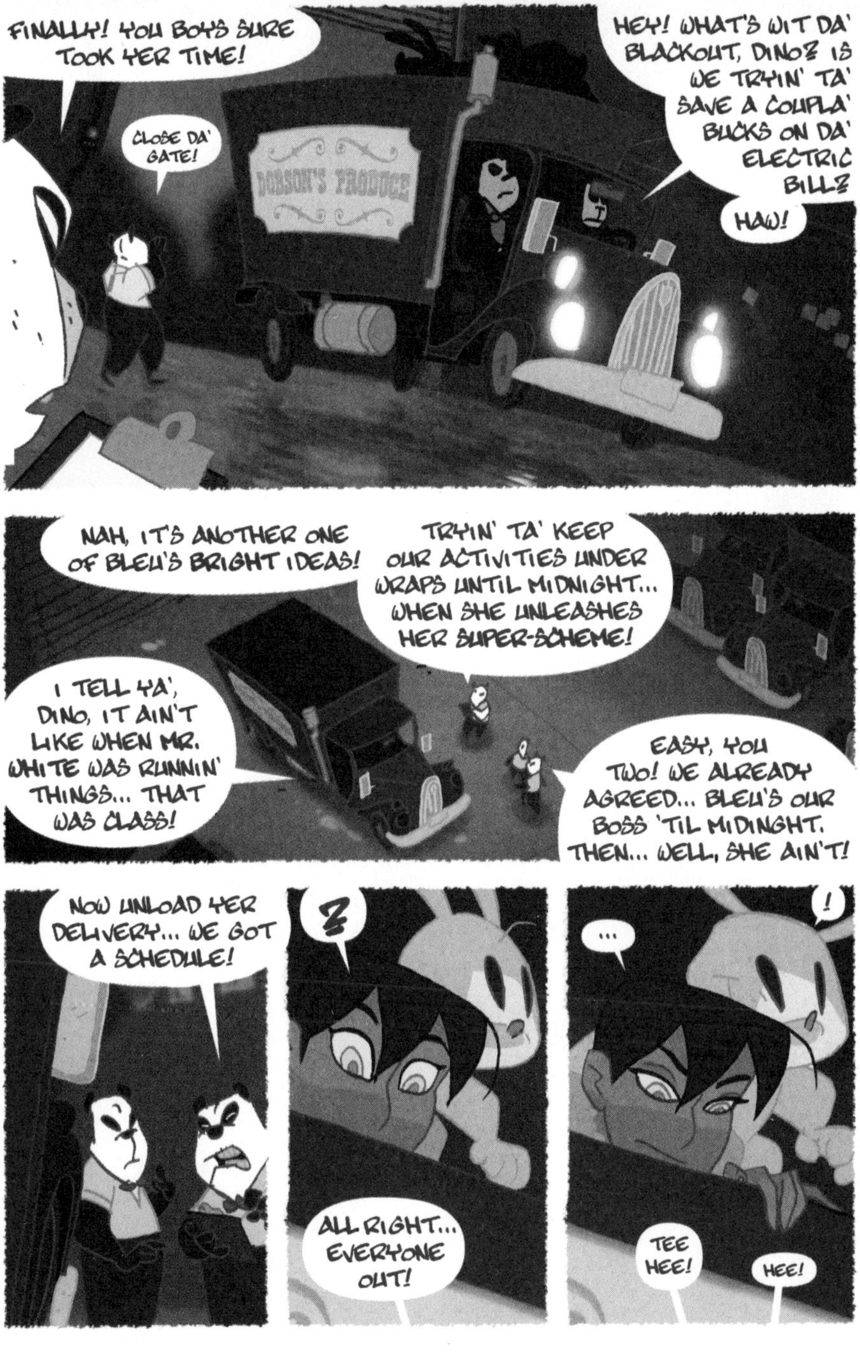
FINALLY! YOU BOYS SURE TOOK YER TIME!
CLOSE DA' GATE!
DOBSON'S PRODUCE
HEY! WHAT'S WIT DA' BLACKOUT, DINO? IS WE TRYIN' TA' SAVE A COUPLA' BUCKS ON DA' ELECTRIC BILL?
HAW!
NAH, IT'S ANOTHER ONE OF BLEU'S BRIGHT IDEAS!
TRYIN' TA' KEEP OUR ACTIVITIES UNDER WRAPS UNTIL MIDNIGHT... WHEN SHE UNLEASHES HER SUPER-SCHEME!
I TELL YA', DINO, IT AIN'T LIKE WHEN MR. WHITE WAS RUNNIN' THINGS... THAT WAS CLASS!
EASY, YOU TWO! WE ALREADY AGREED... BLEU'S OUR BOSS 'TIL MIDINGHT. THEN... WELL, SHE AIN'T!
NOW UNLOAD YER DELIVERY... WE GOT A SCHEDULE!
?
ALL RIGHT... EVERYONE OUT!
...
!
TEE HEE!
HEE!

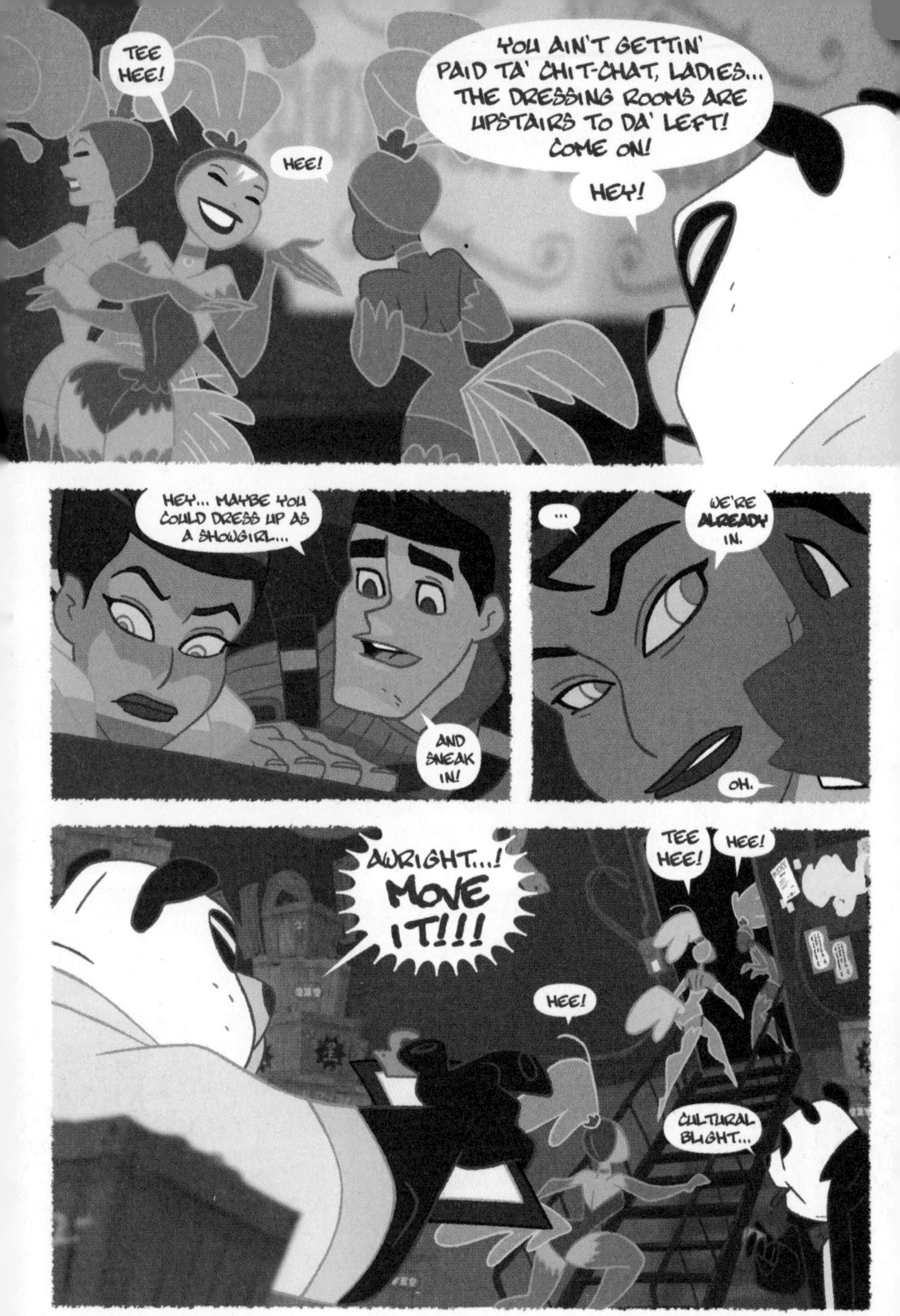
TEE HEE!
HEE!
YOU AIN'T GETTIN' PAID TA' CHIT-CHAT, LADIES... THE DRESSING ROOMS ARE UPSTAIRS TO DA' LEFT! COME ON!
HEY!
HEY... MAYBE YOU COULD DRESS UP AS A SHOWGIRL...
AND SNEAK IN!
...
WE'RE ALREADY IN.
OH.
AWRIGHT...! MOVE IT!!!
TEE HEE!
HEE!
HEE!
CULTURAL BLIGHT...

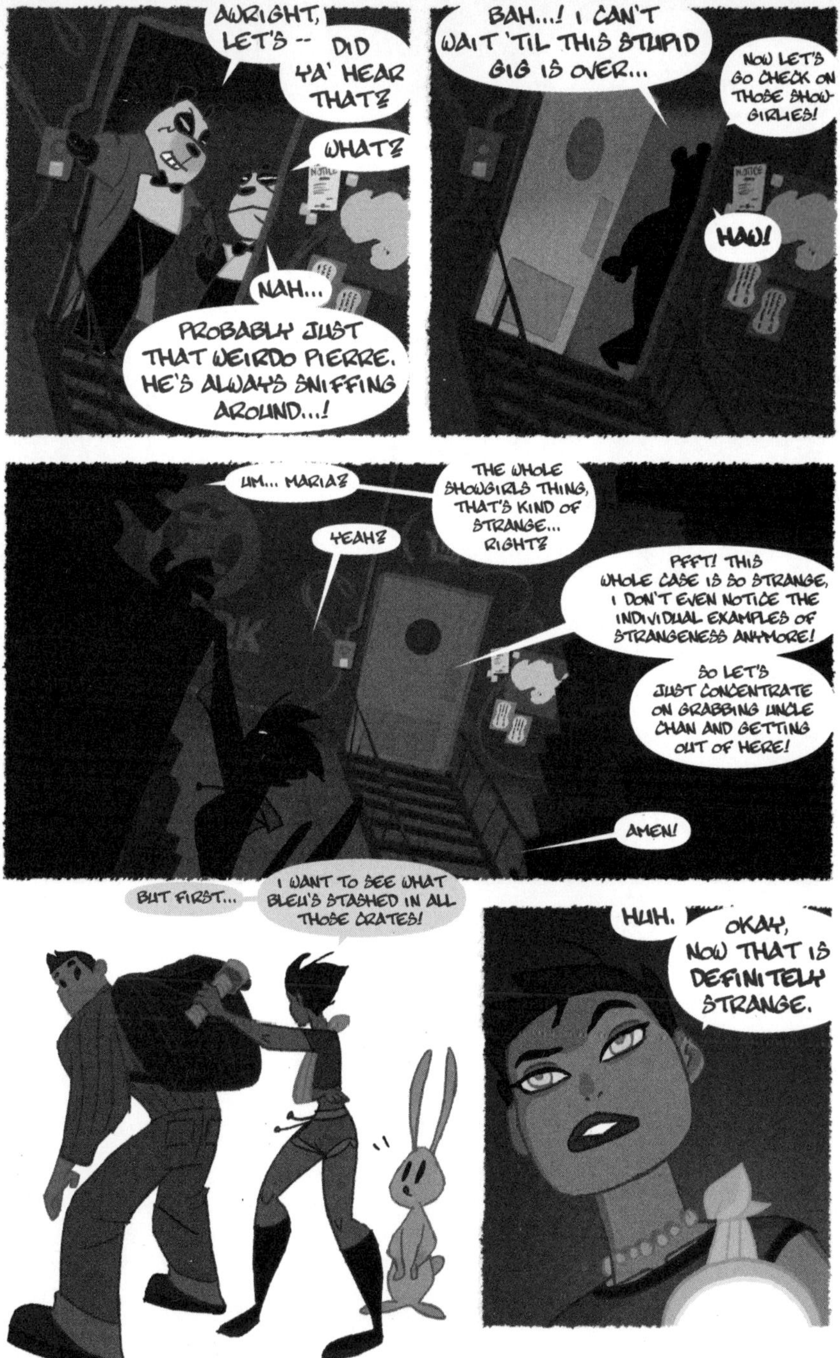
AWRIGHT, LET'S --
DID YA' HEAR THAT?
WHAT?
NAH...
PROBABLY JUST THAT WEIRDO PIERRE. HE'S ALWAYS SNIFFING AROUND...!
BAH...! I CAN'T WAIT 'TIL THIS STUPID GIG IS OVER...
NOW LET'S GO CHECK ON THOSE SHOW-GIRLIES!
HAW!
UM... MARIA?
THE WHOLE SHOWGIRLS THING, THAT'S KIND OF STRANGE... RIGHT?
YEAH?
PFFT! THIS WHOLE CASE IS SO STRANGE, I DON'T EVEN NOTICE THE INDIVIDUAL EXAMPLES OF STRANGENESS ANYMORE!
SO LET'S JUST CONCENTRATE ON GRABBING UNCLE CHAN AND GETTING OUT OF HERE!
AMEN!
BUT FIRST...
I WANT TO SEE WHAT BLEU'S STASHED IN ALL THOSE CRATES!
HUH.
OKAY, NOW THAT IS DEFINITELY STRANGE.

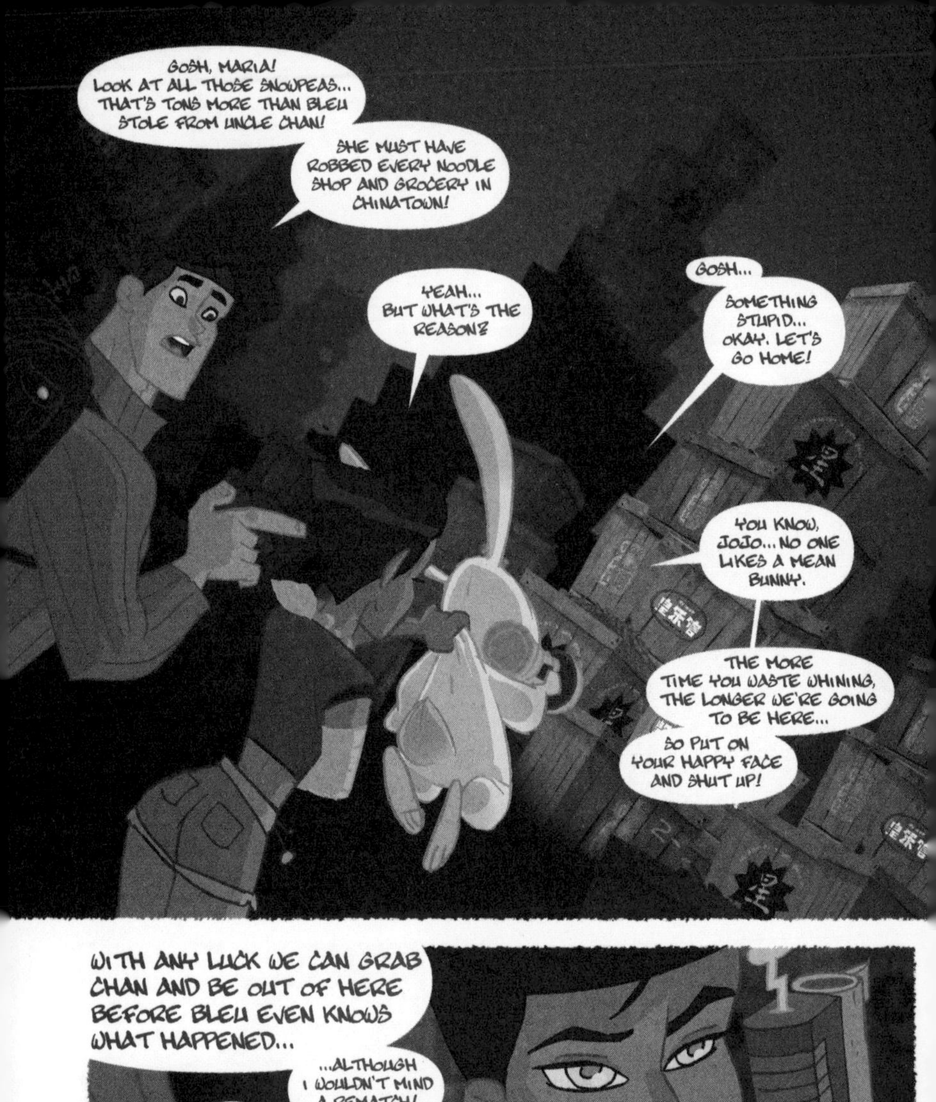
GOSH, MARIA! LOOK AT ALL THOSE SNOWPEAS... THAT'S TONS MORE THAN BLEU STOLE FROM UNCLE CHAN!
SHE MUST HAVE ROBBED EVERY NOODLE SHOP AND GROCERY IN CHINATOWN!
YEAH... BUT WHAT'S THE REASON?
GOSH...
SOMETHING STUPID... OKAY. LET'S GO HOME!
YOU KNOW, JOJO... NO ONE LIKES A MEAN BUNNY.
THE MORE TIME YOU WASTE WHINING, THE LONGER WE'RE GOING TO BE HERE...
SO PUT ON YOUR HAPPY FACE AND SHUT UP!

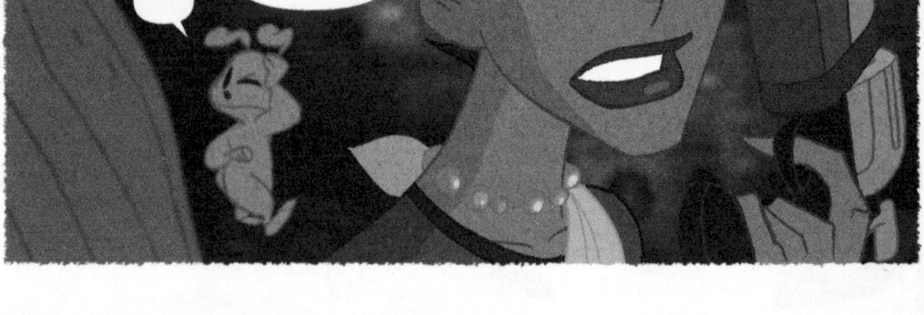
WITH ANY LUCK WE CAN GRAB CHAN AND BE OUT OF HERE BEFORE BLEU EVEN KNOWS WHAT HAPPENED...
...ALTHOUGH I WOULDN'T MIND A REMATCH!
...

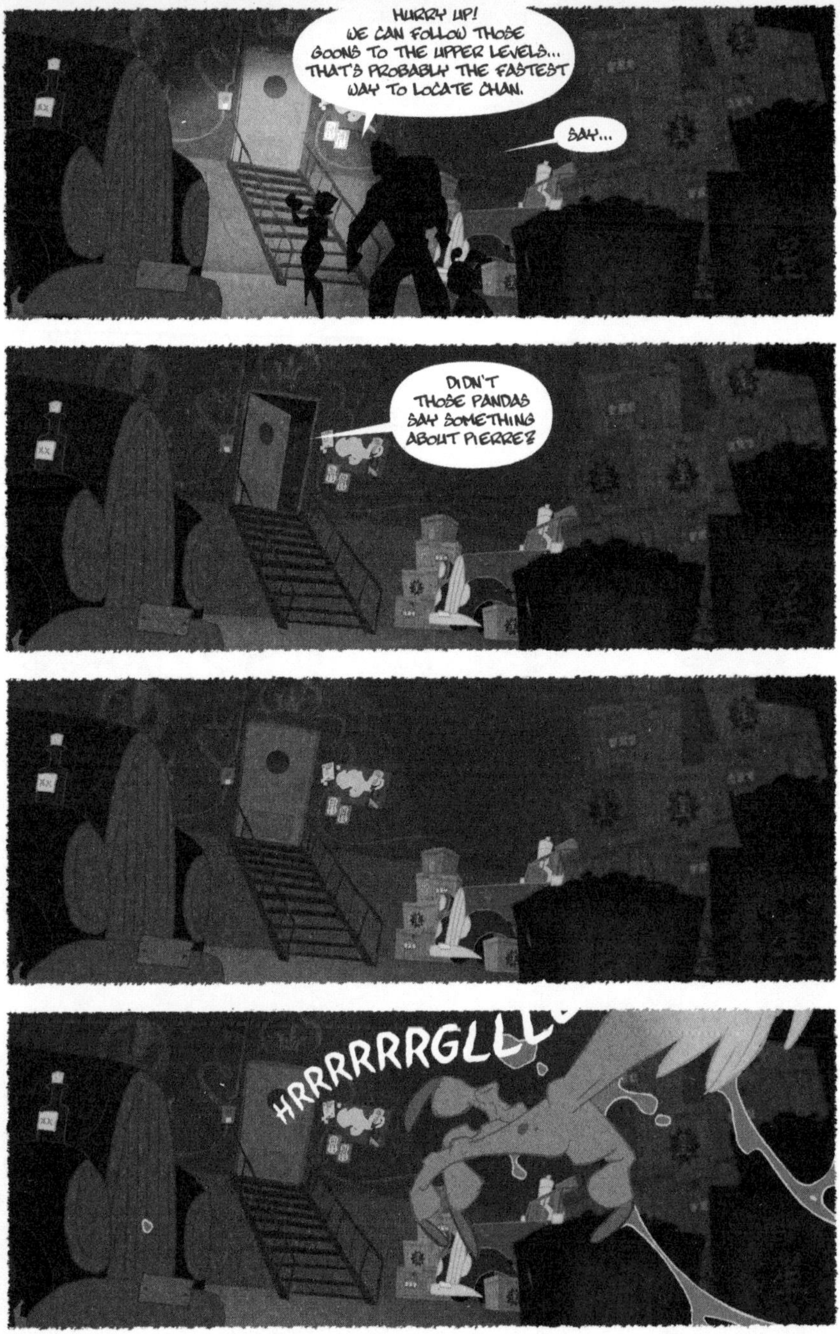
HURRY UP! WE CAN FOLLOW THOSE GOONS TO THE UPPER LEVELS... THAT'S PROBABLY THE FASTEST WAY TO LOCATE CHAN.
SAY...
DIDN'T THOSE PANDAS SAY SOMETHING ABOUT PIERRE?
HRRRRRRGLLL

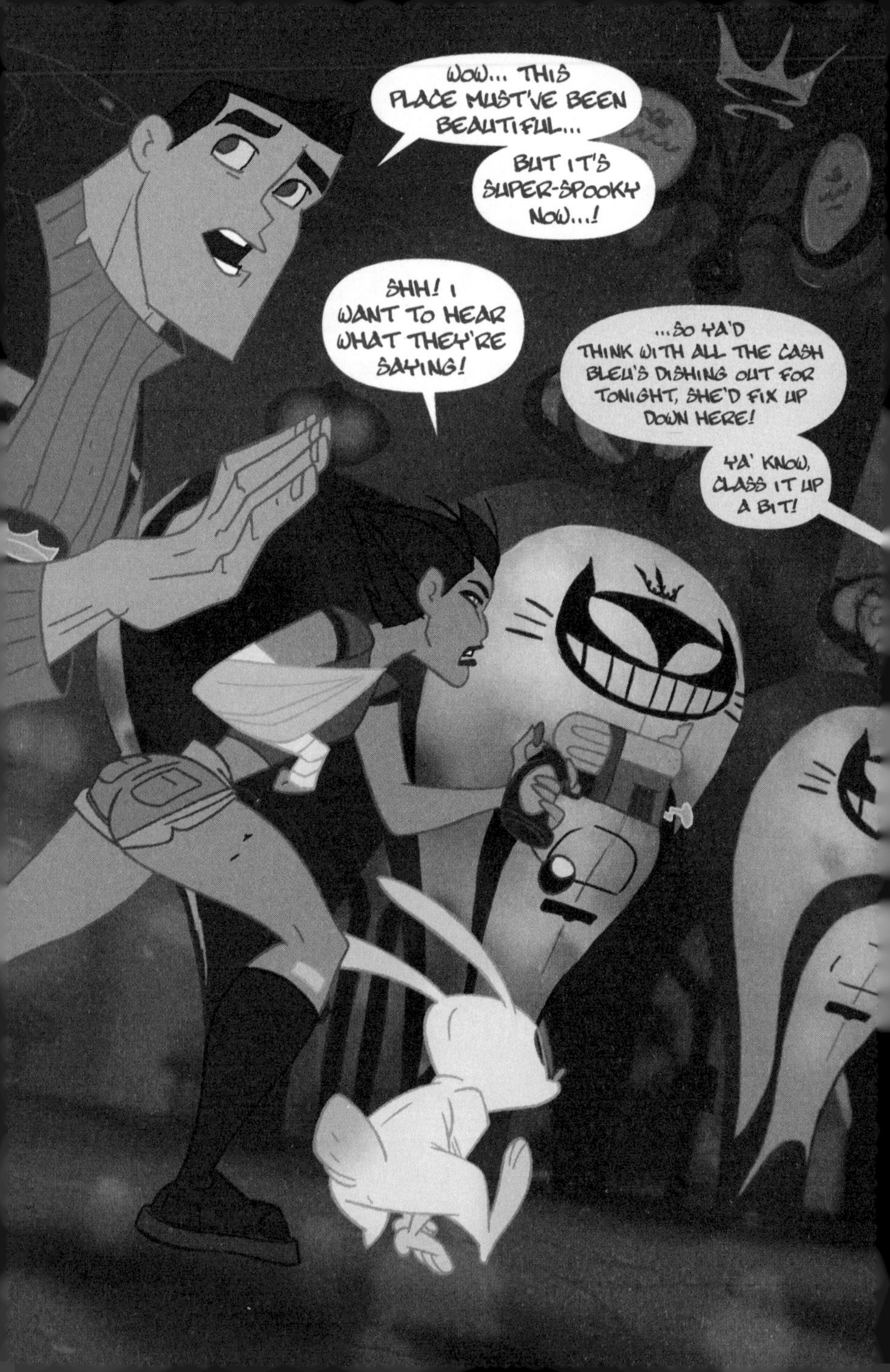
WOW... THIS PLACE MUST'VE BEEN BEAUTIFUL...
BUT IT'S SUPER-SPOOKY NOW...!
SHH! I WANT TO HEAR WHAT THEY'RE SAYING!
...SO YA'D THINK WITH ALL THE CASH BLEU'S DISHING OUT FOR TONIGHT, SHE'D FIX UP DOWN HERE!
YA' KNOW, CLASS IT UP A BIT!

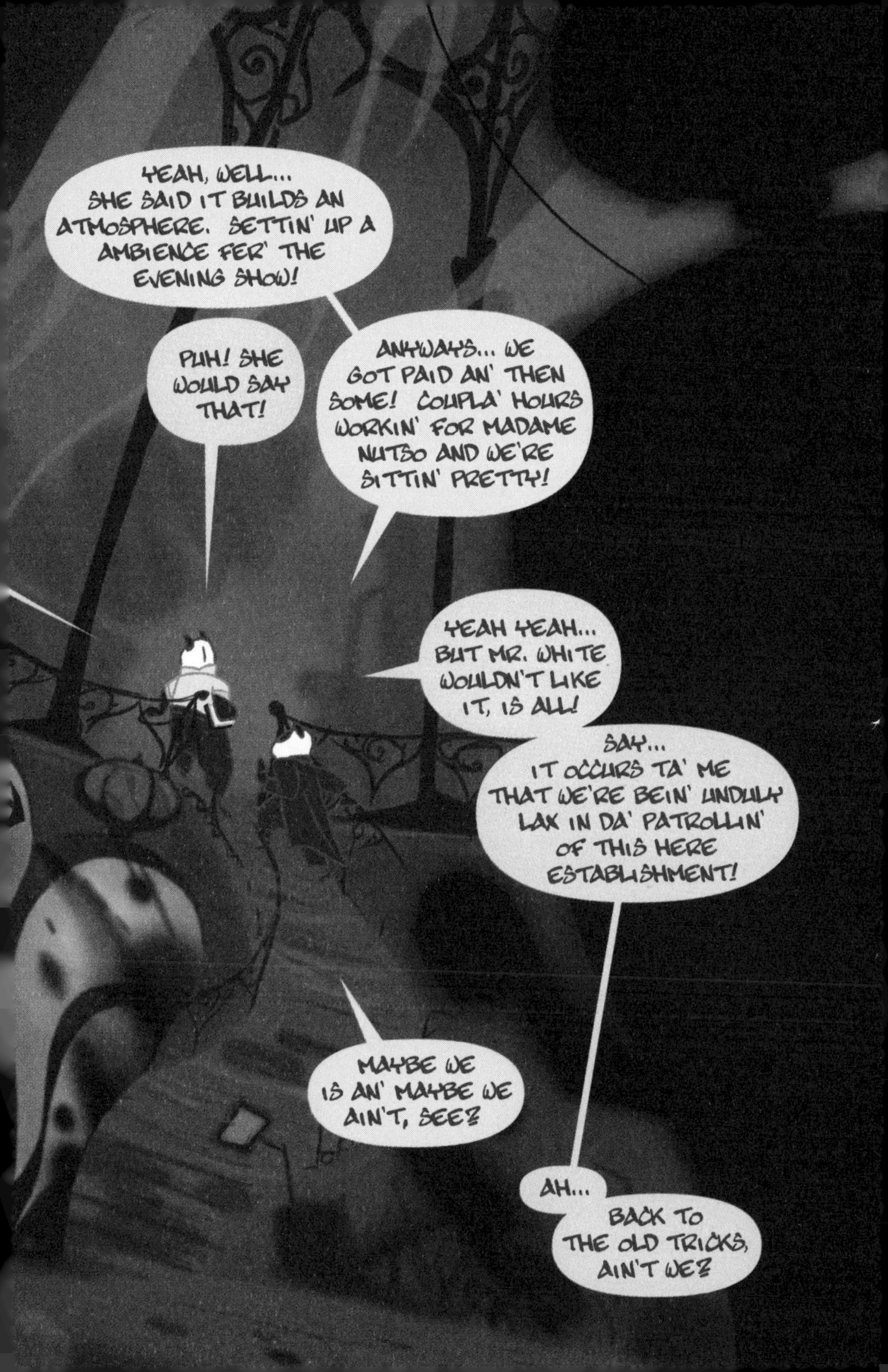
YEAH, WELL... SHE SAID IT BUILDS AN ATMOSPHERE. SETTIN' UP A AMBIENCE FER' THE EVENING SHOW!
PUH! SHE WOULD SAY THAT!
ANYWAYS... WE GOT PAID AN' THEN SOME! COUPLA' HOURS WORKIN' FOR MADAME NUTSO AND WE'RE SITTIN' PRETTY!
YEAH YEAH... BUT MR. WHITE WOULDN'T LIKE IT, IS ALL!
SAY... IT OCCURS TA' ME THAT WE'RE BEIN' UNDULY LAX IN DA' PATROLLIN' OF THIS HERE ESTABLISHMENT!
MAYBE WE IS AN' MAYBE WE AIN'T, SEE?
AH...
BACK TO THE OLD TRICKS, AIN'T WE?

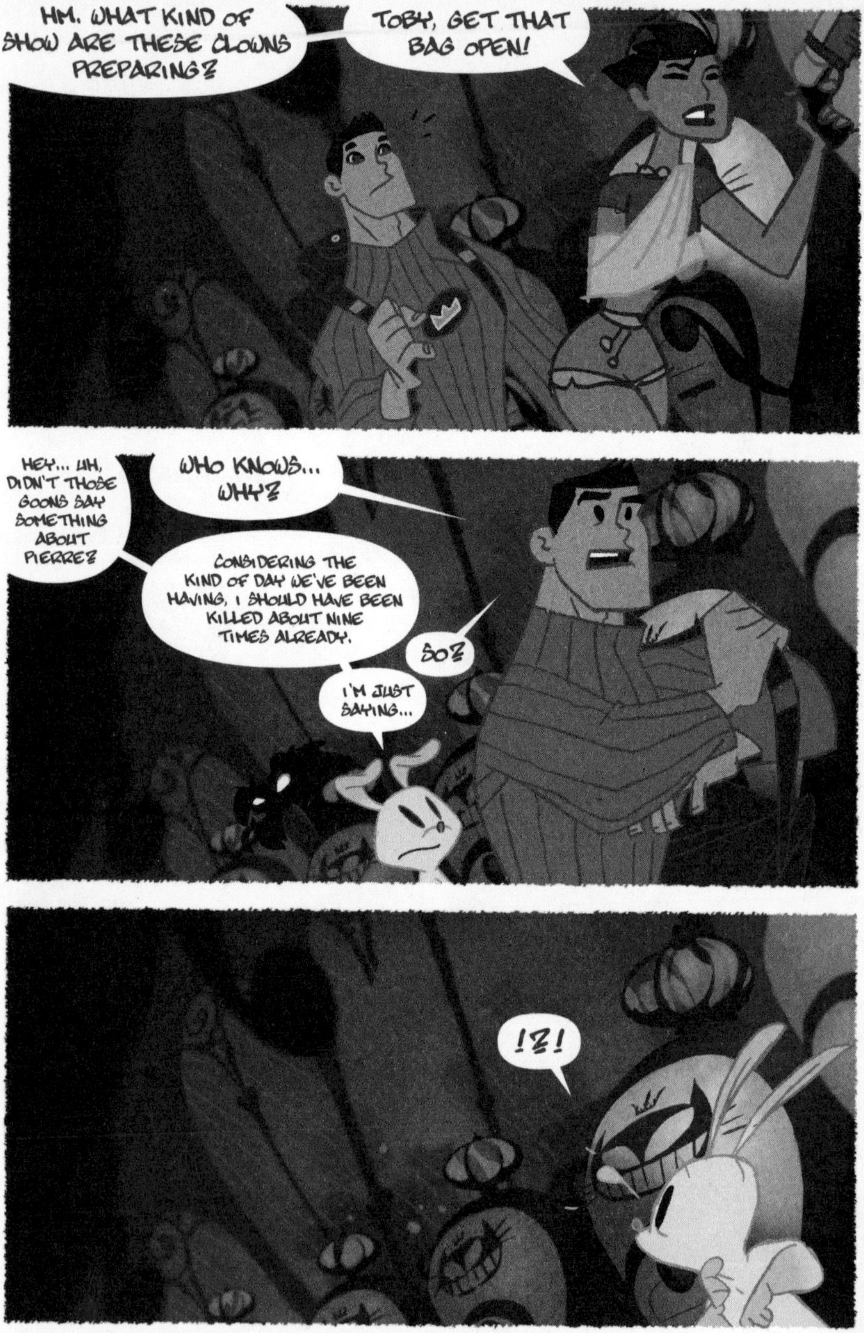
HM. WHAT KIND OF SHOW ARE THESE CLOWNS PREPARING?
TOBY, GET THAT BAG OPEN!
HEY... UH, DIDN'T THOSE GOONS SAY SOMETHING ABOUT PIERRE?
WHO KNOWS... WHY?
CONSIDERING THE KIND OF DAY WE'VE BEEN HAVING, I SHOULD HAVE BEEN KILLED ABOUT NINE TIMES ALREADY.
SO?
I'M JUST SAYING...
!?!

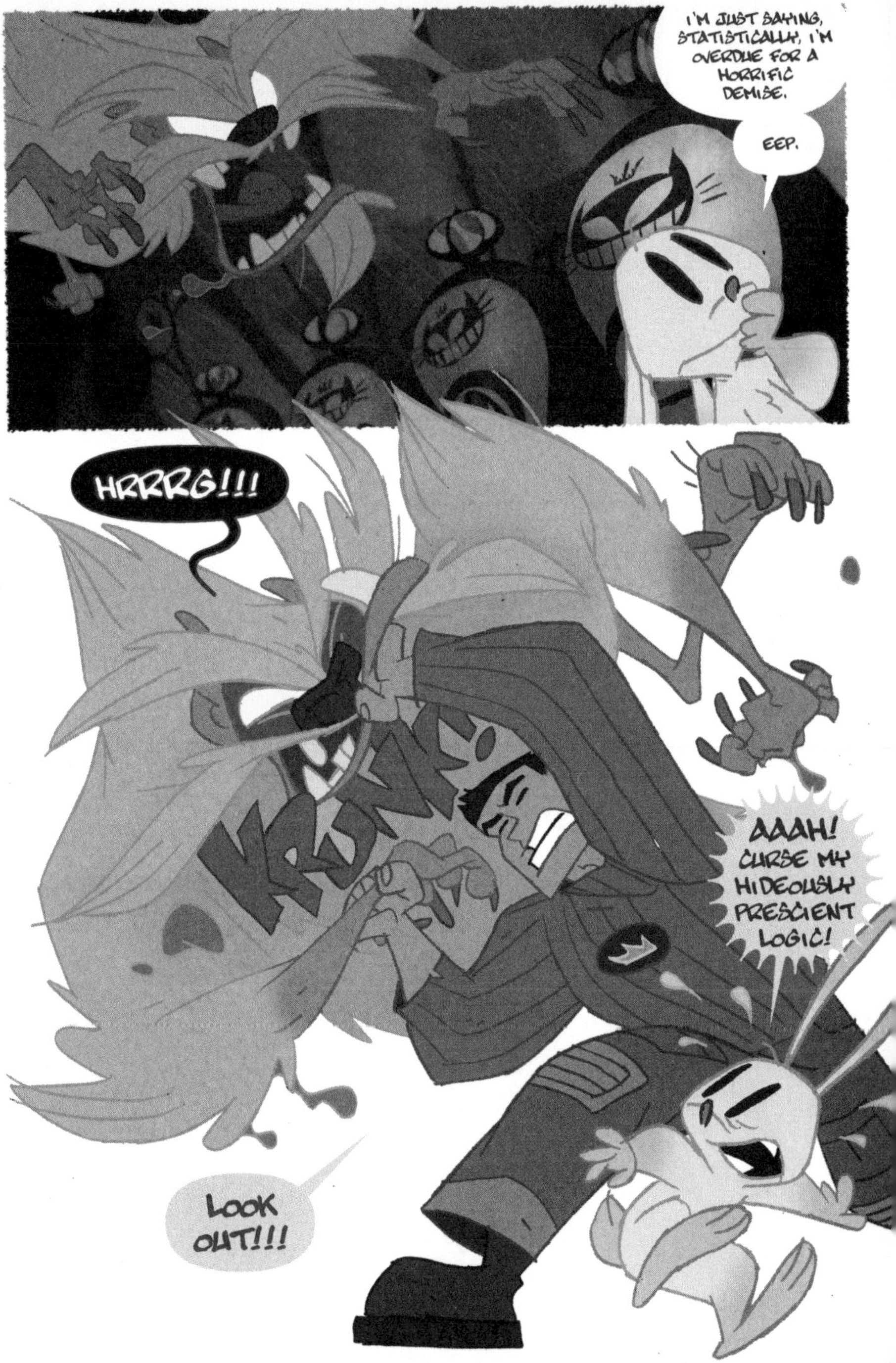
I'M JUST SAYING, STATISTICALLY, I'M OVERDUE FOR A HORRIFIC DEMISE.
EEP.
HRRRG!!!
KRUNK
AAAH! CURSE MY HIDEOUSLY PRESCIENT LOGIC!
LOOK OUT!!!

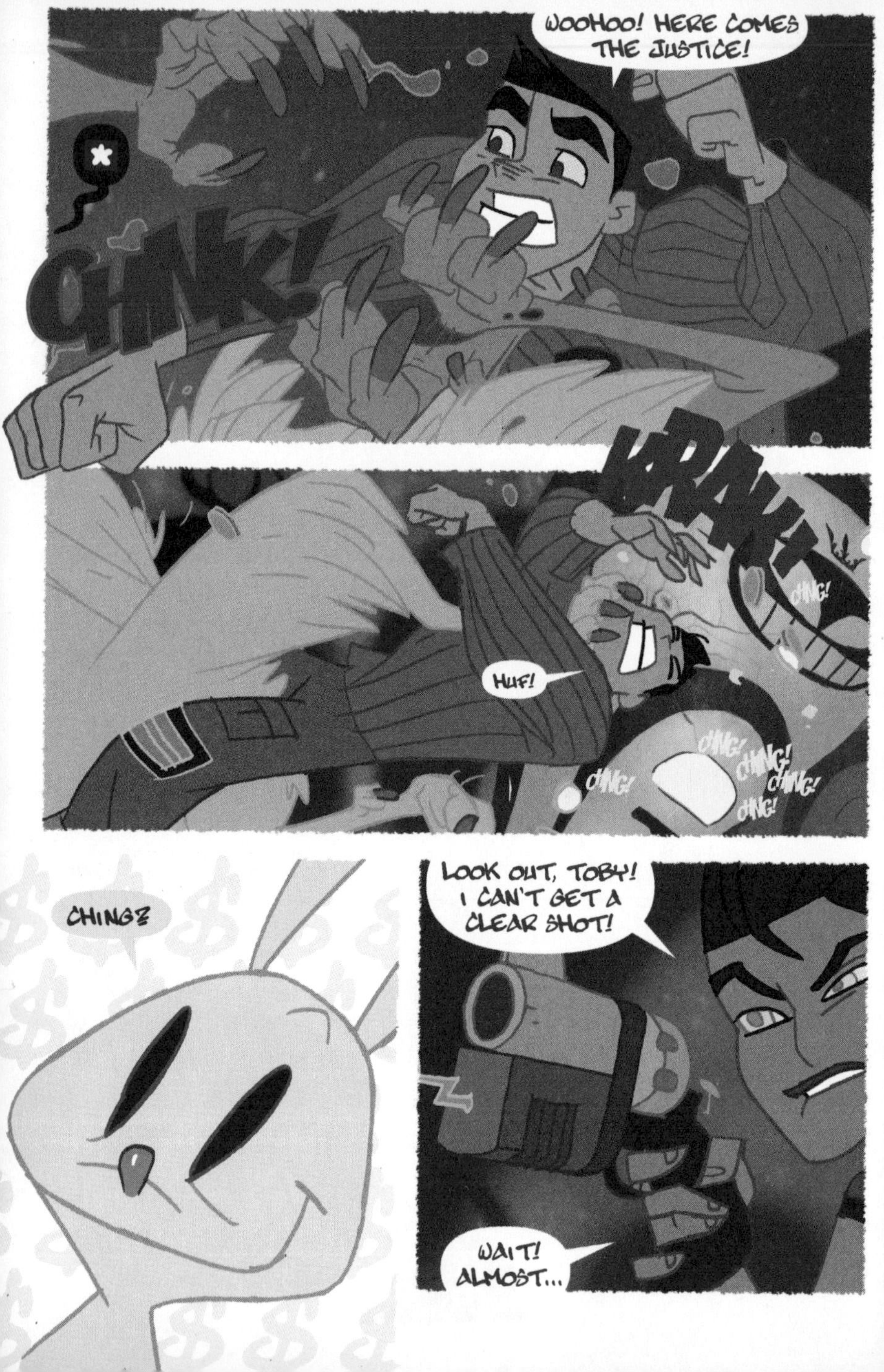
WOOHOO! HERE COMES THE JUSTICE!
CHINK!
KRAK!
CHING!
HUF!
CHING!
CHING!
CHING!
CHING!
CHING!
CHING?
LOOK OUT, TOBY! I CAN'T GET A CLEAR SHOT!
WAIT! ALMOST...

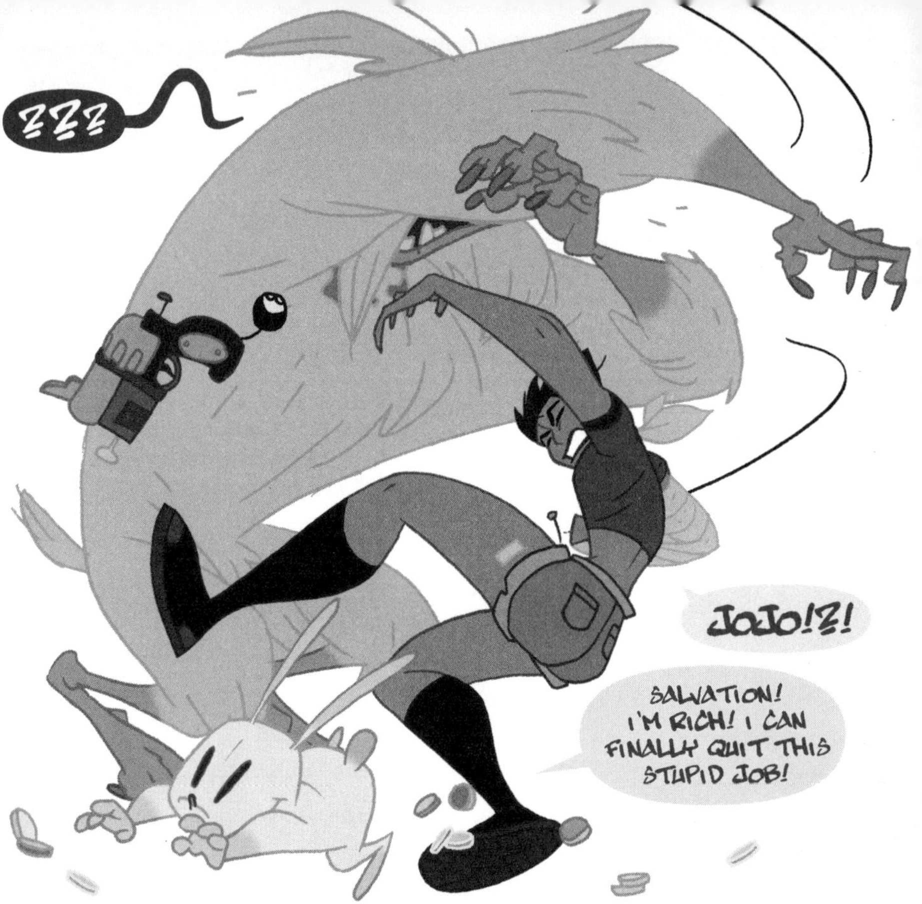
ZZZ
JOJO!?!
SALVATION! I'M RICH! I CAN FINALLY QUIT THIS STUPID JOB!

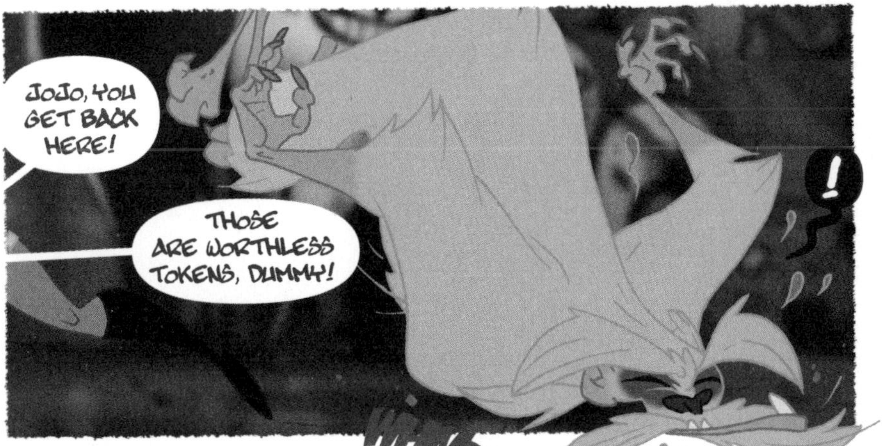
JOJO, YOU GET BACK HERE!
THOSE ARE WORTHLESS TOKENS, DUMMY!
!
WHMP!

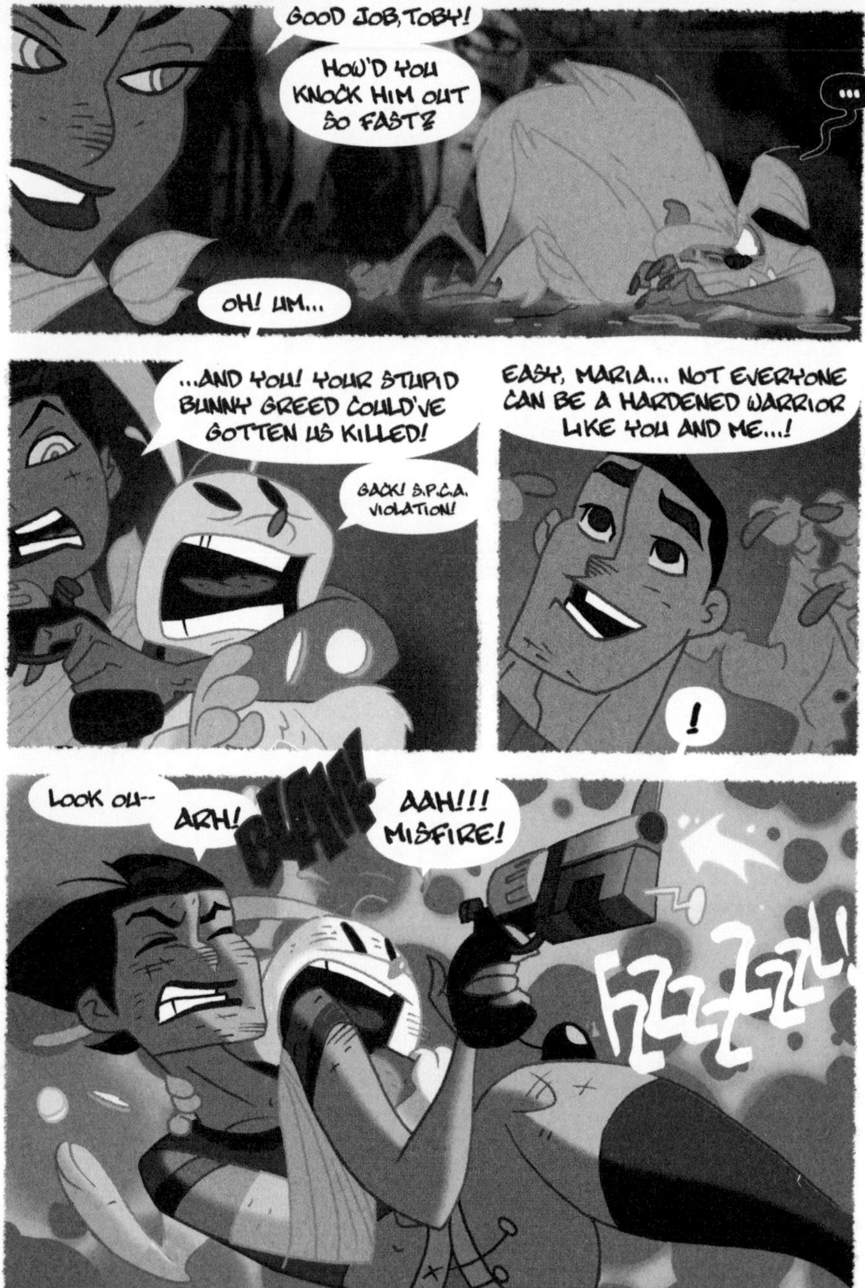
GOOD JOB, TOBY!
HOW'D YOU KNOCK HIM OUT SO FAST?
...
OH! UM...
...AND YOU! YOUR STUPID BUNNY GREED COULD'VE GOTTEN US KILLED!
GACK! S.P.C.A. VIOLATION!
EASY, MARIA... NOT EVERYONE CAN BE A HARDENED WARRIOR LIKE YOU AND ME...!
!
LOOK OU--
ARH!
BLAM!
AAH!!! MISFIRE!
FZZZZZZL!

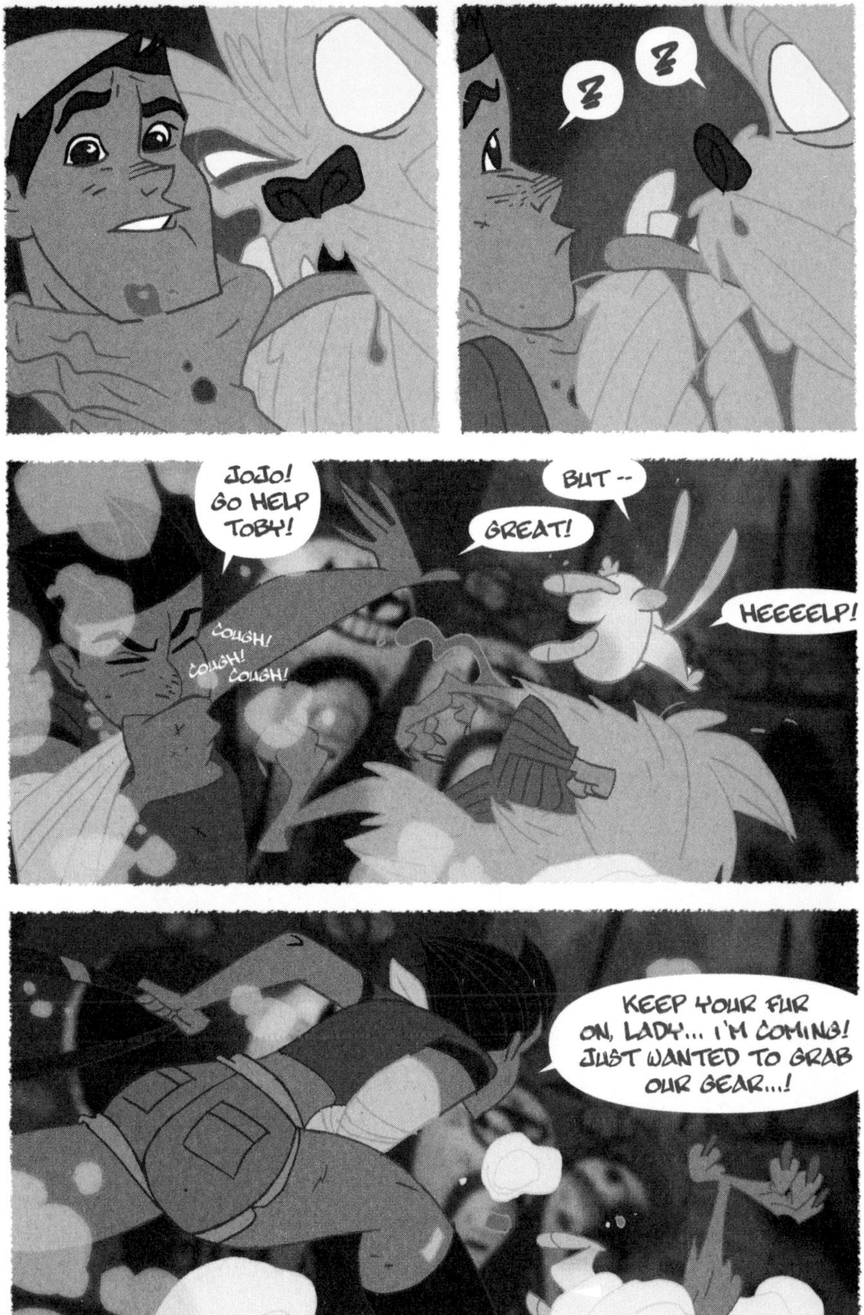
Z
Z
JOJO! GO HELP TOBY!
BUT --
GREAT!
COUGH! COUGH! COUGH!
HEEEELP!
KEEP YOUR FUR ON, LADY... I'M COMING! JUST WANTED TO GRAB OUR GEAR...!

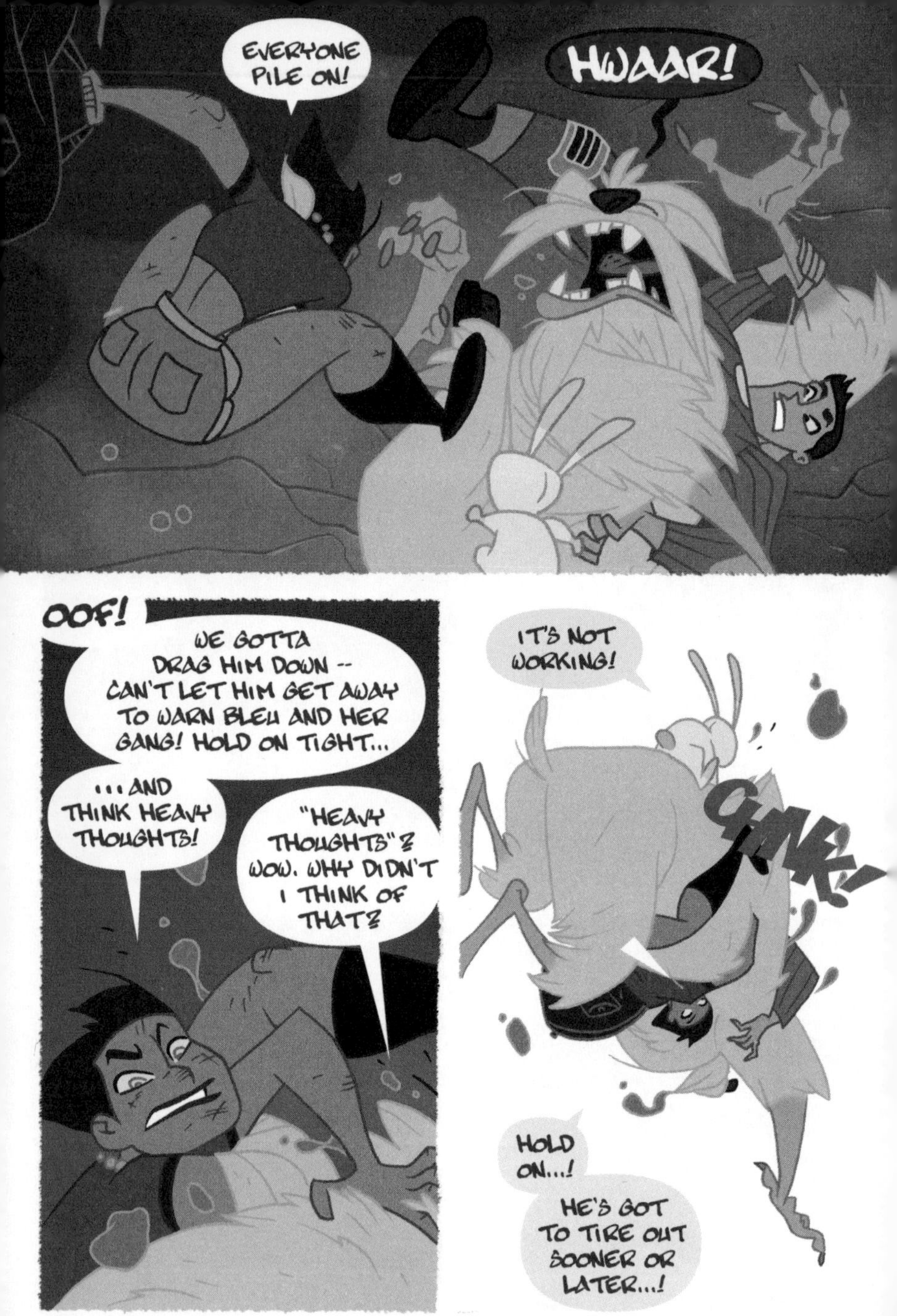
EVERYONE PILE ON!
HWAAR!
OOF!
WE GOTTA DRAG HIM DOWN -- CAN'T LET HIM GET AWAY TO WARN BLEU AND HER GANG! HOLD ON TIGHT...
...AND THINK HEAVY THOUGHTS!
"HEAVY THOUGHTS"? WOW. WHY DIDN'T I THINK OF THAT?
IT'S NOT WORKING!
GHAK!
HOLD ON...!
HE'S GOT TO TIRE OUT SOONER OR LATER...!

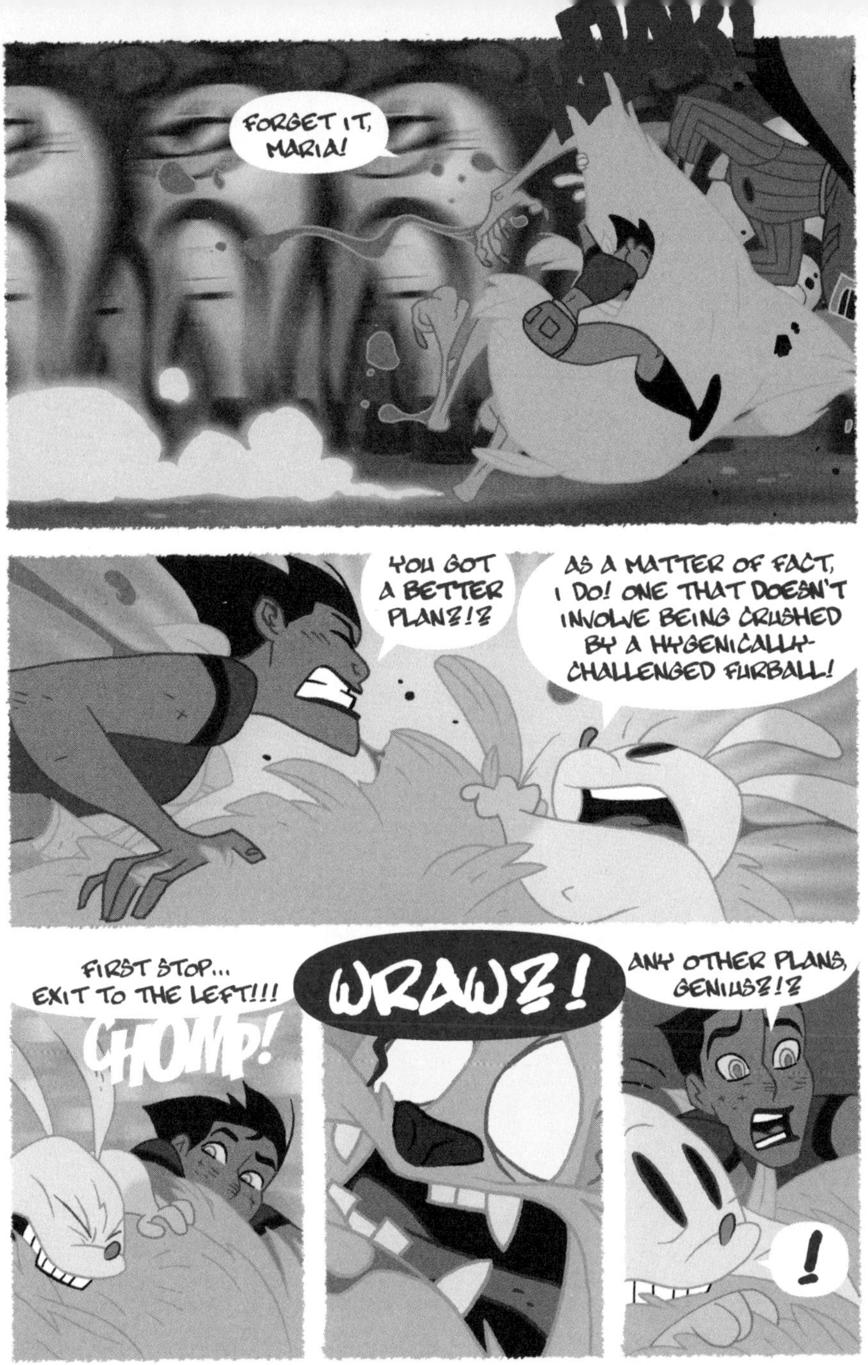
FORGET IT, MARIA!
YOU GOT A BETTER PLAN?!?
AS A MATTER OF FACT, I DO! ONE THAT DOESN'T INVOLVE BEING CRUSHED BY A HYGENICALLY-CHALLENGED FURBALL!
FIRST STOP... EXIT TO THE LEFT!!!
CHOMP!
WRAWZ!
ANY OTHER PLANS, GENIUS?!?
!

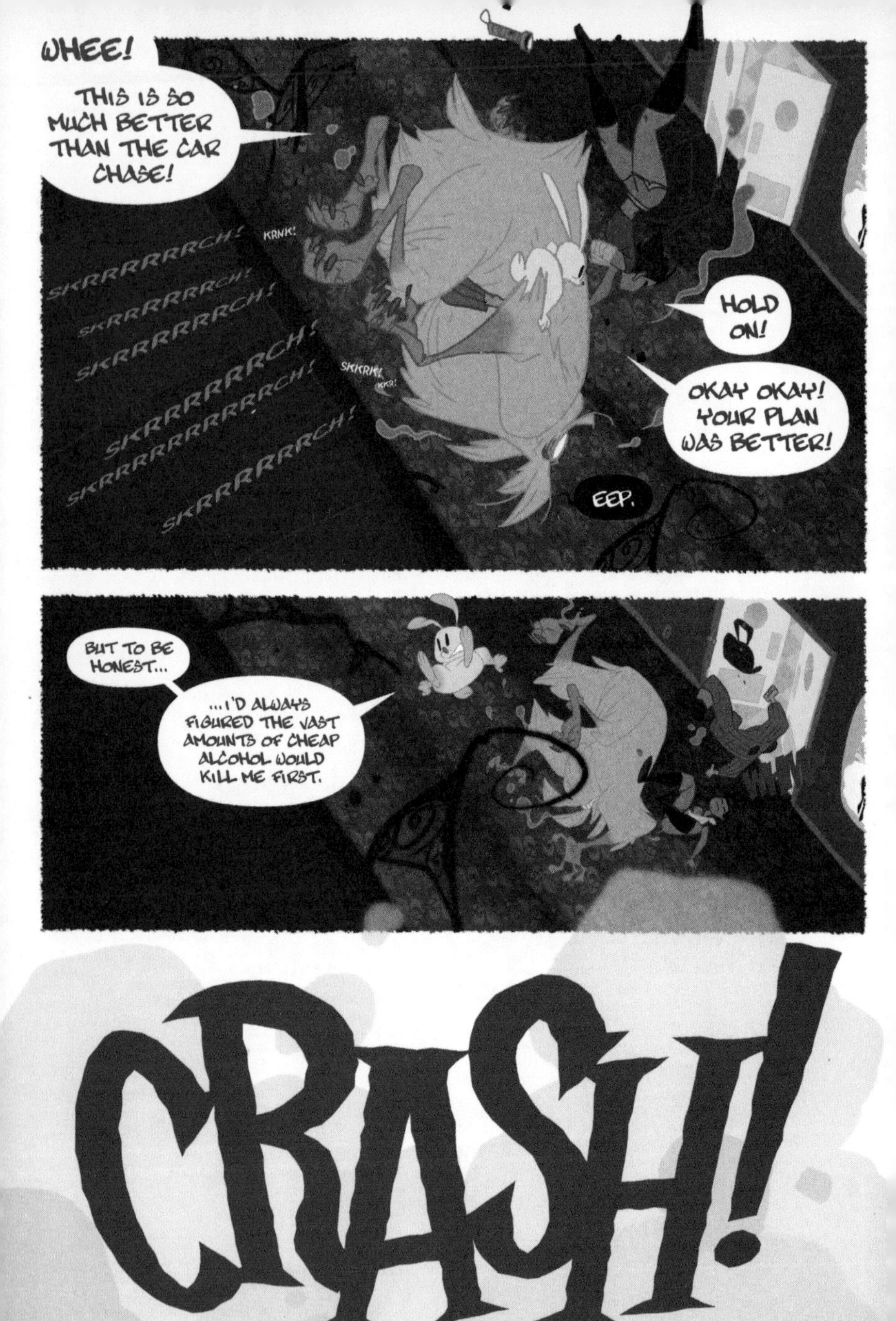
WHEE!
THIS IS SO MUCH BETTER THAN THE CAR CHASE!
KRNK!
SKRRRRRRCH!
SKRRRRRRRCH!
SKRRRRRRRCH!
SKRRRRRRRCH!
SKKRK!
KKR!
SKRRRRRRRRRCH!
SKRRRRRRRCH!
HOLD ON!
OKAY OKAY! YOUR PLAN WAS BETTER!
EEP.
BUT TO BE HONEST...
...I'D ALWAYS FIGURED THE VAST AMOUNTS OF CHEAP ALCOHOL WOULD KILL ME FIRST.
CRASH!

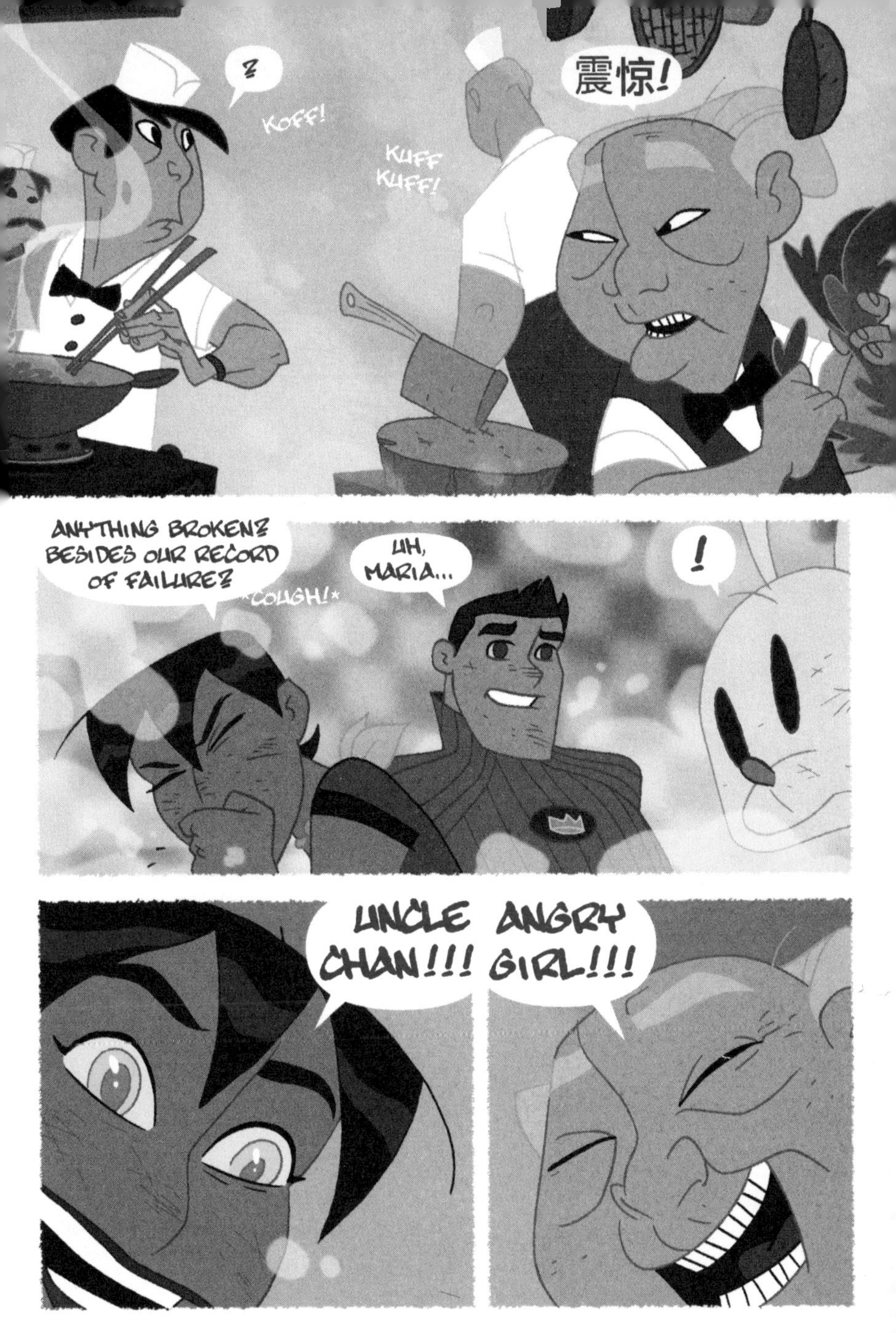
?
KOFF!
KUFF KUFF!
震惊!
ANYTHING BROKEN? BESIDES OUR RECORD OF FAILURE?
COUGH!
UH, MARIA...
!
UNCLE CHAN!!!
ANGRY GIRL!!!

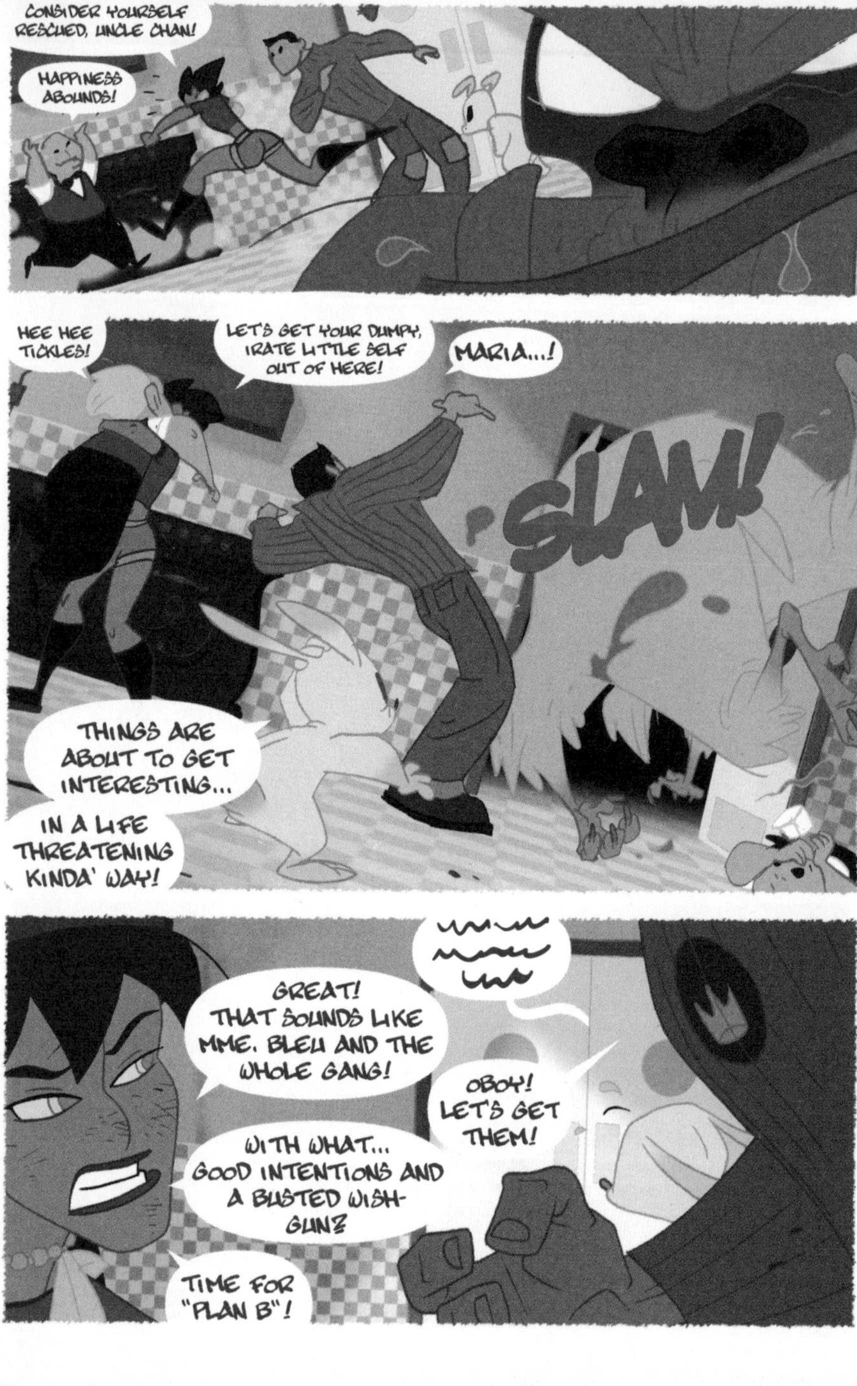
CONSIDER YOURSELF RESCUED, UNCLE CHAN!
HAPPINESS ABOUNDS!
HEE HEE TICKLES!
LET'S GET YOUR DUMPY, IRATE LITTLE SELF OUT OF HERE!
MARIA...!
SLAM!
THINGS ARE ABOUT TO GET INTERESTING...
IN A LIFE THREATENING KINDA' WAY!
GREAT! THAT SOUNDS LIKE MME. BLEU AND THE WHOLE GANG!
OBOY! LET'S GET THEM!
WITH WHAT... GOOD INTENTIONS AND A BUSTED WISH-GUN?
TIME FOR "PLAN B"!

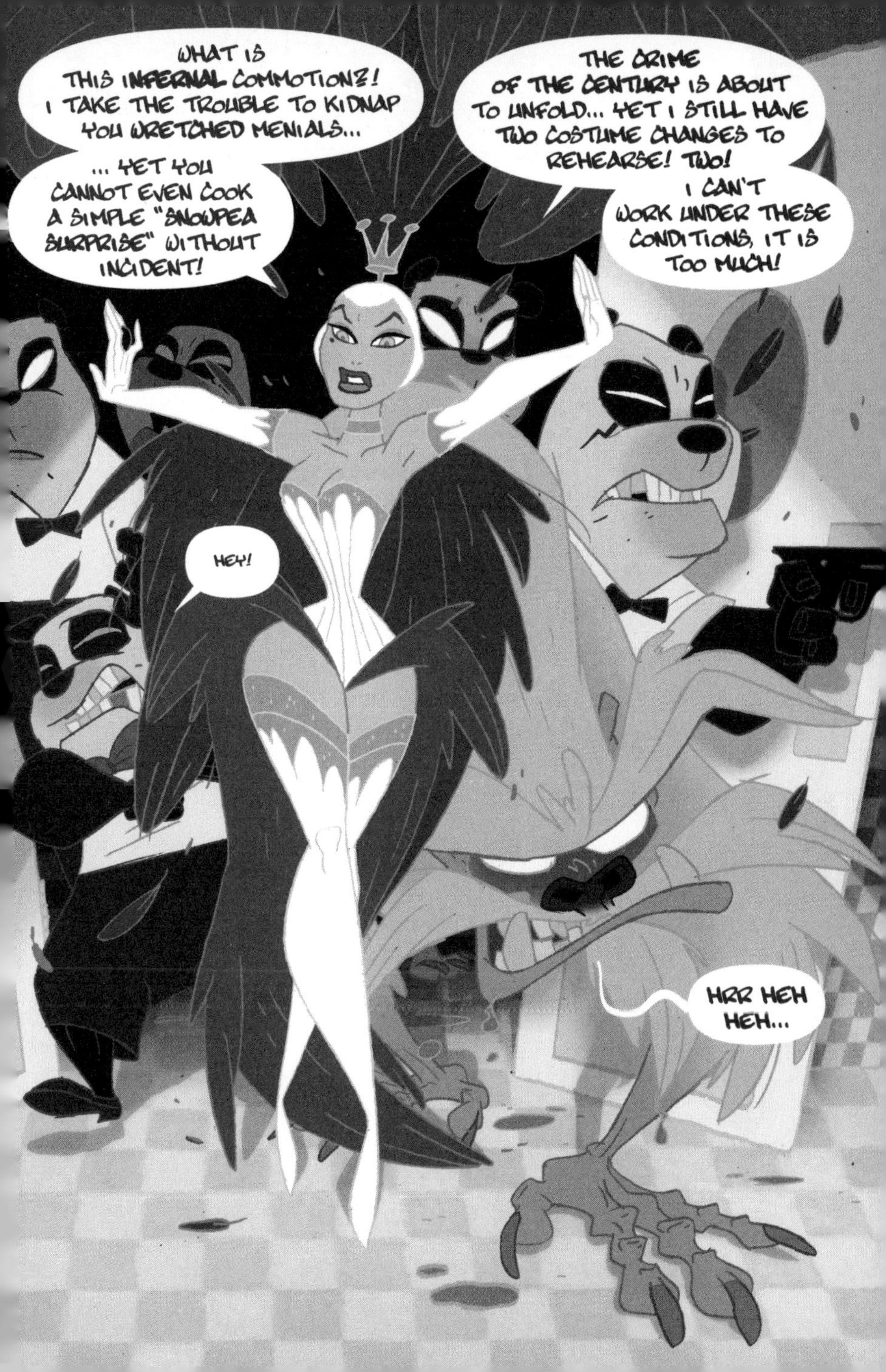
WHAT IS THIS INFERNAL COMMOTION?! I TAKE THE TROUBLE TO KIDNAP YOU WRETCHED MENIALS...
... YET YOU CANNOT EVEN COOK A SIMPLE "SNOWPEA SURPRISE" WITHOUT INCIDENT!
THE CRIME OF THE CENTURY IS ABOUT TO UNFOLD... YET I STILL HAVE TWO COSTUME CHANGES TO REHEARSE! TWO!
I CAN'T WORK UNDER THESE CONDITIONS, IT IS TOO MUCH!
HEY!
HRR HEH HEH...

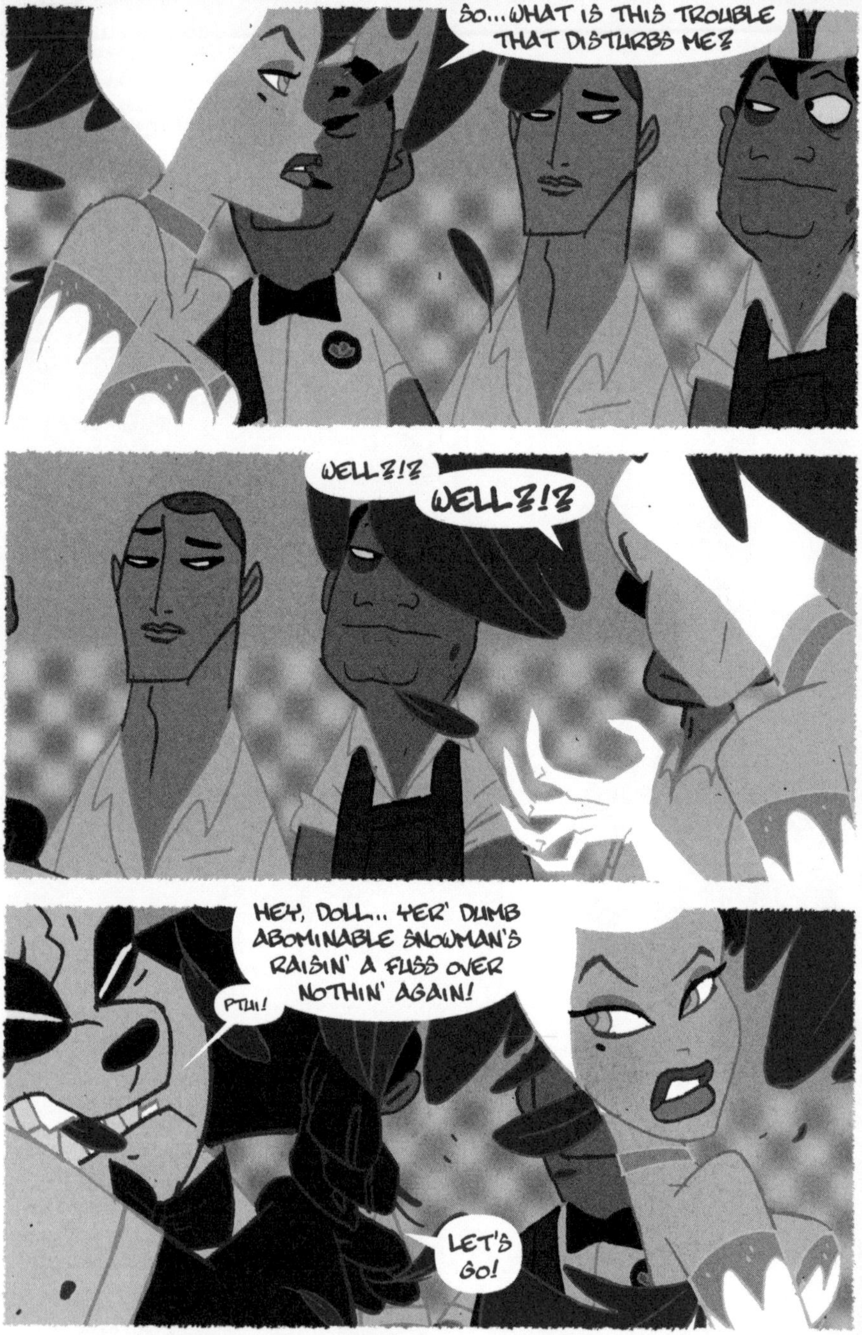
SO... WHAT IS THIS TROUBLE THAT DISTURBS ME?
WELL?!?
WELL?!?
HEY, DOLL... YER' DUMB ABOMINABLE SNOWMAN'S RAISIN' A FUSS OVER NOTHIN' AGAIN!
PTUI!
LET'S GO!

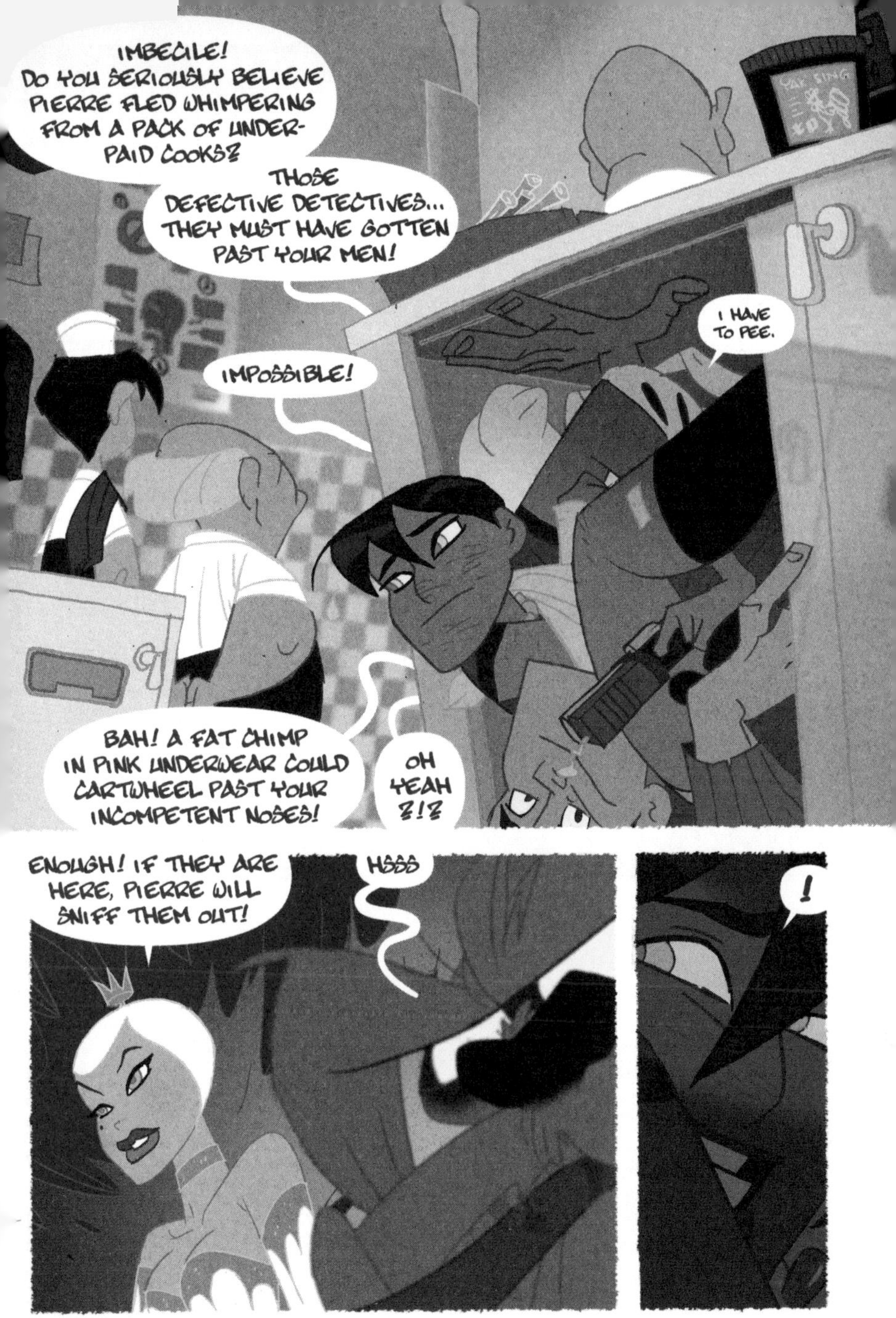
IMBECILE! DO YOU SERIOUSLY BELIEVE PIERRE FLED WHIMPERING FROM A PACK OF UNDER-PAID COOKS?!
THOSE DEFECTIVE DETECTIVES... THEY MUST HAVE GOTTEN PAST YOUR MEN!
I HAVE TO PEE.
IMPOSSIBLE!
BAH! A FAT CHIMP IN PINK UNDERWEAR COULD CARTWHEEL PAST YOUR INCOMPETENT NOSES!
OH YEAH ?!?
ENOUGH! IF THEY ARE HERE, PIERRE WILL SNIFF THEM OUT!
HSSS
!

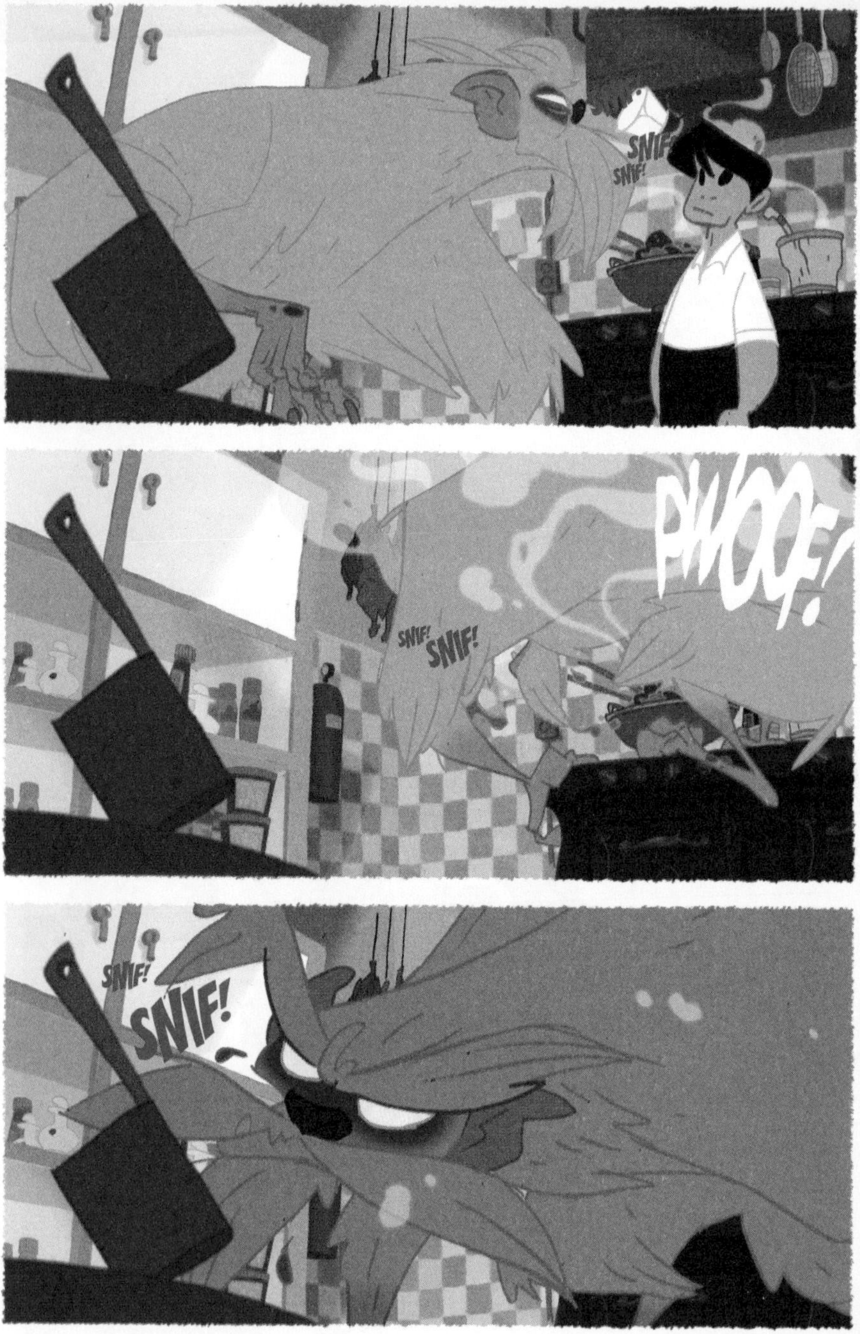
SNIF!
SNIF!
SNIF!
SNIF!
PHOOF!
SNIF!
SNIF!

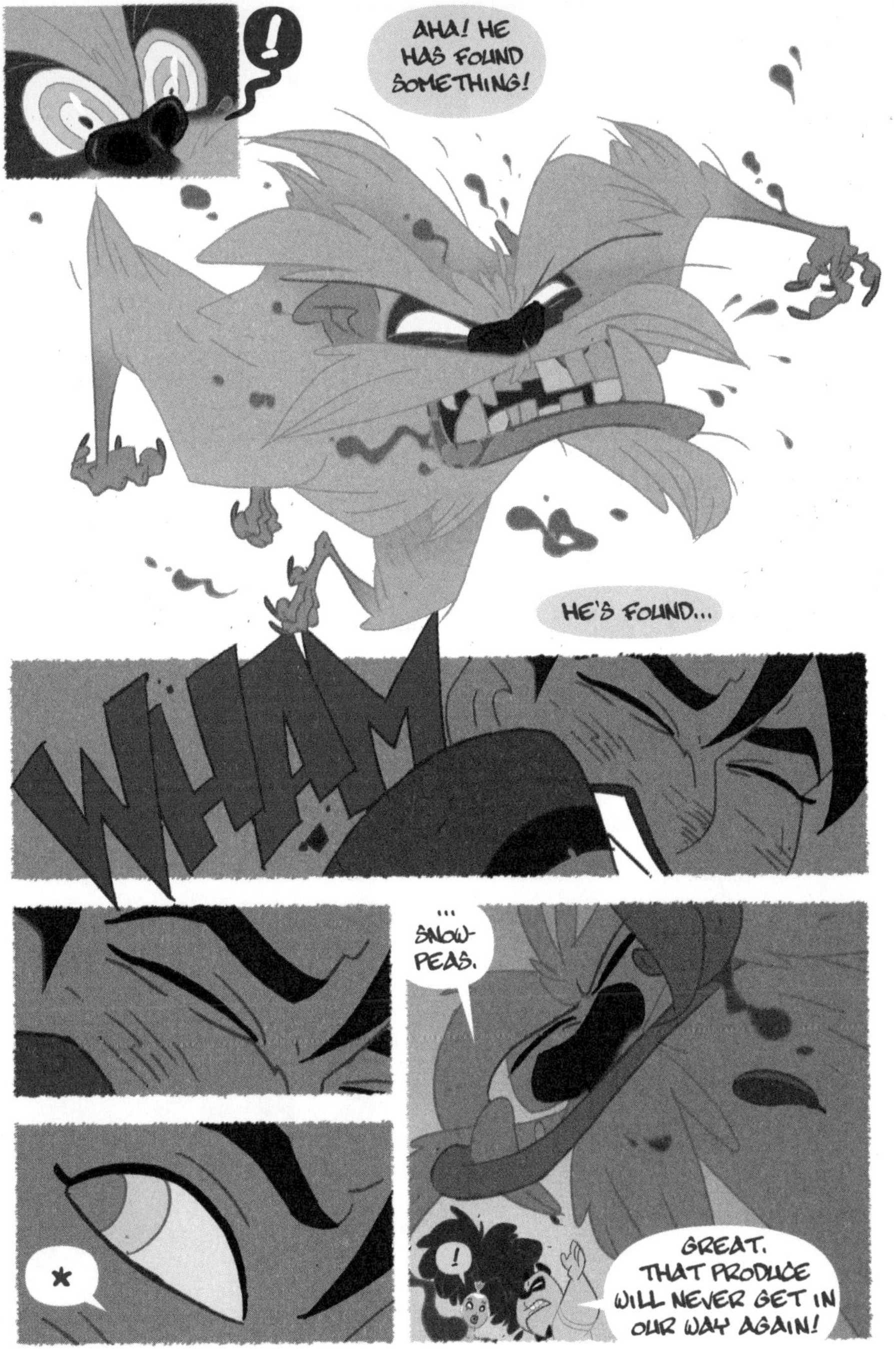
!
AHA! HE HAS FOUND SOMETHING!
HE'S FOUND...
WHAM
... SNOW-PEAS.
*
!
GREAT. THAT PRODUCE WILL NEVER GET IN OUR WAY AGAIN!

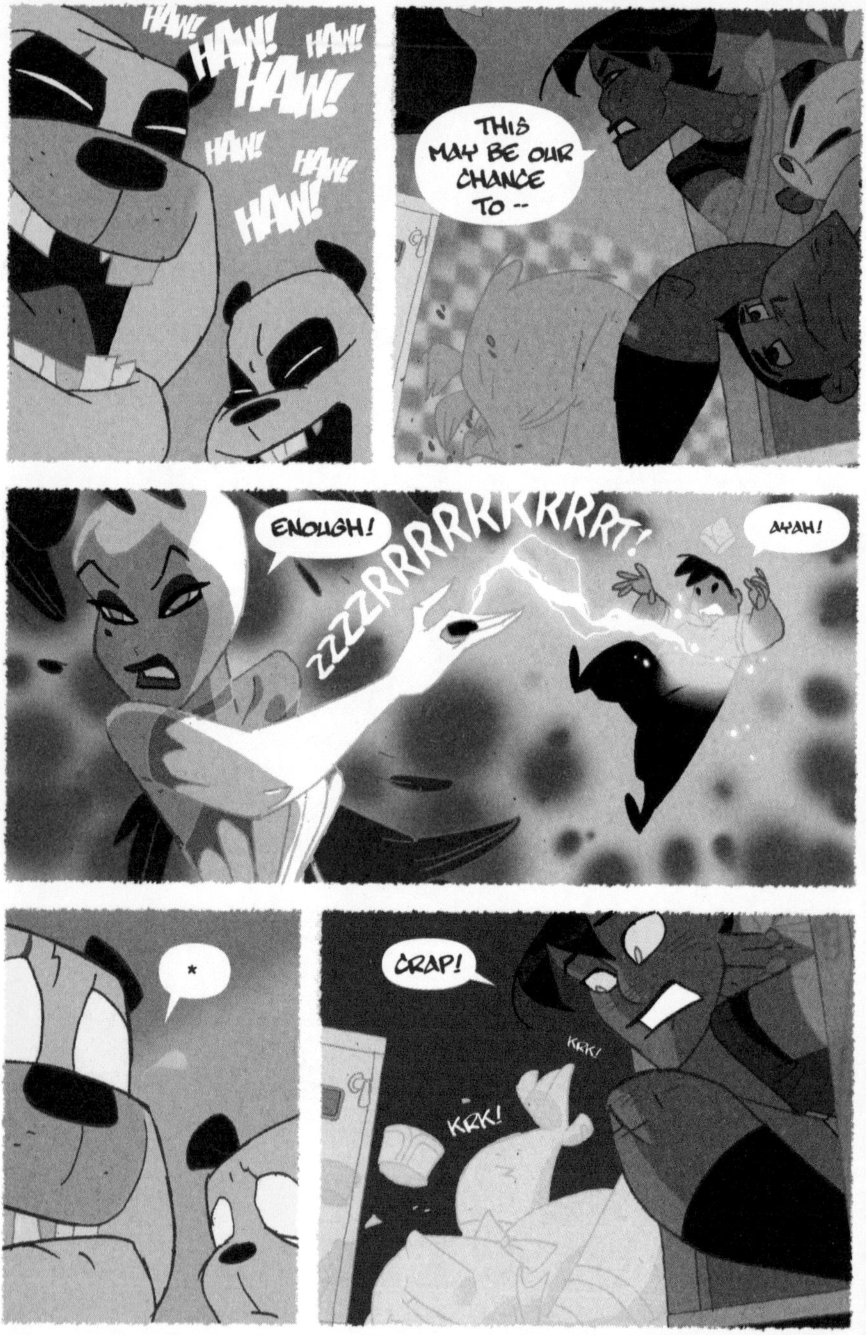
HAW!
HAW!
HAW!
HAW!
HAW!
HAW!
HAW!
THIS MAY BE OUR CHANCE TO --
ENOUGH!
ZZZZRRRRRKKRRRT!
AYAH!
*
CRAP!
KRK!
KRK!

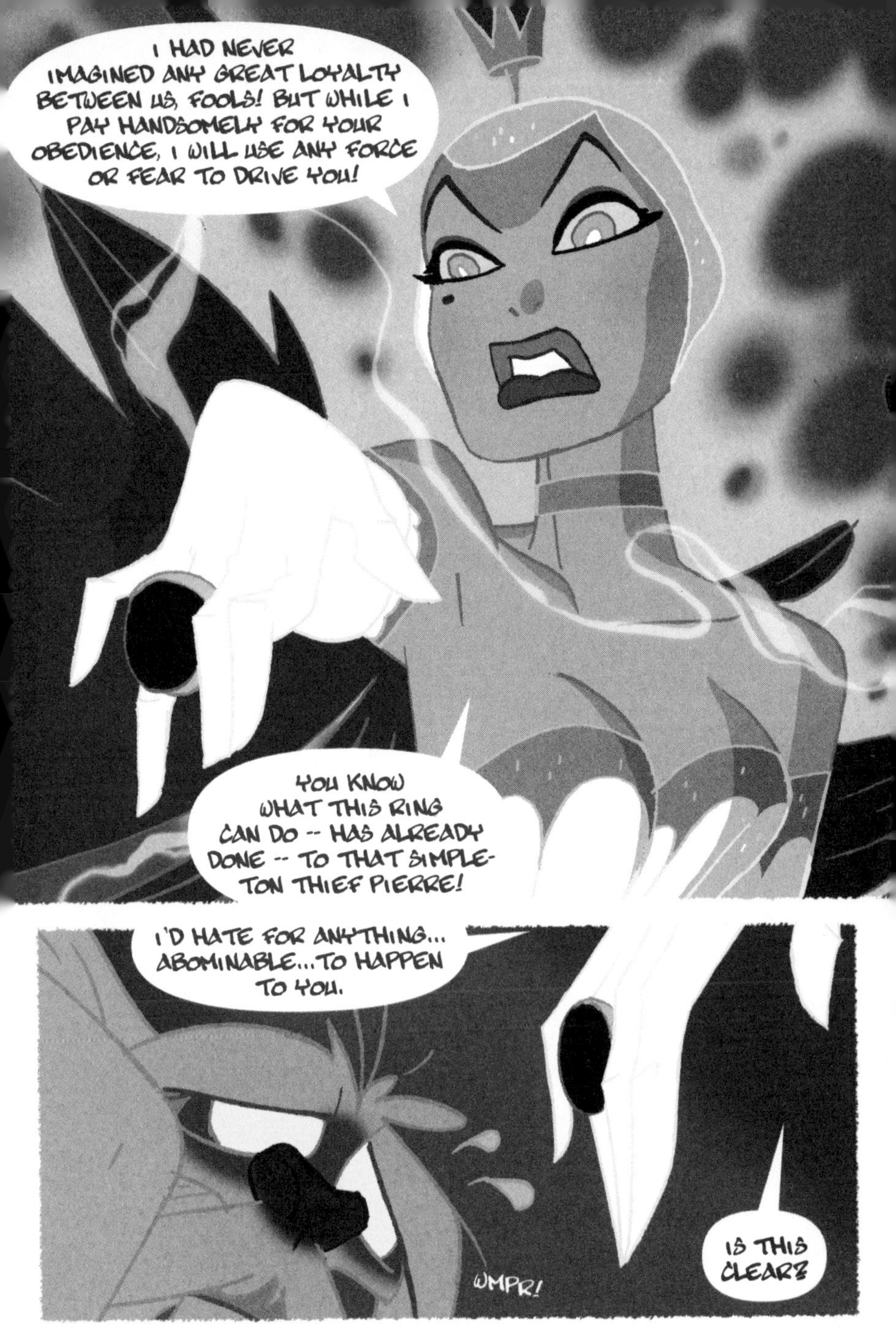
I HAD NEVER IMAGINED ANY GREAT LOYALTY BETWEEN US, FOOLS! BUT WHILE I PAY HANDSOMELY FOR YOUR OBEDIENCE, I WILL USE ANY FORCE OR FEAR TO DRIVE YOU!
YOU KNOW WHAT THIS RING CAN DO -- HAS ALREADY DONE -- TO THAT SIMPLE-TON THIEF PIERRE!
I'D HATE FOR ANYTHING... ABOMINABLE... TO HAPPEN TO YOU.
WMPR!
IS THIS CLEAR?

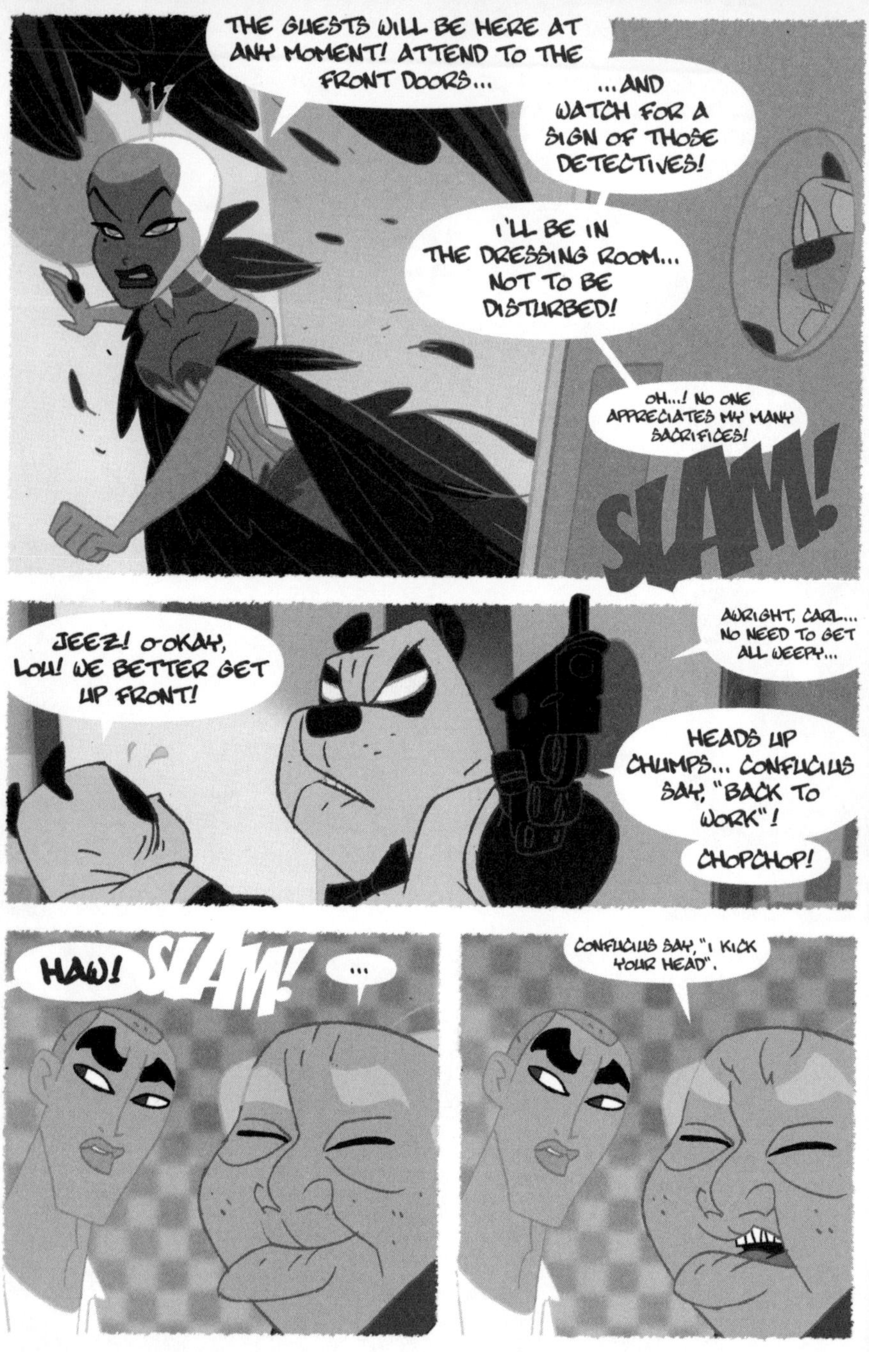
THE GUESTS WILL BE HERE AT ANY MOMENT! ATTEND TO THE FRONT DOORS...
...AND WATCH FOR A SIGN OF THOSE DETECTIVES!
I'LL BE IN THE DRESSING ROOM... NOT TO BE DISTURBED!
OH...! NO ONE APPRECIATES MY MANY SACRIFICES!
SLAM!
JEEZ! O-OKAY, LOU! WE BETTER GET UP FRONT!
AWRIGHT, CARL... NO NEED TO GET ALL WEEPY...
HEADS UP CHUMPS... CONFUCIUS SAY, "BACK TO WORK"!
CHOPCHOP!
HAW!
SLAM!
...
CONFUCIUS SAY, "I KICK YOUR HEAD".

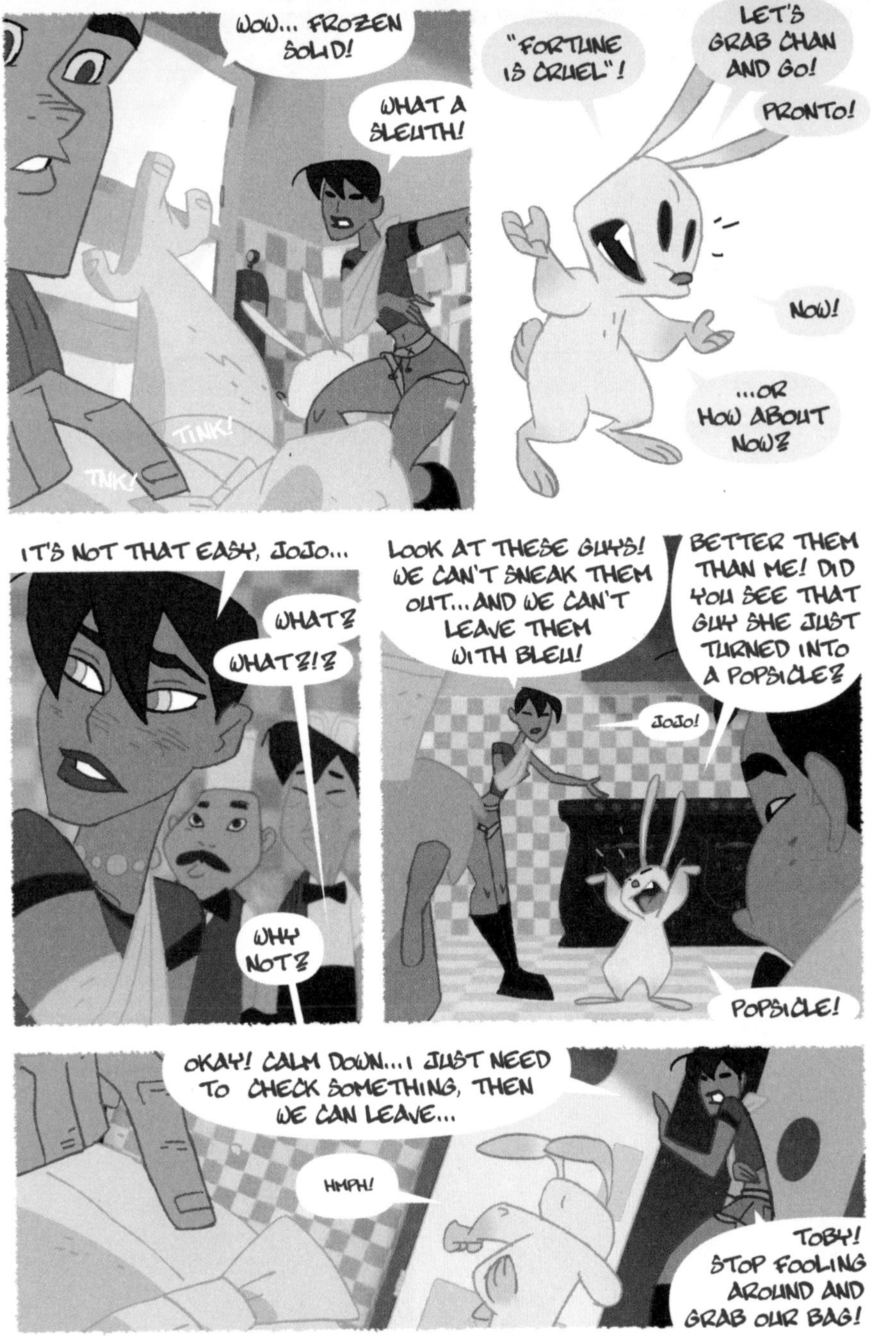
WOW... FROZEN SOLID!
WHAT A SLEUTH!
TINK!
TINK!
"FORTUNE IS CRUEL"!
LET'S GRAB CHAN AND GO!
PRONTO!
NOW!
...OR HOW ABOUT NOW?
IT'S NOT THAT EASY, JOJO...
WHAT?
WHAT?!?
WHY NOT?
LOOK AT THESE GUYS! WE CAN'T SNEAK THEM OUT...AND WE CAN'T LEAVE THEM WITH BLEU!
BETTER THEM THAN ME! DID YOU SEE THAT GUY SHE JUST TURNED INTO A POPSICLE?
JOJO!
POPSICLE!
OKAY! CALM DOWN...I JUST NEED TO CHECK SOMETHING, THEN WE CAN LEAVE...
HMPH!
TOBY! STOP FOOLING AROUND AND GRAB OUR BAG!

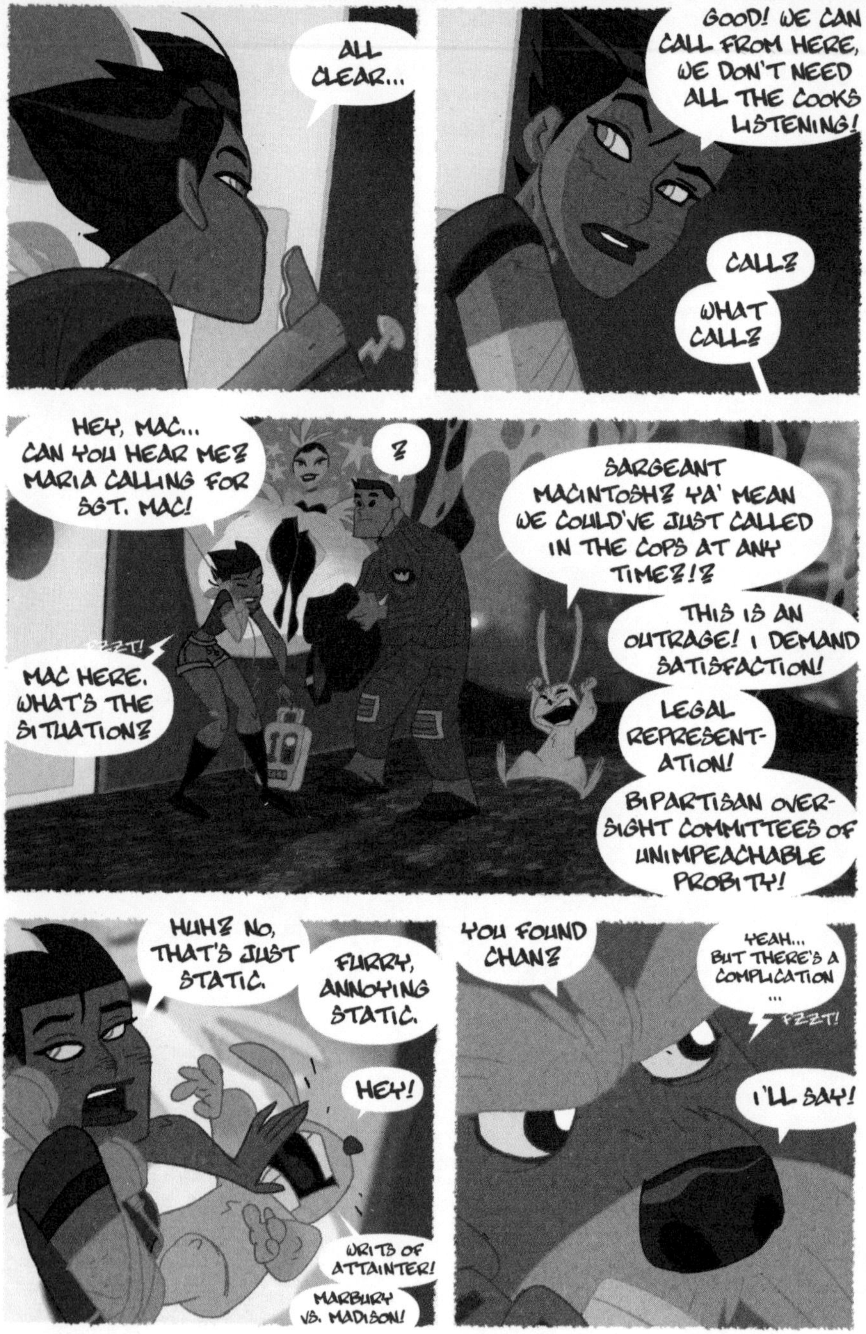
ALL CLEAR...
GOOD! WE CAN CALL FROM HERE, WE DON'T NEED ALL THE COOKS LISTENING!
CALL?
WHAT CALL?
HEY, MAC... CAN YOU HEAR ME? MARIA CALLING FOR SGT. MAC!
?
SARGEANT MACINTOSH? YA' MEAN WE COULD'VE JUST CALLED IN THE COPS AT ANY TIME?!?
FZZT!
MAC HERE. WHAT'S THE SITUATION?
THIS IS AN OUTRAGE! I DEMAND SATISFACTION!
LEGAL REPRESENT-ATION!
BIPARTISAN OVER-SIGHT COMMITTEES OF UNIMPEACHABLE PROBITY!
HUH? NO, THAT'S JUST STATIC.
FURRY, ANNOYING STATIC.
HEY!
WRITS OF ATTAINTER!
MARBURY VS. MADISON!
YOU FOUND CHAN?
YEAH... BUT THERE'S A COMPLICATION ...
FZZT!
I'LL SAY!

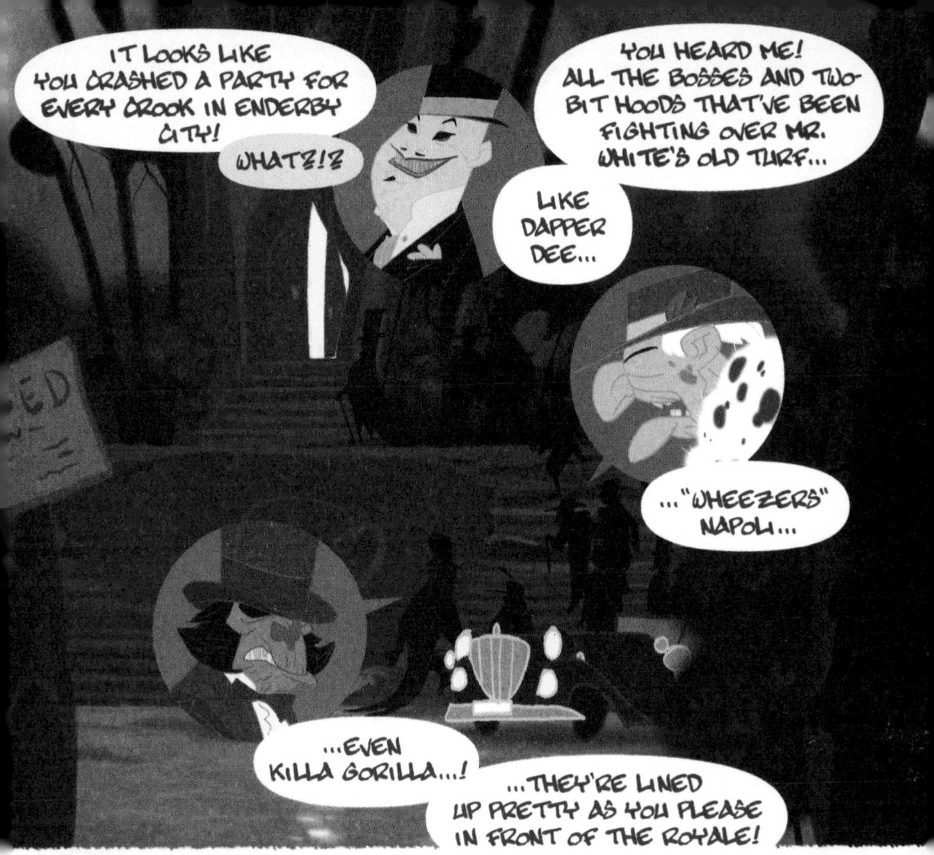
IT LOOKS LIKE YOU CRASHED A PARTY FOR EVERY CROOK IN ENDERBY CITY!
WHAT?!?
YOU HEARD ME! ALL THE BOSSES AND TWO-BIT HOODS THAT'VE BEEN FIGHTING OVER MR. WHITE'S OLD TURF...
LIKE DAPPER DEE...
..."WHEEZERS" NAPOLI...
...EVEN KILLA GORILLA...!
...THEY'RE LINED UP PRETTY AS YOU PLEASE IN FRONT OF THE ROYALE!
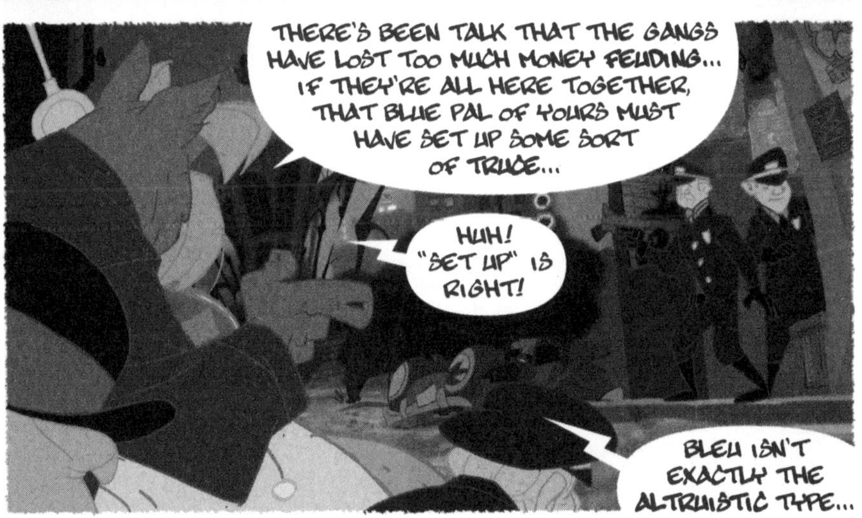
THERE'S BEEN TALK THAT THE GANGS HAVE LOST TOO MUCH MONEY FEUDING... IF THEY'RE ALL HERE TOGETHER, THAT BLUE PAL OF YOURS MUST HAVE SET UP SOME SORT OF TRUCE...
HUH! "SET UP" IS RIGHT!
BLEU ISN'T EXACTLY THE ALTRUISTIC TYPE...

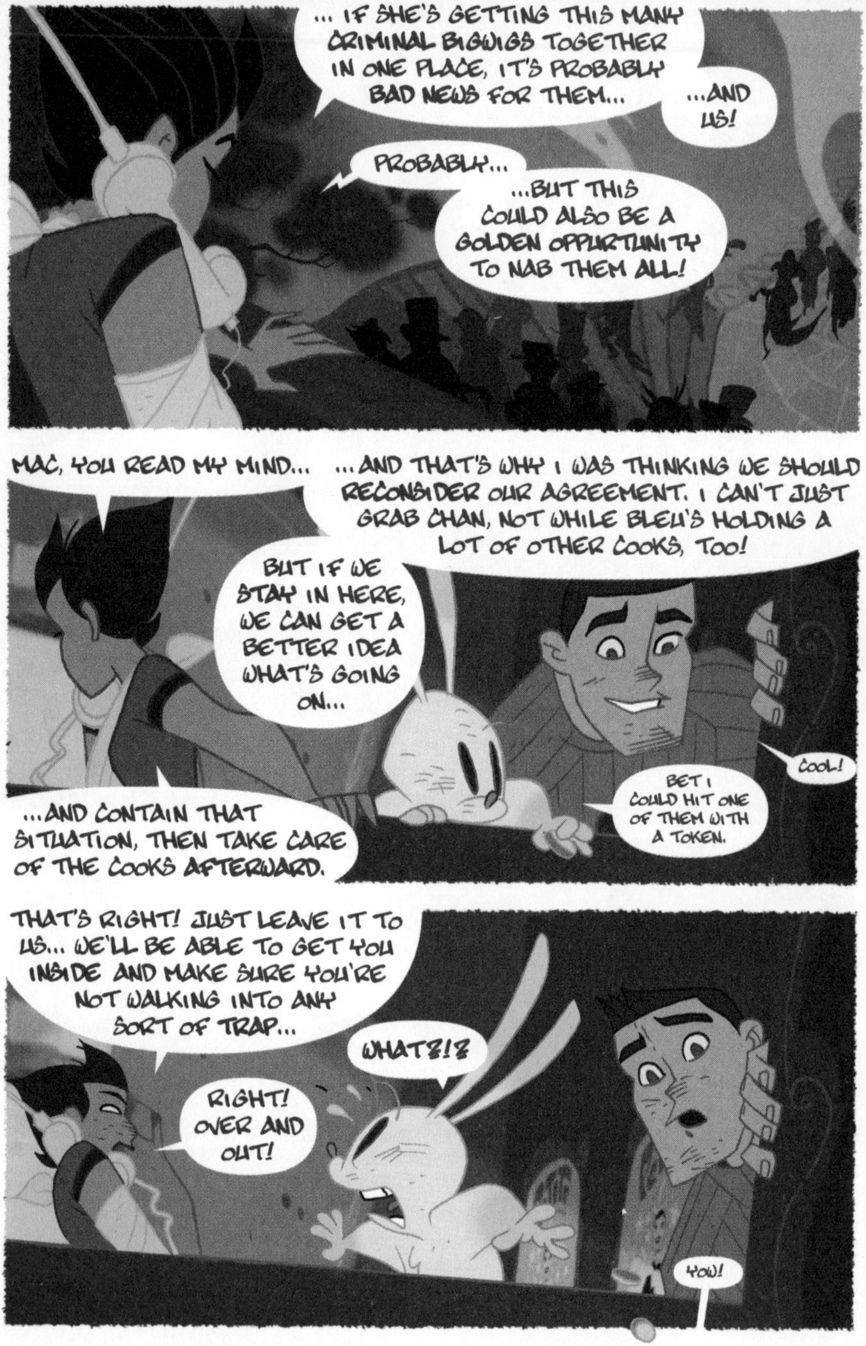
... IF SHE'S GETTING THIS MANY CRIMINAL BIGWIGS TOGETHER IN ONE PLACE, IT'S PROBABLY BAD NEWS FOR THEM...
...AND US!
PROBABLY...
...BUT THIS COULD ALSO BE A GOLDEN OPPURTUNITY TO NAB THEM ALL!
MAC, YOU READ MY MIND...
...AND THAT'S WHY I WAS THINKING WE SHOULD RECONSIDER OUR AGREEMENT. I CAN'T JUST GRAB CHAN, NOT WHILE BLEU'S HOLDING A LOT OF OTHER COOKS, TOO!
BUT IF WE STAY IN HERE, WE CAN GET A BETTER IDEA WHAT'S GOING ON...
...AND CONTAIN THAT SITUATION, THEN TAKE CARE OF THE COOKS AFTERWARD.
COOL!
BET I COULD HIT ONE OF THEM WITH A TOKEN.
THAT'S RIGHT! JUST LEAVE IT TO US... WE'LL BE ABLE TO GET YOU INSIDE AND MAKE SURE YOU'RE NOT WALKING INTO ANY SORT OF TRAP...
WHAT?!?
RIGHT! OVER AND OUT!
YOW!

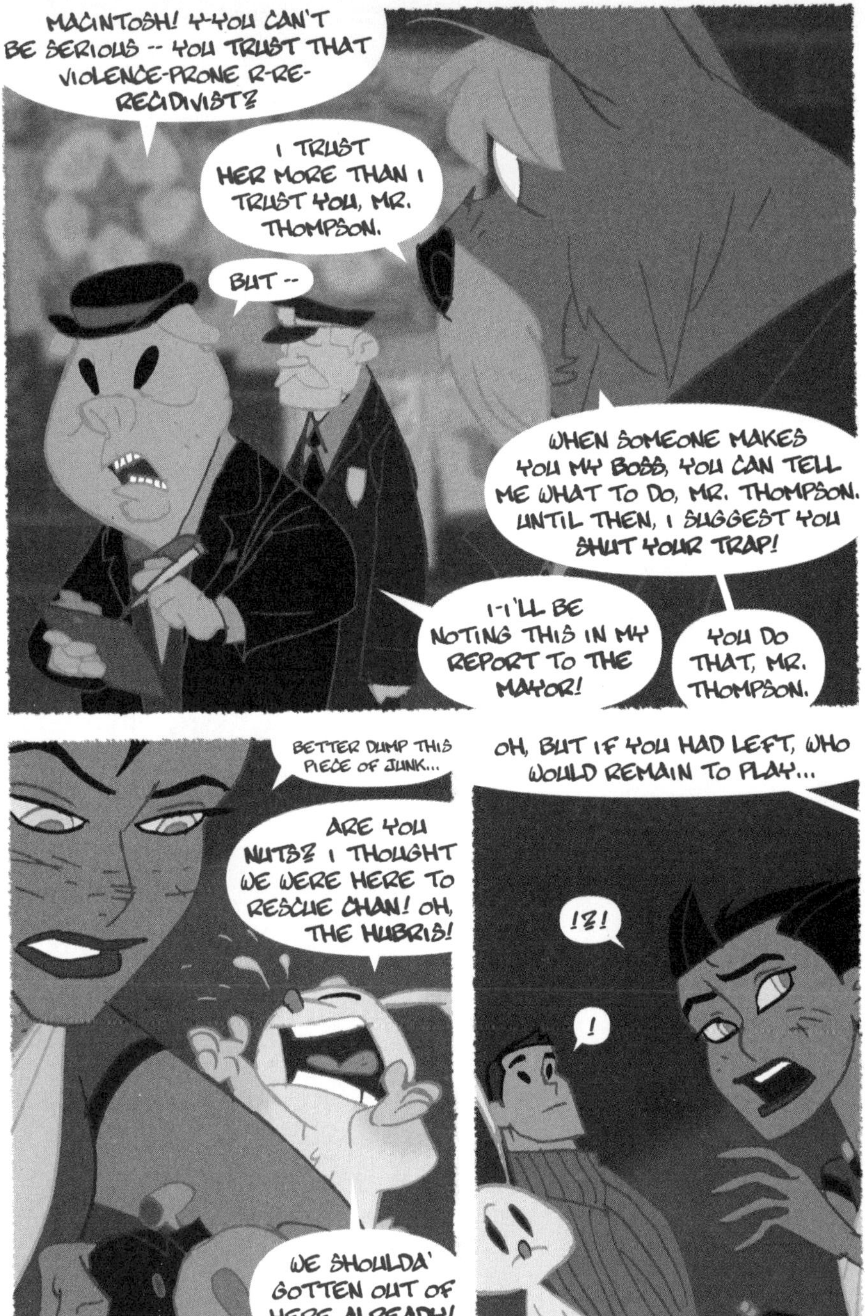
MACINTOSH! Y-YOU CAN'T BE SERIOUS -- YOU TRUST THAT VIOLENCE-PRONE R-RE-RECIDIVIST?
I TRUST HER MORE THAN I TRUST YOU, MR. THOMPSON.
BUT --
WHEN SOMEONE MAKES YOU MY BOSS, YOU CAN TELL ME WHAT TO DO, MR. THOMPSON. UNTIL THEN, I SUGGEST YOU SHUT YOUR TRAP!
I-I'LL BE NOTING THIS IN MY REPORT TO THE MAYOR!
YOU DO THAT, MR. THOMPSON.
BETTER DUMP THIS PIECE OF JUNK...
ARE YOU NUTS? I THOUGHT WE WERE HERE TO RESCUE CHAN! OH, THE HUBRIS!
WE SHOULDA' GOTTEN OUT OF HERE ALREADY!
OH, BUT IF YOU HAD LEFT, WHO WOULD REMAIN TO PLAY...
!?!
!

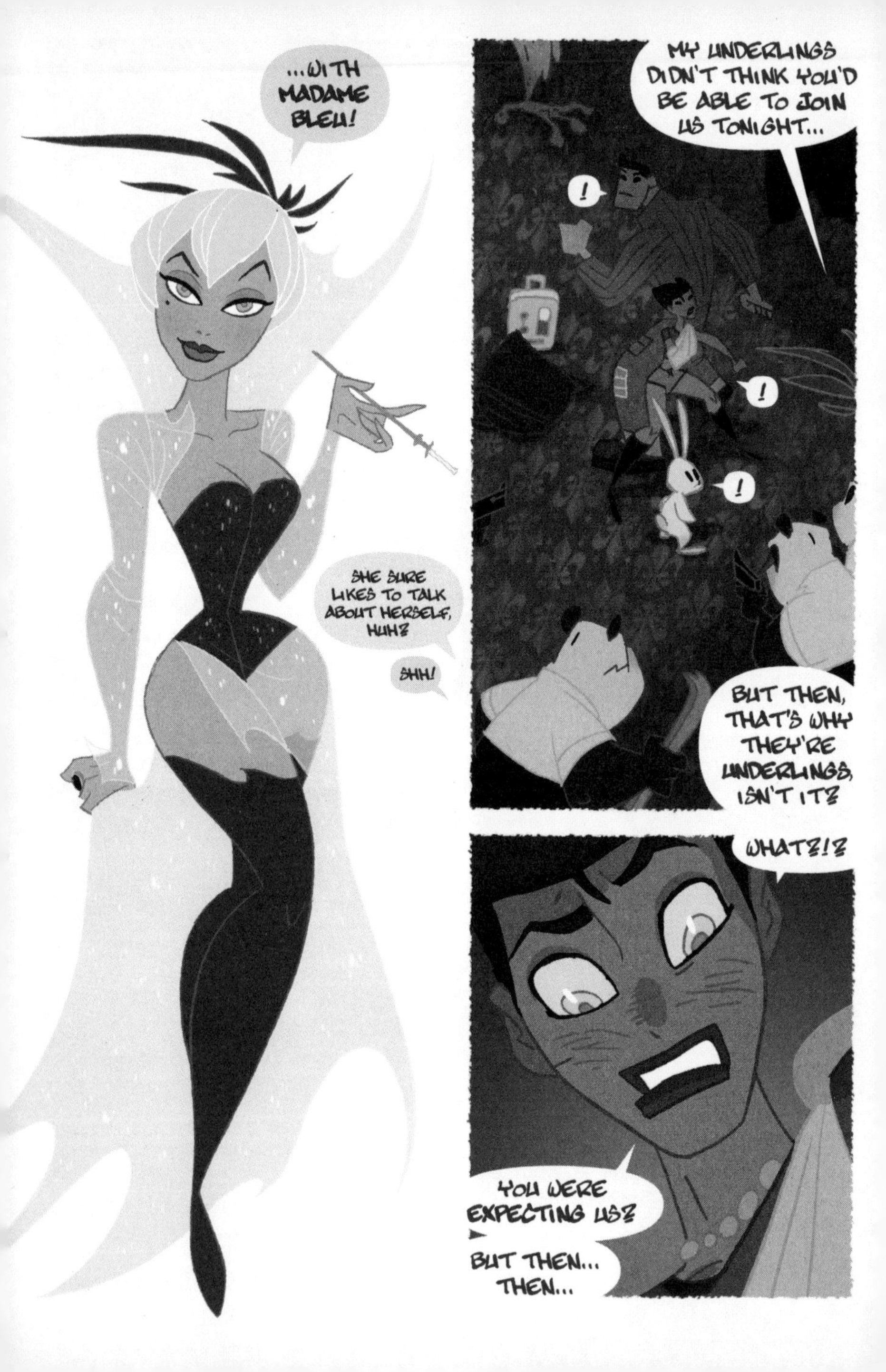
...WITH MADAME BLEU!
SHE SURE LIKES TO TALK ABOUT HERSELF, HUH?
SHH!
MY UNDERLINGS DIDN'T THINK YOU'D BE ABLE TO JOIN US TONIGHT...
!
!
!
BUT THEN, THAT'S WHY THEY'RE UNDERLINGS, ISN'T IT?
WHAT?!?
YOU WERE EXPECTING US?
BUT THEN... THEN...

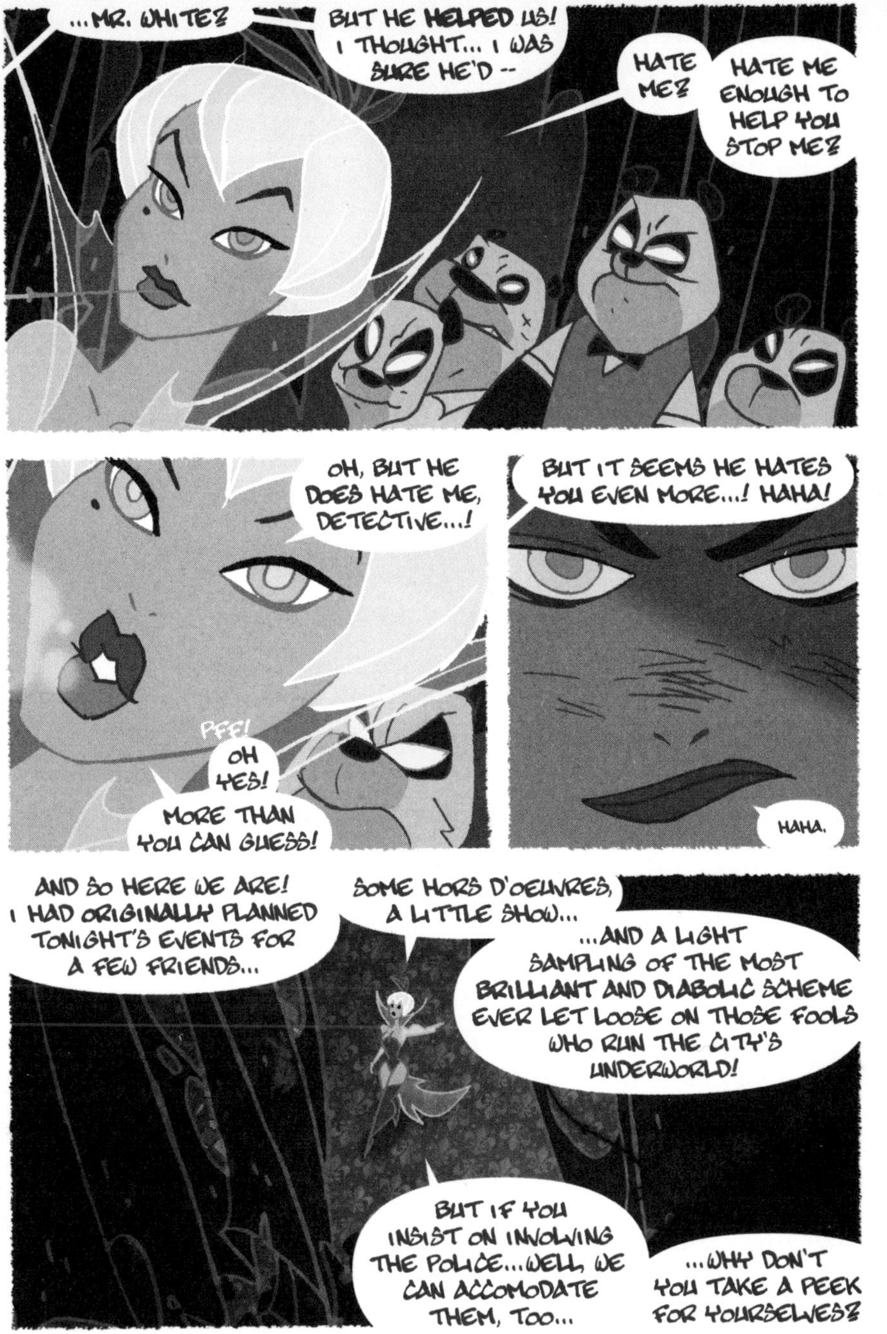
...MR. WHITE?
BUT HE HELPED US! I THOUGHT... I WAS SURE HE'D --
HATE ME?
HATE ME ENOUGH TO HELP YOU STOP ME?
OH, BUT HE DOES HATE ME, DETECTIVE...!
PFE!
OH YES!
MORE THAN YOU CAN GUESS!
BUT IT SEEMS HE HATES YOU EVEN MORE...! HAHA!
HAHA.
AND SO HERE WE ARE! I HAD ORIGINALLY PLANNED TONIGHT'S EVENTS FOR A FEW FRIENDS...
SOME HORS D'OEUVRES, A LITTLE SHOW...
...AND A LIGHT SAMPLING OF THE MOST BRILLIANT AND DIABOLIC SCHEME EVER LET LOOSE ON THOSE FOOLS WHO RUN THE CITY'S UNDERWORLD!
BUT IF YOU INSIST ON INVOLVING THE POLICE...WELL, WE CAN ACCOMODATE THEM, TOO...
...WHY DON'T YOU TAKE A PEEK FOR YOURSELVES?

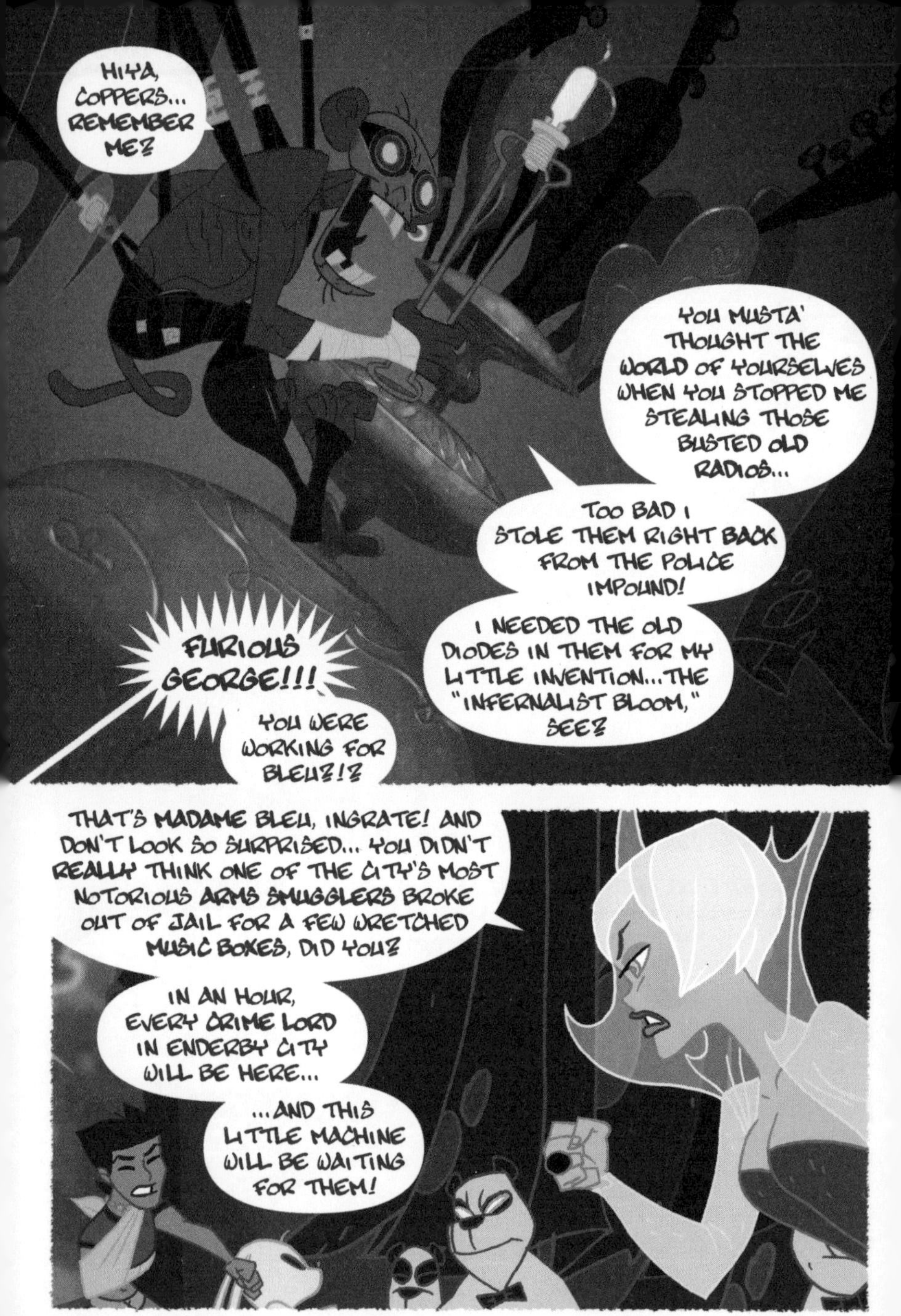
HIYA, COPPERS... REMEMBER ME?
YOU MUSTA' THOUGHT THE WORLD OF YOURSELVES WHEN YOU STOPPED ME STEALING THOSE BUSTED OLD RADIOS...
TOO BAD I STOLE THEM RIGHT BACK FROM THE POLICE IMPOUND!
I NEEDED THE OLD DIODES IN THEM FOR MY LITTLE INVENTION... THE "INFERNALIST BLOOM," SEE?
FURIOUS GEORGE!!!
YOU WERE WORKING FOR BLEU?!?
THAT'S MADAME BLEU, INGRATE! AND DON'T LOOK SO SURPRISED... YOU DIDN'T REALLY THINK ONE OF THE CITY'S MOST NOTORIOUS ARMS SMUGGLERS BROKE OUT OF JAIL FOR A FEW WRETCHED MUSIC BOXES, DID YOU?
IN AN HOUR, EVERY CRIME LORD IN ENDERBY CITY WILL BE HERE...
...AND THIS LITTLE MACHINE WILL BE WAITING FOR THEM!

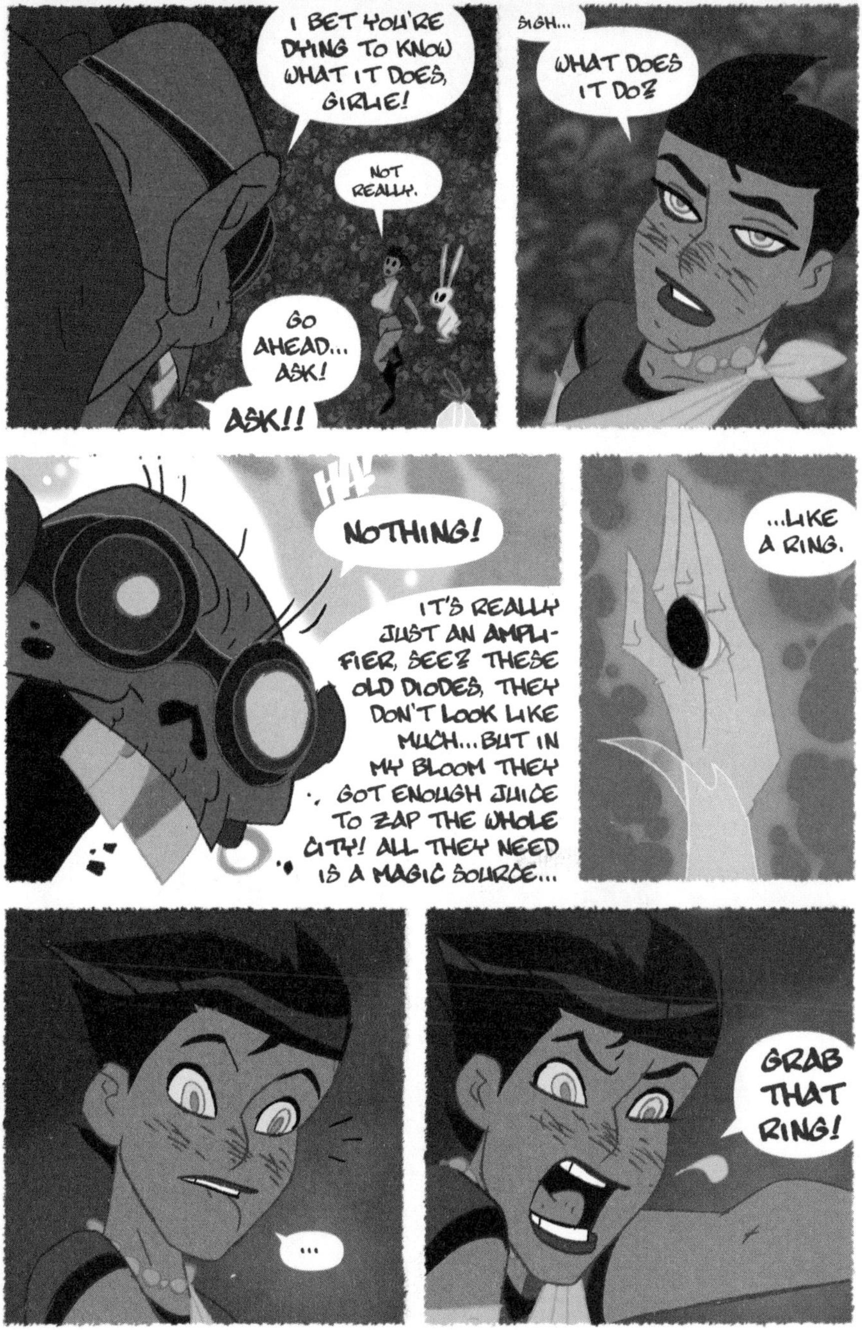
I BET YOU'RE DYING TO KNOW WHAT IT DOES, GIRLIE!
NOT REALLY.
GO AHEAD... ASK!
ASK!!
SIGH...
WHAT DOES IT DO?
HA!
NOTHING!
IT'S REALLY JUST AN AMPLIFIER, SEE? THESE OLD DIODES, THEY DON'T LOOK LIKE MUCH... BUT IN MY BLOOM THEY GOT ENOUGH JUICE TO ZAP THE WHOLE CITY! ALL THEY NEED IS A MAGIC SOURCE...
...LIKE A RING.
...
GRAB THAT RING!

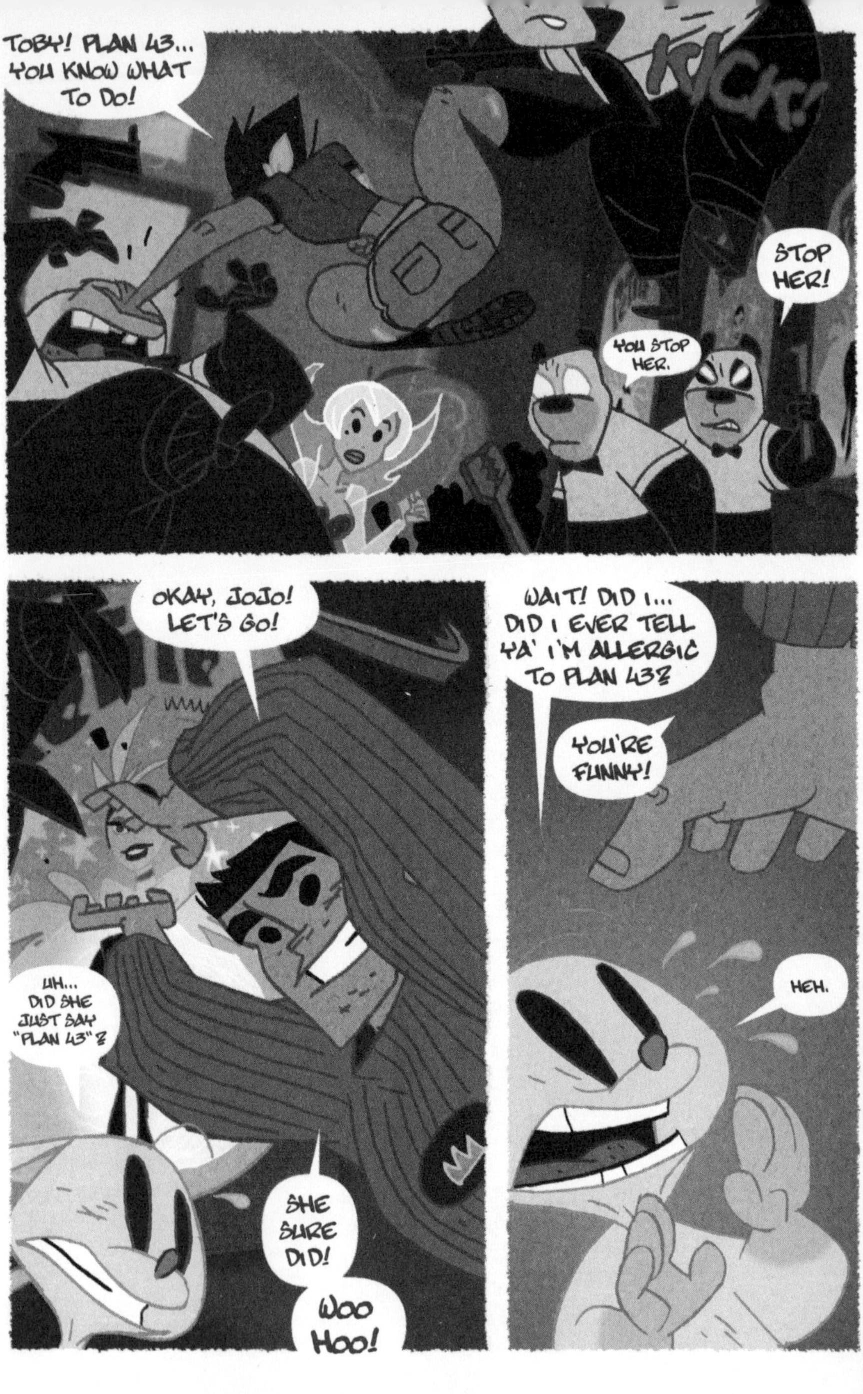

TOBY! PLAN 43...
YOU KNOW WHAT TO DO!
KICK!
STOP HER!
YOU STOP HER.
OKAY, JOJO! LET'S GO!
UH... DID SHE JUST SAY "PLAN 43"?
SHE SURE DID!
WOO HOO!
WAIT! DID I... DID I EVER TELL YA' I'M ALLERGIC TO PLAN 43?
YOU'RE FUNNY!
HEH.

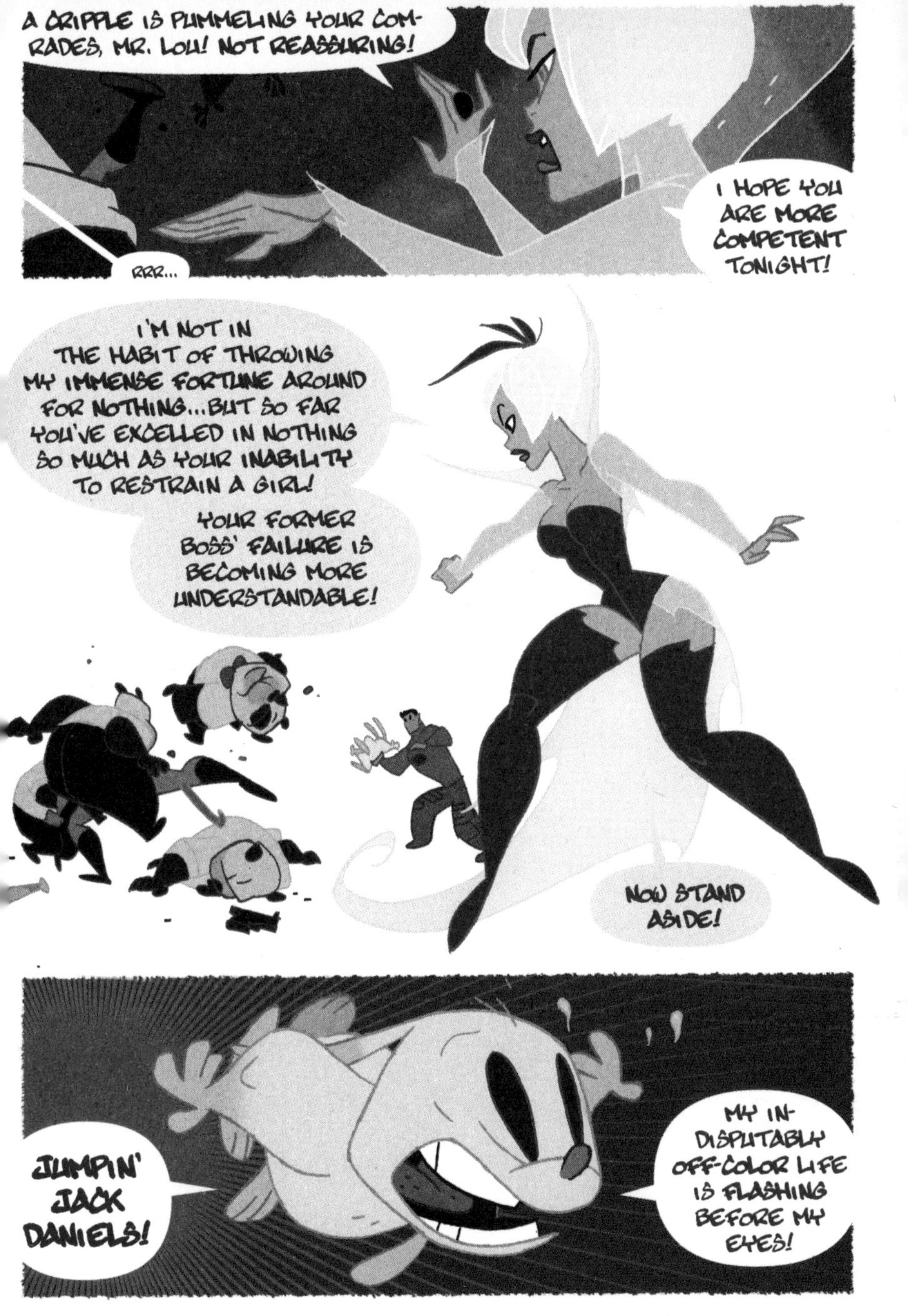
A CRIPPLE IS PUMMELING YOUR COMRADES, MR. LOU! NOT REASSURING!
RRR...
I HOPE YOU ARE MORE COMPETENT TONIGHT!
I'M NOT IN THE HABIT OF THROWING MY IMMENSE FORTUNE AROUND FOR NOTHING...BUT SO FAR YOU'VE EXCELLED IN NOTHING SO MUCH AS YOUR INABILITY TO RESTRAIN A GIRL!
YOUR FORMER BOSS' FAILURE IS BECOMING MORE UNDERSTANDABLE!
NOW STAND ASIDE!
JUMPIN' JACK DANIELS!
MY INDISPUTABLY OFF-COLOR LIFE IS FLASHING BEFORE MY EYES!

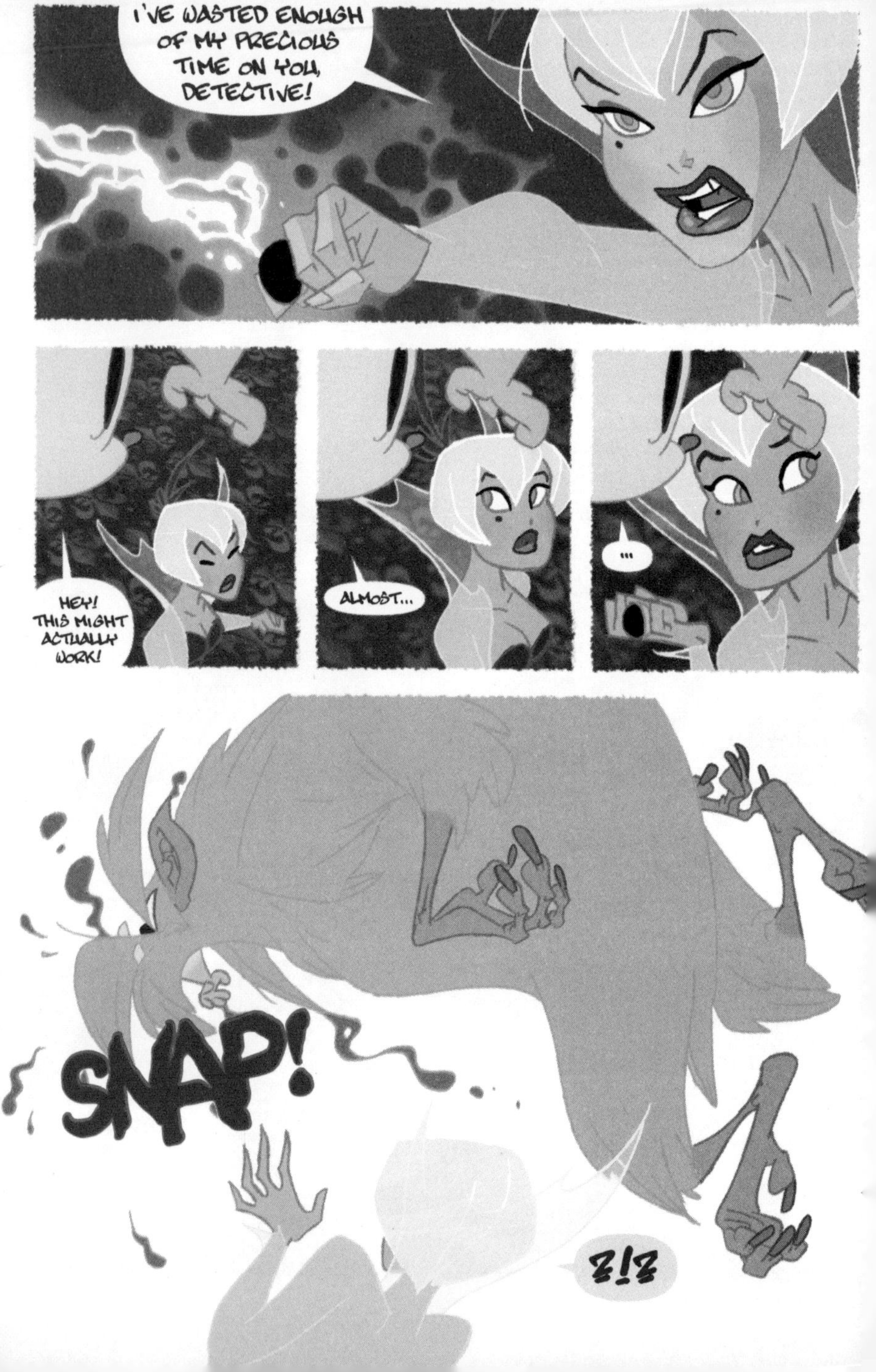
I'VE WASTED ENOUGH OF MY PRECIOUS TIME ON YOU, DETECTIVE!
HEY! THIS MIGHT ACTUALLY WORK!
ALMOST...
...
SNAP!
?!?

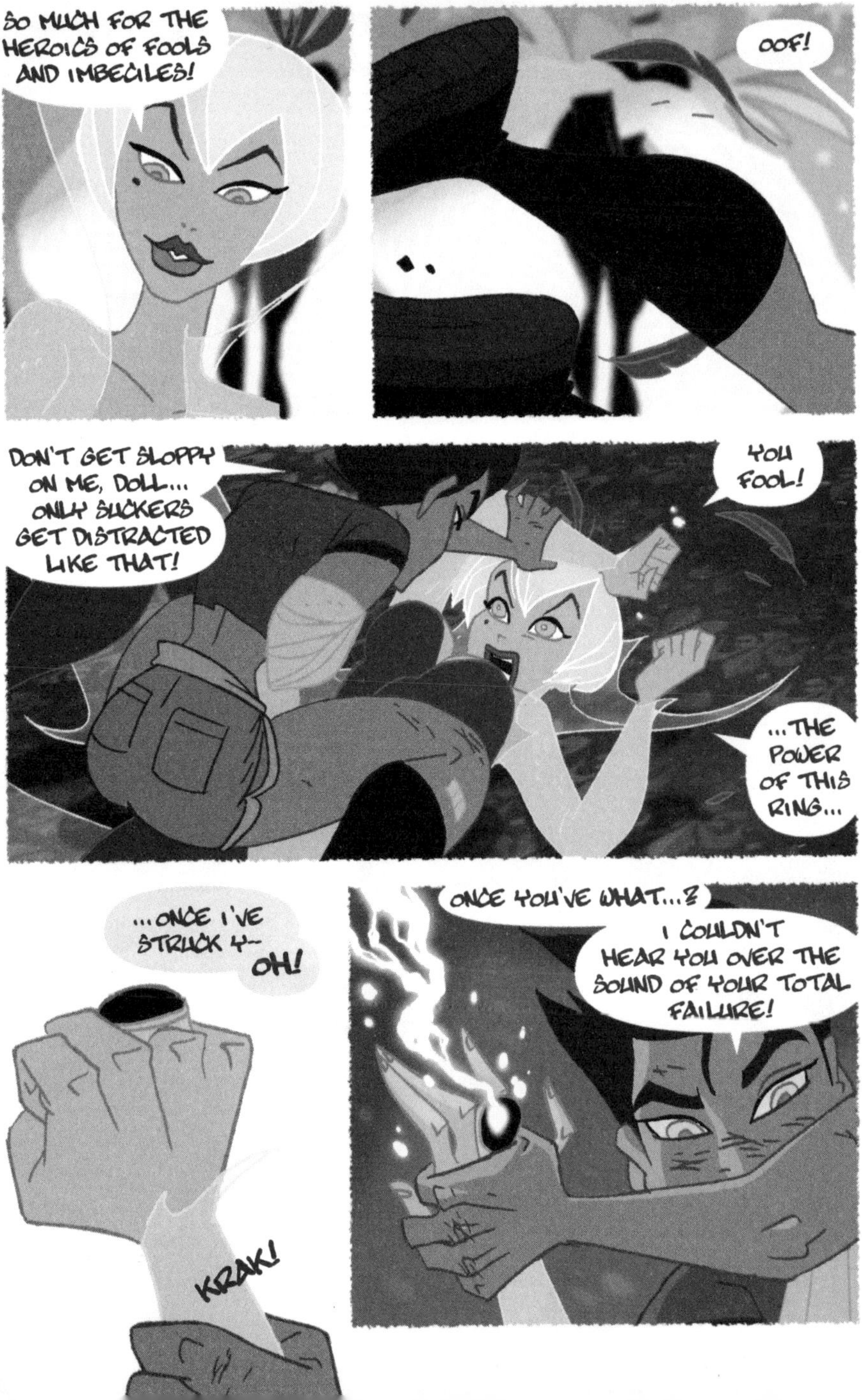
SO MUCH FOR THE HEROICS OF FOOLS AND IMBECILES!
OOF!
DON'T GET SLOPPY ON ME, DOLL... ONLY SUCKERS GET DISTRACTED LIKE THAT!
YOU FOOL!
...THE POWER OF THIS RING...
...ONCE I'VE STRUCK Y-
OH!
KRAK!
ONCE YOU'VE WHAT...?
I COULDN'T HEAR YOU OVER THE SOUND OF YOUR TOTAL FAILURE!

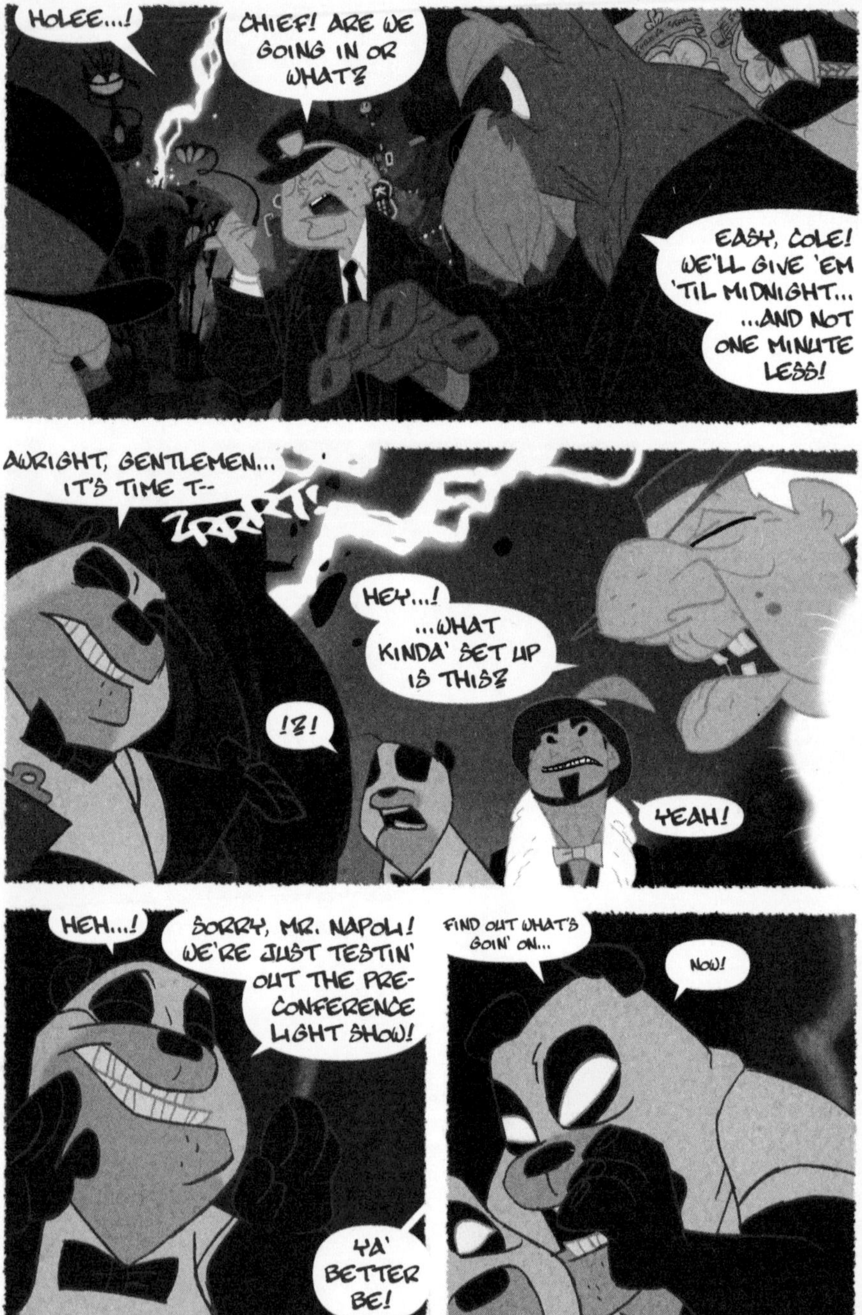
HOLEE...!
CHIEF! ARE WE GOING IN OR WHAT?
EASY, COLE! WE'LL GIVE 'EM 'TIL MIDNIGHT... ...AND NOT ONE MINUTE LESS!
AWRIGHT, GENTLEMEN... IT'S TIME T--
ZZRRRT!
HEY...! ...WHAT KINDA' SET UP IS THIS?
!?!
YEAH!
HEH...!
SORRY, MR. NAPOLI! WE'RE JUST TESTIN' OUT THE PRE-CONFERENCE LIGHT SHOW!
YA' BETTER BE!
FIND OUT WHAT'S GOIN' ON...
NOW!

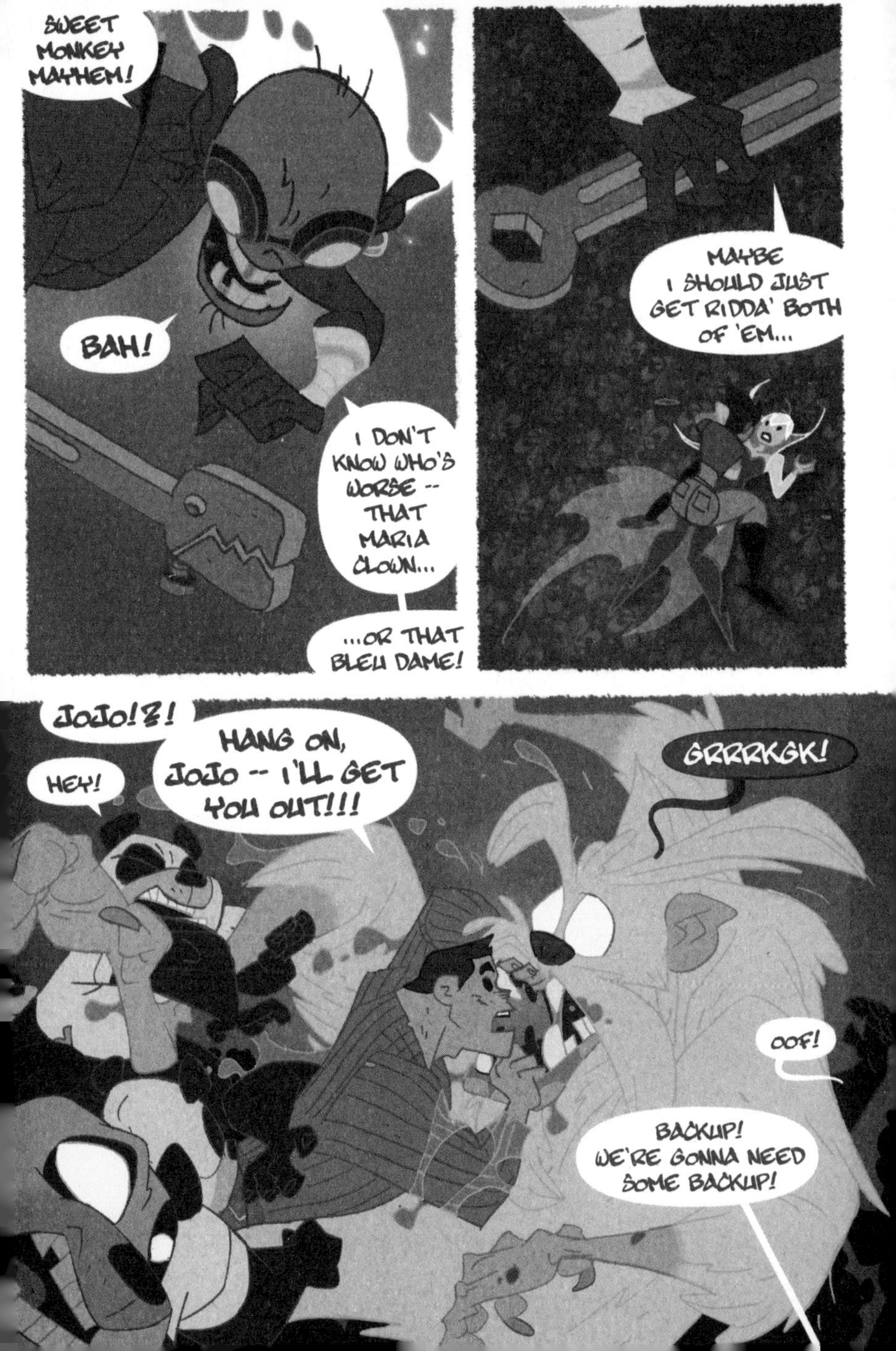
SWEET MONKEY MAYHEM!
BAH!
I DON'T KNOW WHO'S WORSE -- THAT MARIA CLOWN...
...OR THAT BLEU DAME!
MAYBE I SHOULD JUST GET RIDDA' BOTH OF 'EM...
JOJO!?!
HEY!
HANG ON, JOJO -- I'LL GET YOU OUT!!!
GRRRKGK!
OOF!
BACKUP! WE'RE GONNA NEED SOME BACKUP!

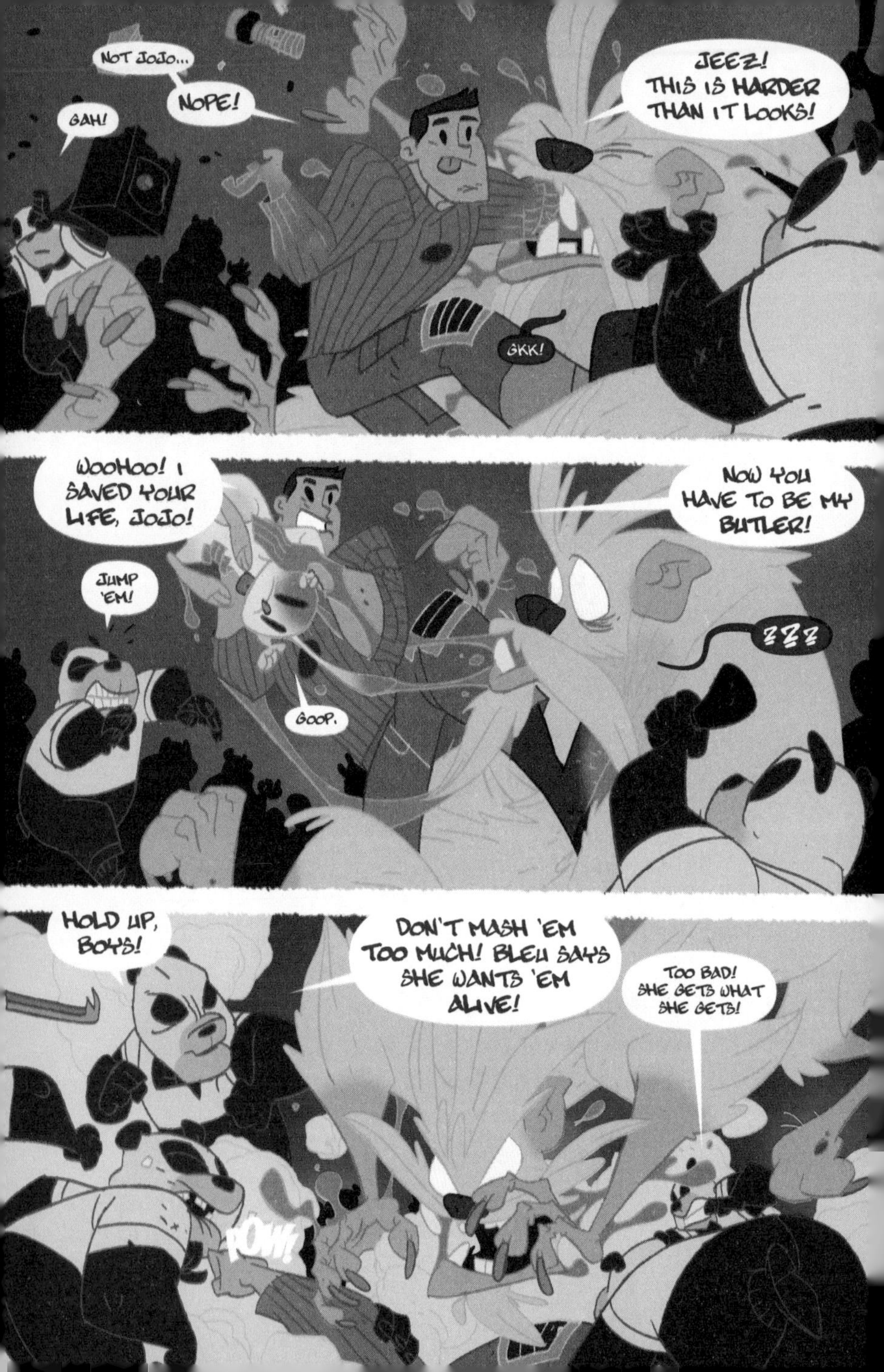
NOT JOJO...
NOPE!
GAH!
JEEZ! THIS IS HARDER THAN IT LOOKS!
GKK!
WOOHOO! I SAVED YOUR LIFE, JOJO!
NOW YOU HAVE TO BE MY BUTLER!
JUMP 'EM!
ZZZ
GOOP.
HOLD UP, BOYS!
DON'T MASH 'EM TOO MUCH! BLEU SAYS SHE WANTS 'EM ALIVE!
TOO BAD! SHE GETS WHAT SHE GETS!
POW!

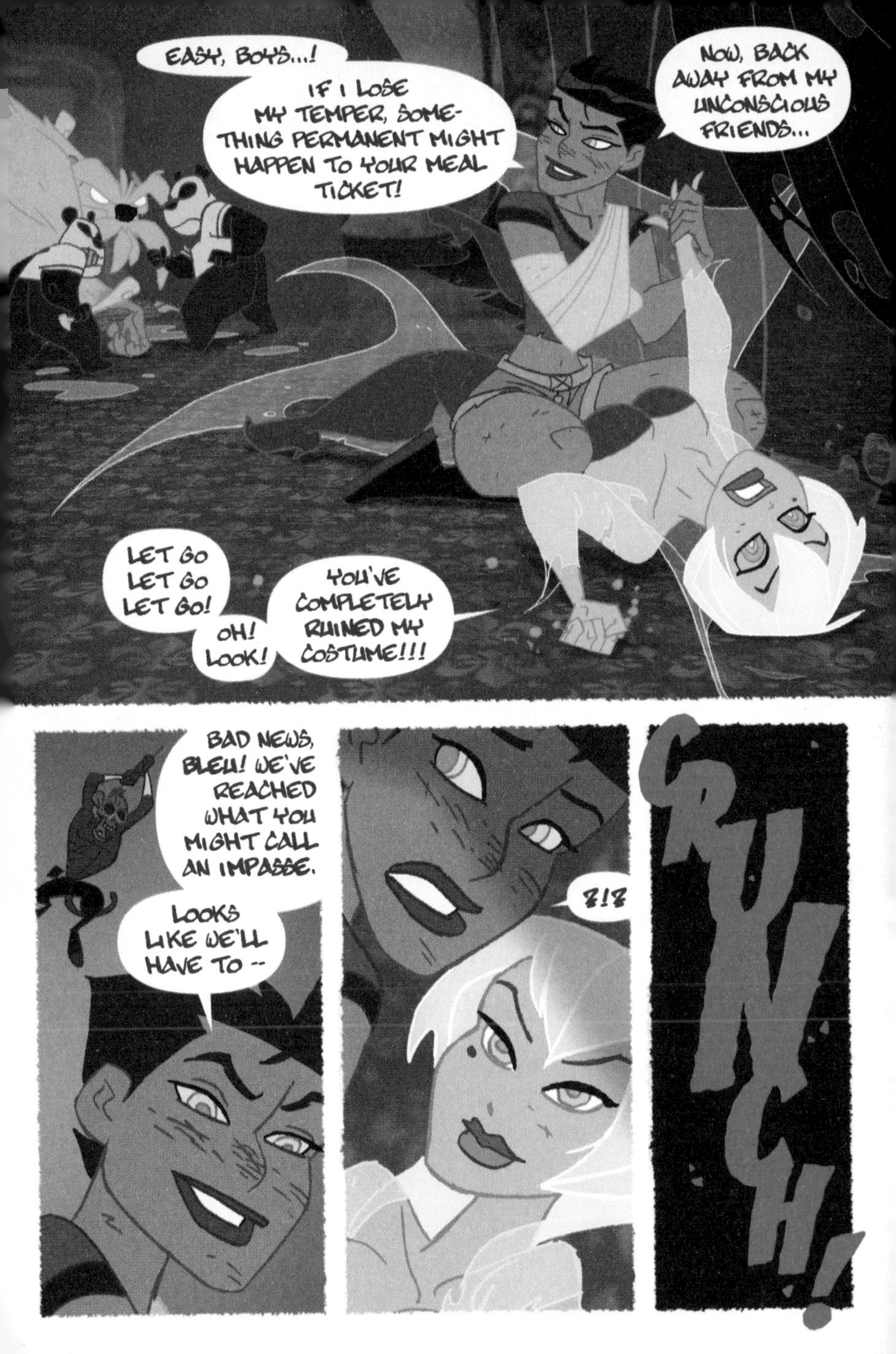

EASY, BOYS...!
IF I LOSE MY TEMPER, SOME-THING PERMANENT MIGHT HAPPEN TO YOUR MEAL TICKET!
NOW, BACK AWAY FROM MY UNCONSCIOUS FRIENDS...
LET GO LET GO LET GO!
OH! LOOK!
YOU'VE COMPLETELY RUINED MY COSTUME!!!
BAD NEWS, BLEU! WE'VE REACHED WHAT YOU MIGHT CALL AN IMPASSE.
LOOKS LIKE WE'LL HAVE TO --
?!?
CRUNCH!!

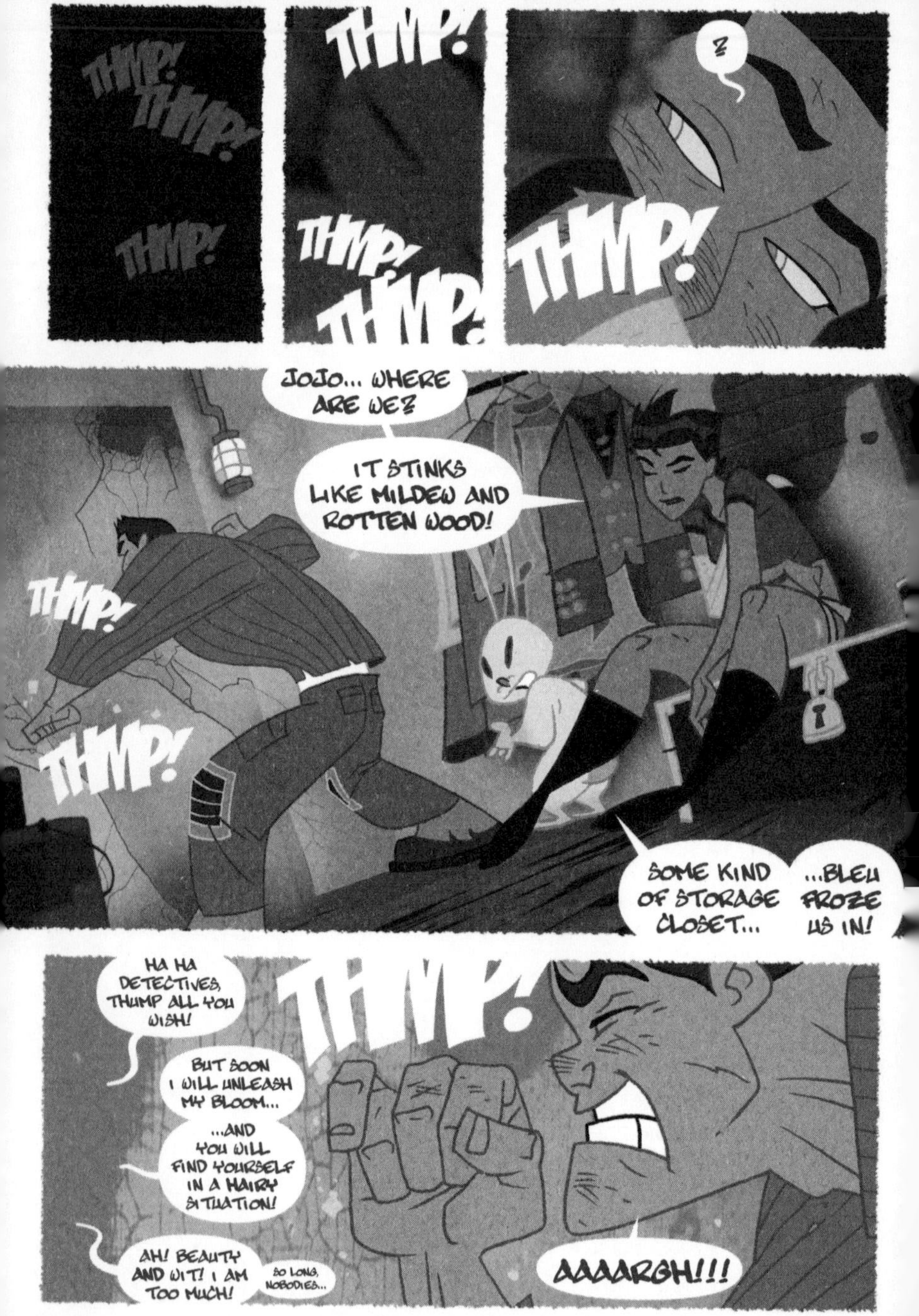
THMP! THMP!
THMP!
THMP!
THMP!
THMP!
?
THMP!
JOJO... WHERE ARE WE?
IT STINKS LIKE MILDEW AND ROTTEN WOOD!
THMP!
THMP!
SOME KIND OF STORAGE CLOSET...
...BLEU FROZE US IN!
HA HA DETECTIVES, THUMP ALL YOU WISH!
THMP!
BUT SOON I WILL UNLEASH MY BLOOM...
...AND YOU WILL FIND YOURSELF IN A HAIRY SITUATION!
AH! BEAUTY AND WIT! I AM TOO MUCH!
SO LONG, NOBODIES...
AAAARGH!!!

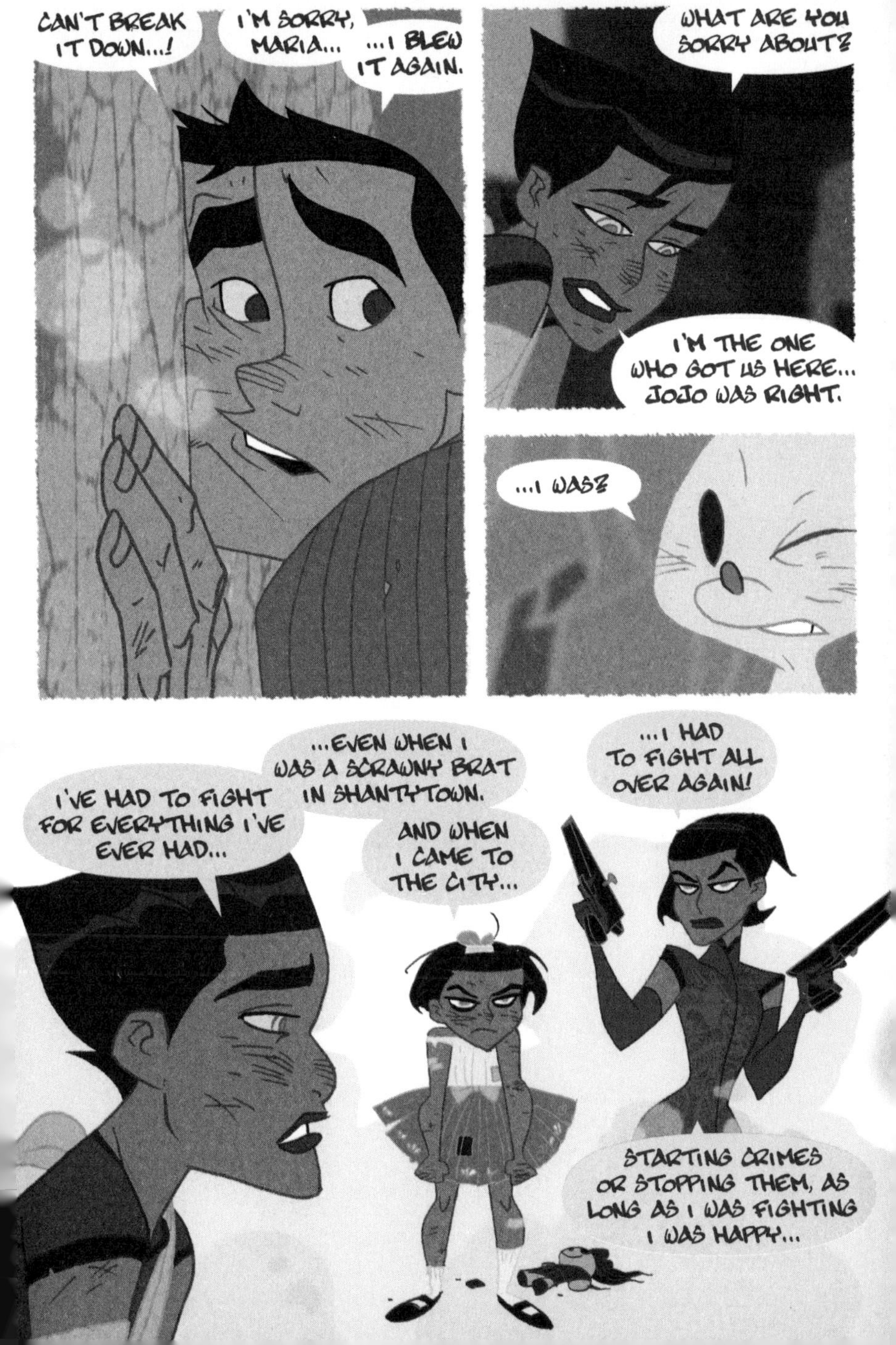
CAN'T BREAK IT DOWN...!
I'M SORRY, MARIA...
...I BLEW IT AGAIN.
WHAT ARE YOU SORRY ABOUT?
I'M THE ONE WHO GOT US HERE... JOJO WAS RIGHT.
...I WAS?
I'VE HAD TO FIGHT FOR EVERYTHING I'VE EVER HAD...
...EVEN WHEN I WAS A SCRAWNY BRAT IN SHANTYTOWN.
AND WHEN I CAME TO THE CITY...
...I HAD TO FIGHT ALL OVER AGAIN!
STARTING CRIMES OR STOPPING THEM, AS LONG AS I WAS FIGHTING I WAS HAPPY...

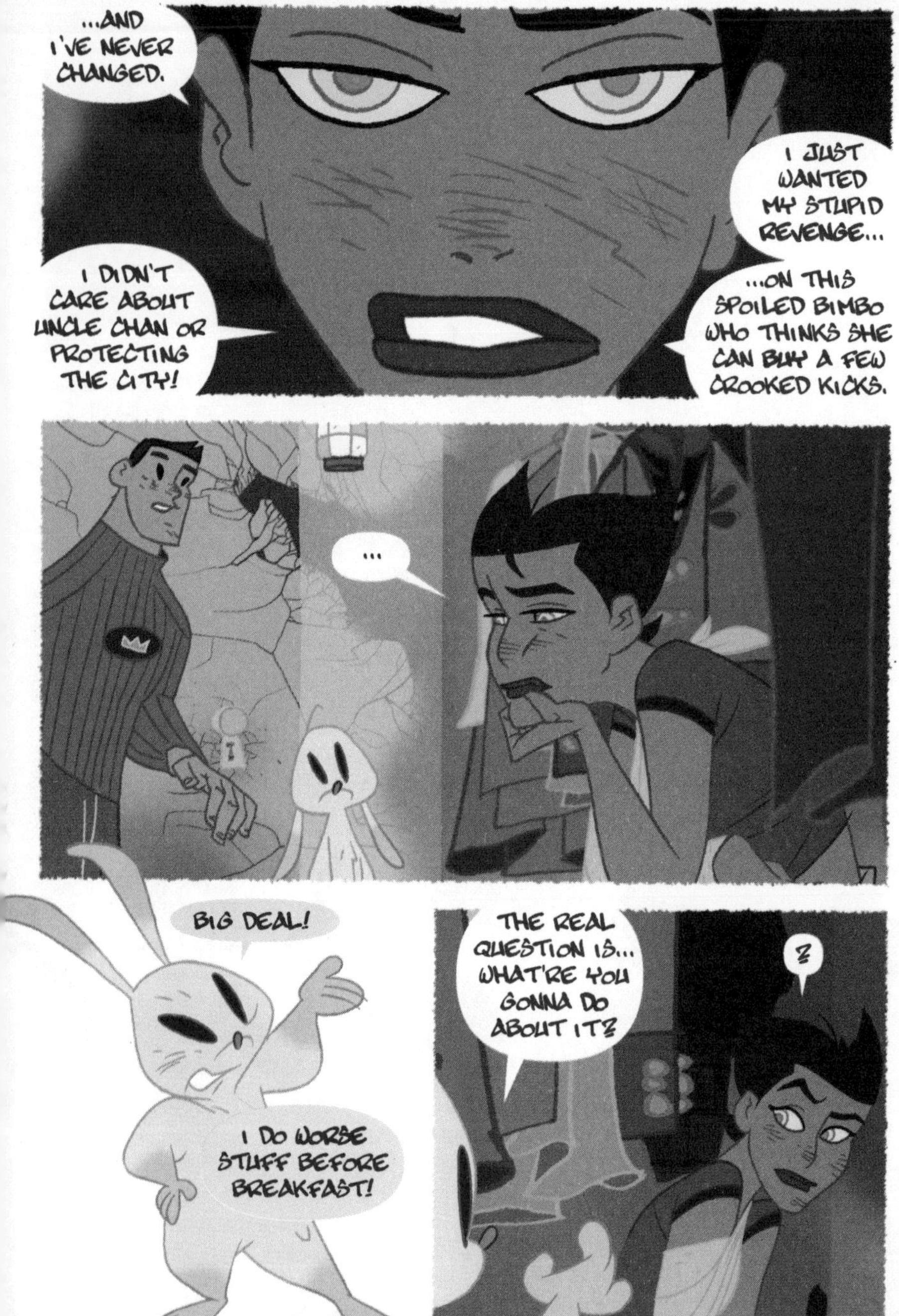
...AND I'VE NEVER CHANGED.
I JUST WANTED MY STUPID REVENGE...
I DIDN'T CARE ABOUT UNCLE CHAN OR PROTECTING THE CITY!
...ON THIS SPOILED BIMBO WHO THINKS SHE CAN BUY A FEW CROOKED KICKS.
...
BIG DEAL!
I DO WORSE STUFF BEFORE BREAKFAST!
THE REAL QUESTION IS... WHAT'RE YOU GONNA DO ABOUT IT?
?

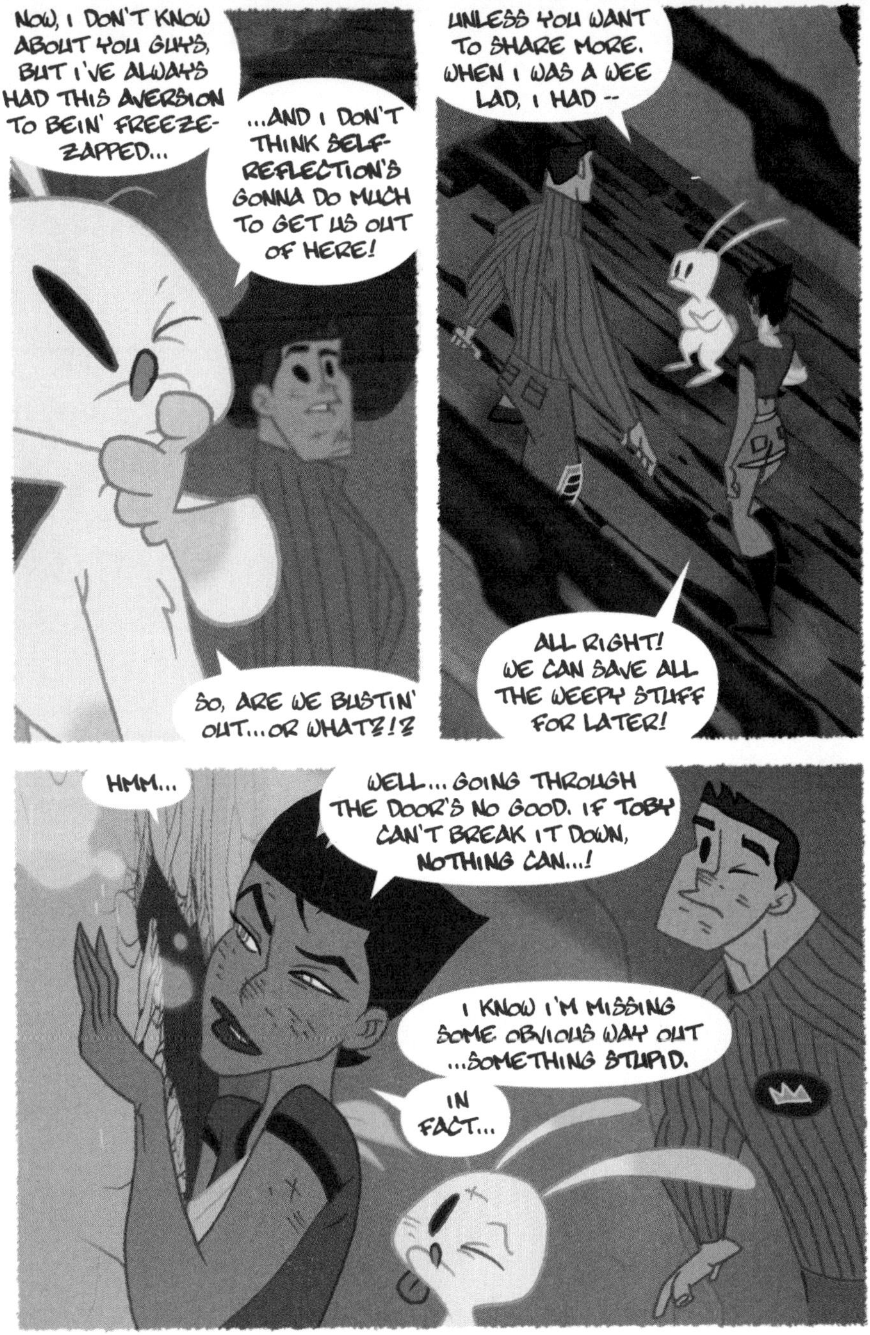
NOW, I DON'T KNOW ABOUT YOU GUYS, BUT I'VE ALWAYS HAD THIS AVERSION TO BEIN' FREEZE-ZAPPED...
...AND I DON'T THINK SELF-REFLECTION'S GONNA DO MUCH TO GET US OUT OF HERE!
SO, ARE WE BUSTIN' OUT...OR WHAT?!?
UNLESS YOU WANT TO SHARE MORE. WHEN I WAS A WEE LAD, I HAD --
ALL RIGHT! WE CAN SAVE ALL THE WEEPY STUFF FOR LATER!
HMM...
WELL... GOING THROUGH THE DOOR'S NO GOOD. IF TOBY CAN'T BREAK IT DOWN, NOTHING CAN...!
I KNOW I'M MISSING SOME OBVIOUS WAY OUT ...SOMETHING STUPID.
IN FACT...

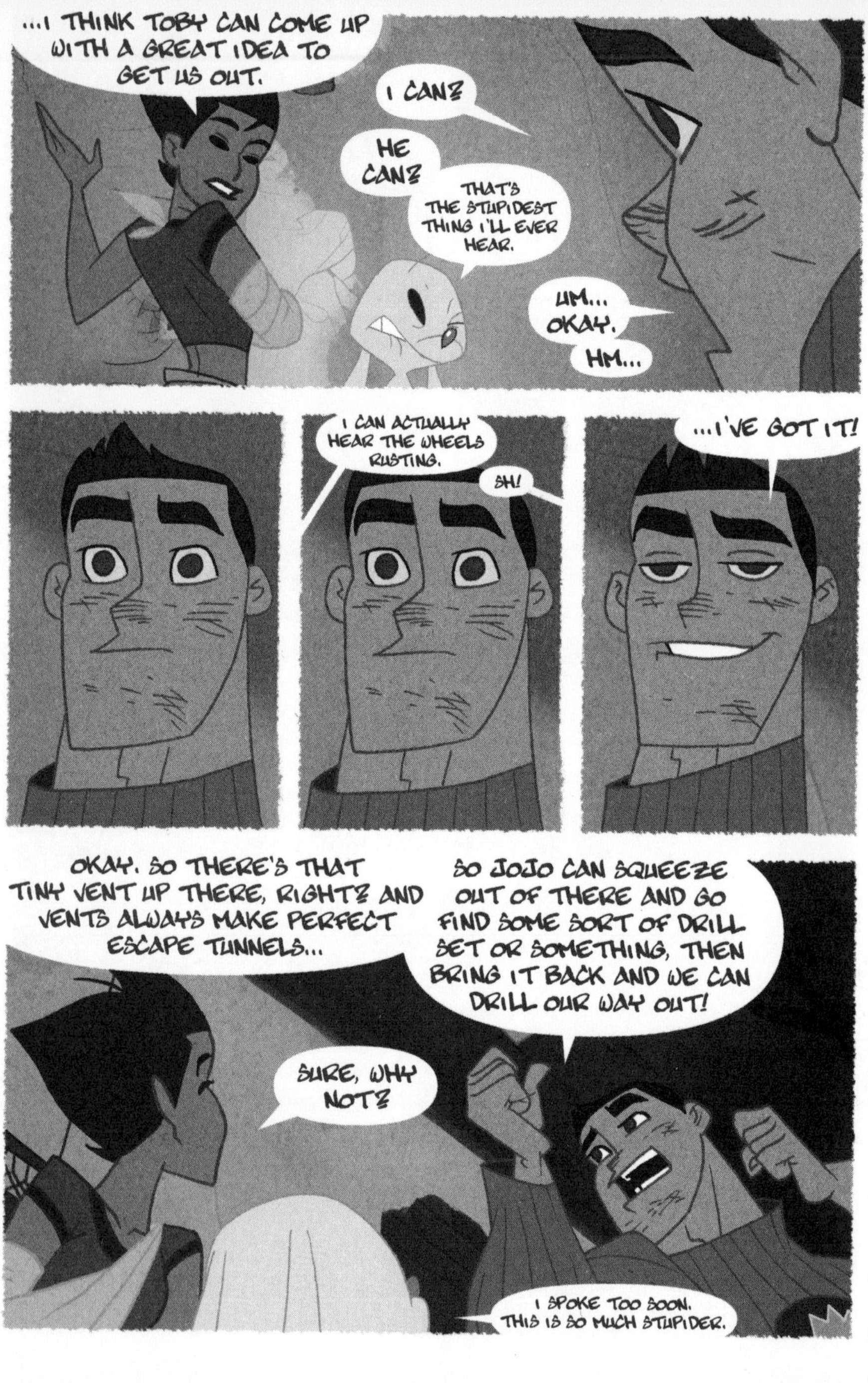
...I THINK TOBY CAN COME UP WITH A GREAT IDEA TO GET US OUT.
I CAN?
HE CAN?
THAT'S THE STUPIDEST THING I'LL EVER HEAR.
UM... OKAY.
HM...
I CAN ACTUALLY HEAR THE WHEELS RUSTING.
SH!
...I'VE GOT IT!
OKAY. SO THERE'S THAT TINY VENT UP THERE, RIGHT? AND VENTS ALWAYS MAKE PERFECT ESCAPE TUNNELS...
SO JOJO CAN SQUEEZE OUT OF THERE AND GO FIND SOME SORT OF DRILL SET OR SOMETHING, THEN BRING IT BACK AND WE CAN DRILL OUR WAY OUT!
SURE, WHY NOT?
I SPOKE TOO SOON. THIS IS SO MUCH STUPIDER.

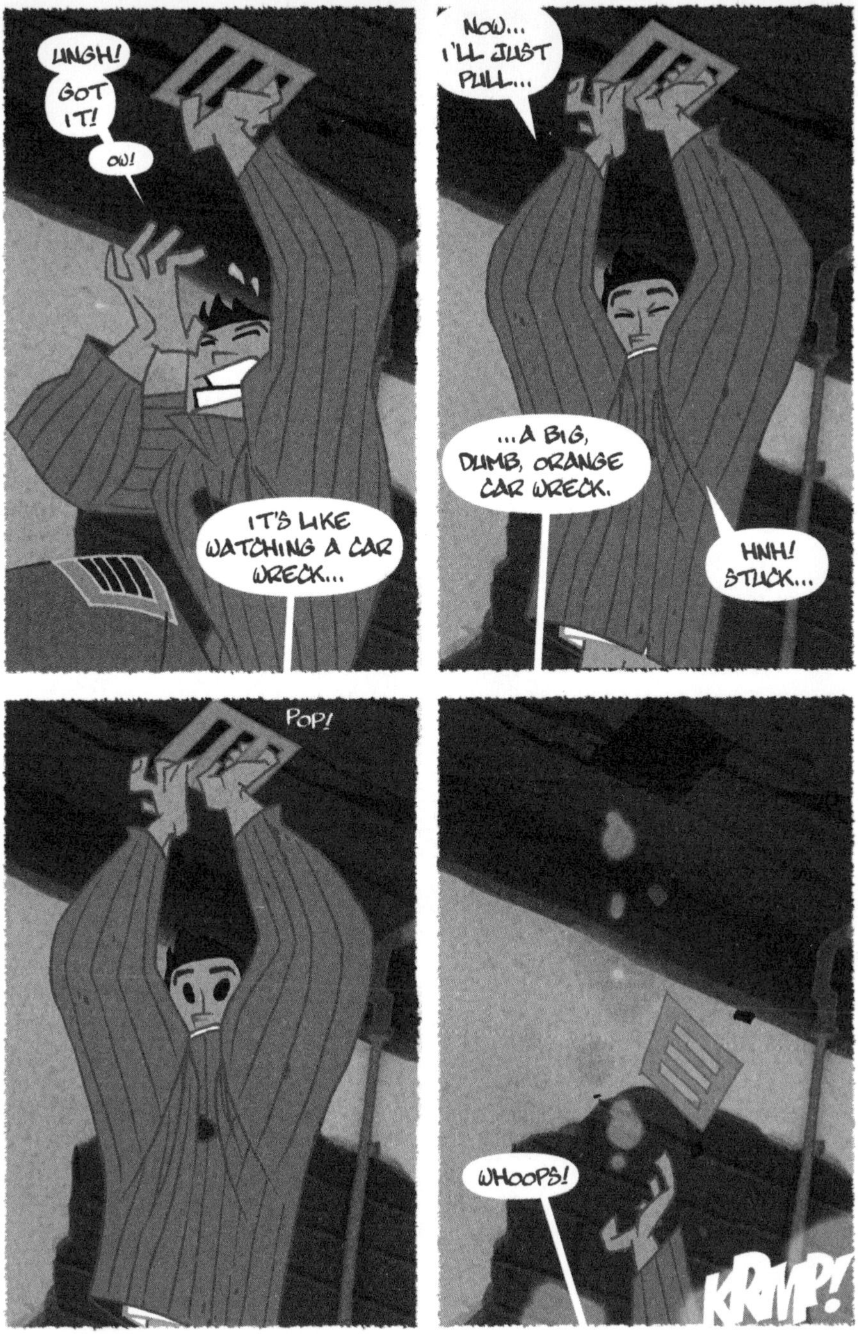
UNGH!
GOT IT!
OW!
IT'S LIKE WATCHING A CAR WRECK...
NOW... I'LL JUST PULL...
...A BIG, DUMB, ORANGE CAR WRECK.
HNH! STUCK...
POP!
WHOOPS!
KRMP!

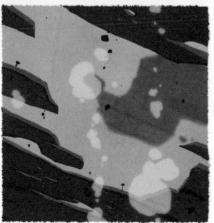

PERFECT...THIS TURNED OUT EVEN BETTER THAN I FIGURED.

? YOU PLANNED THIS?!?

WELL, THINK ABOUT IT...

...THIS IS THE STUPIDEST CASE WE'VE EVER HAD, RIGHT, JOJO?

OH DEFINITELY.

LOGIC AND PLANNING HAVE FAILED...

SO WHY NOT FIGHT STUPID WITH MORE STUPID?

AND TOBY IS PRACTICALLY AN IDIOT SAVANT.

SANS SAVANT...

UH, GUYS?

HEY, GUYS! I THINK I BROKE MY SWEATER!

I FIGURED IF WE LEFT TOBY ENOUGH ROOM TO DO SOMETHING DUMB...

...AND LOOK! WE'RE BACK AT THE GARAGE, JUST LIKE THAT!

NOW...

YOU CAN SLIP OUT UNDER THE FENCE... WARN MACINTOSH.

GO ON! I WON'T HOLD IT AGAINST YOU!

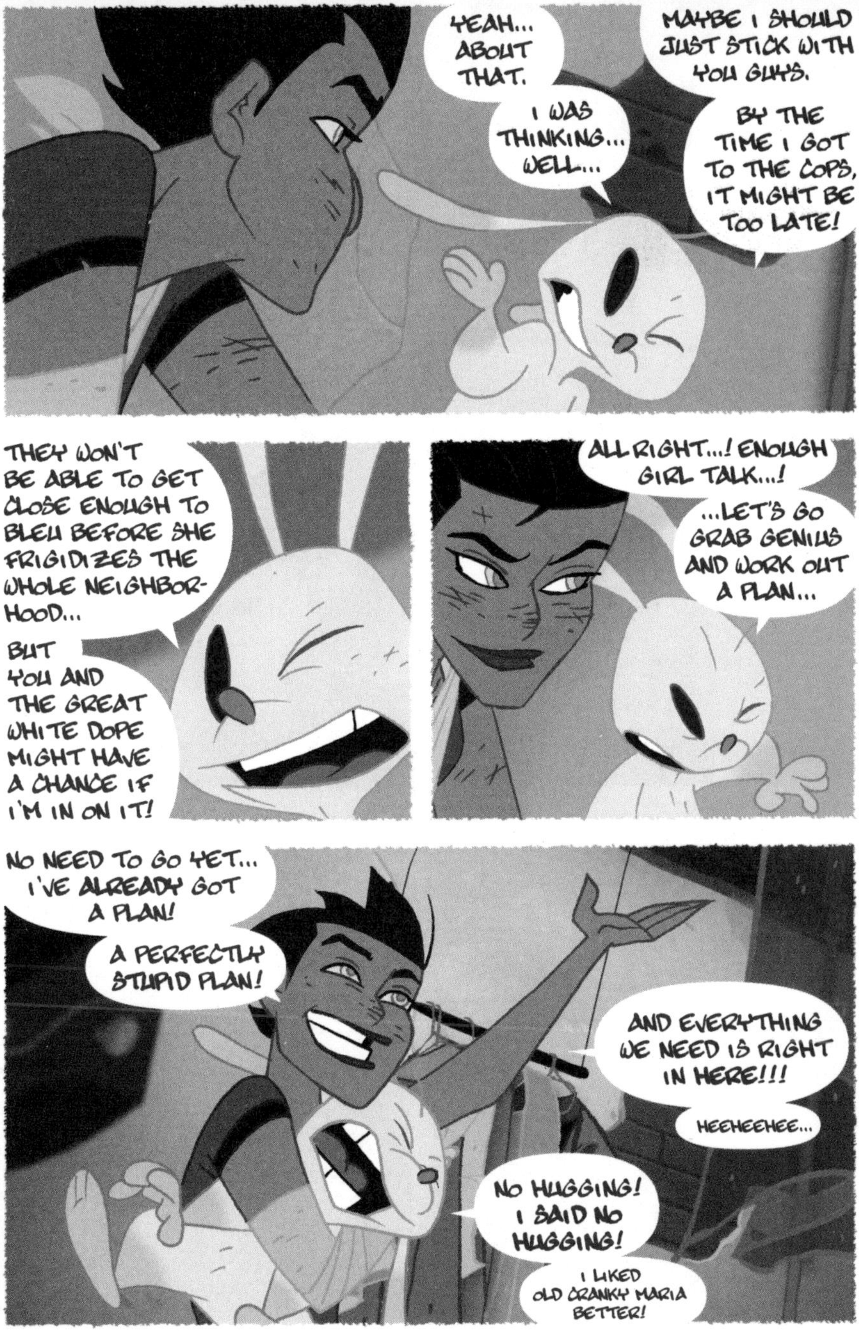
YEAH... ABOUT THAT.
I WAS THINKING... WELL...
MAYBE I SHOULD JUST STICK WITH YOU GUYS.
BY THE TIME I GOT TO THE COPS, IT MIGHT BE TOO LATE!
THEY WON'T BE ABLE TO GET CLOSE ENOUGH TO BLEU BEFORE SHE FRIGIDIZES THE WHOLE NEIGHBOR-HOOD...
BUT YOU AND THE GREAT WHITE DOPE MIGHT HAVE A CHANCE IF I'M IN ON IT!
ALL RIGHT...! ENOUGH GIRL TALK...!
...LET'S GO GRAB GENIUS AND WORK OUT A PLAN...
NO NEED TO GO YET... I'VE ALREADY GOT A PLAN!
A PERFECTLY STUPID PLAN!
AND EVERYTHING WE NEED IS RIGHT IN HERE!!!
HEEHEEHEE...
NO HUGGING! I SAID NO HUGGING!
I LIKED OLD CRANKY MARIA BETTER!

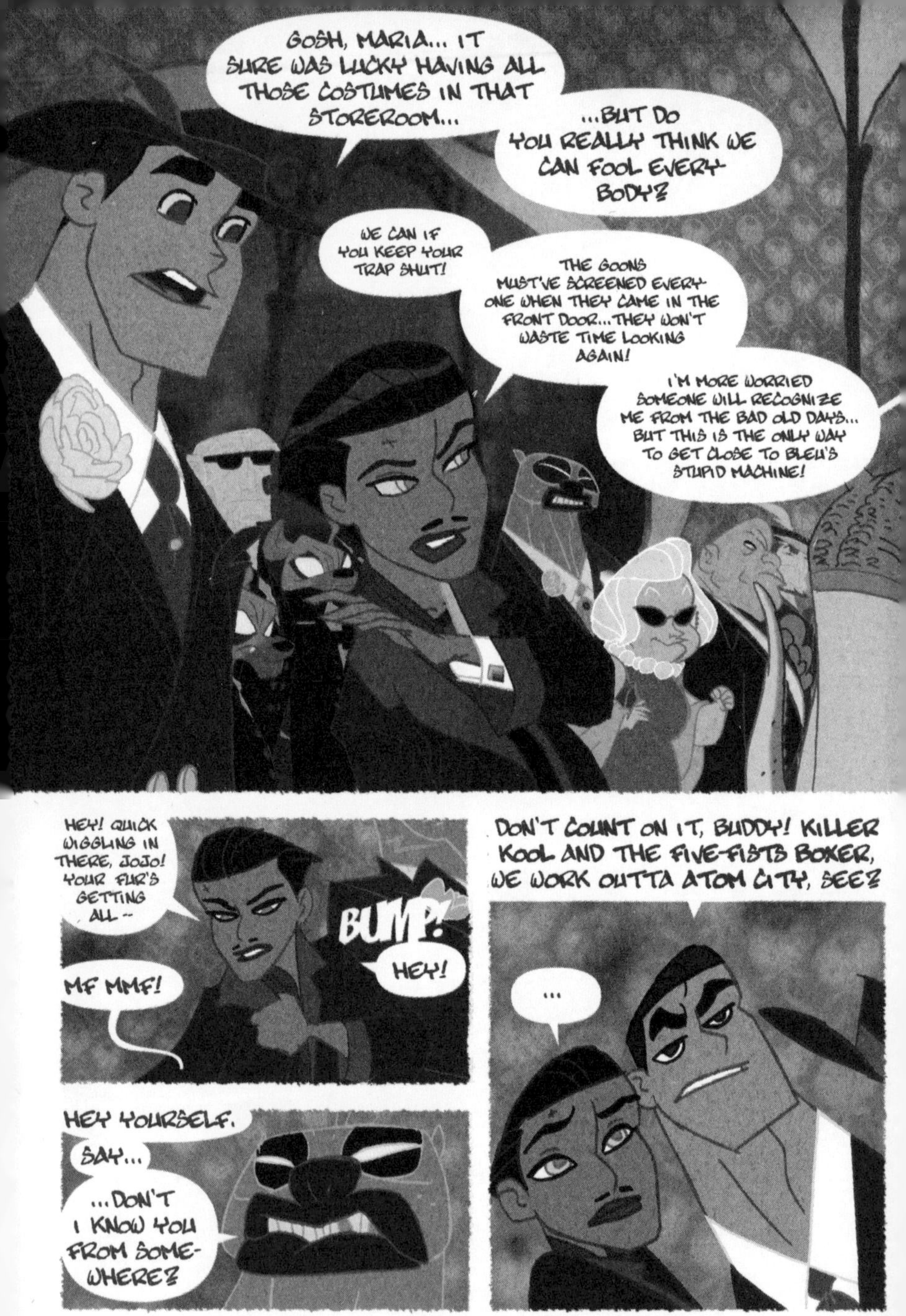
GOSH, MARIA... IT SURE WAS LUCKY HAVING ALL THOSE COSTUMES IN THAT STOREROOM...
...BUT DO YOU REALLY THINK WE CAN FOOL EVERY-BODY?
WE CAN IF YOU KEEP YOUR TRAP SHUT!
THE GOONS MUST'VE SCREENED EVERY-ONE WHEN THEY CAME IN THE FRONT DOOR...THEY WON'T WASTE TIME LOOKING AGAIN!
I'M MORE WORRIED SOMEONE WILL RECOGNIZE ME FROM THE BAD OLD DAYS... BUT THIS IS THE ONLY WAY TO GET CLOSE TO BLEU'S STUPID MACHINE!
HEY! QUICK WIGGLING IN THERE, JOJO! YOUR FUR'S GETTING ALL --
BUMP!
HEY!
MF MMF!
HEY YOURSELF.
SAY...
...DON'T I KNOW YOU FROM SOME-WHERE?
DON'T COUNT ON IT, BUDDY! KILLER KOOL AND THE FIVE-FISTS BOXER, WE WORK OUTTA ATOM CITY, SEE?
...

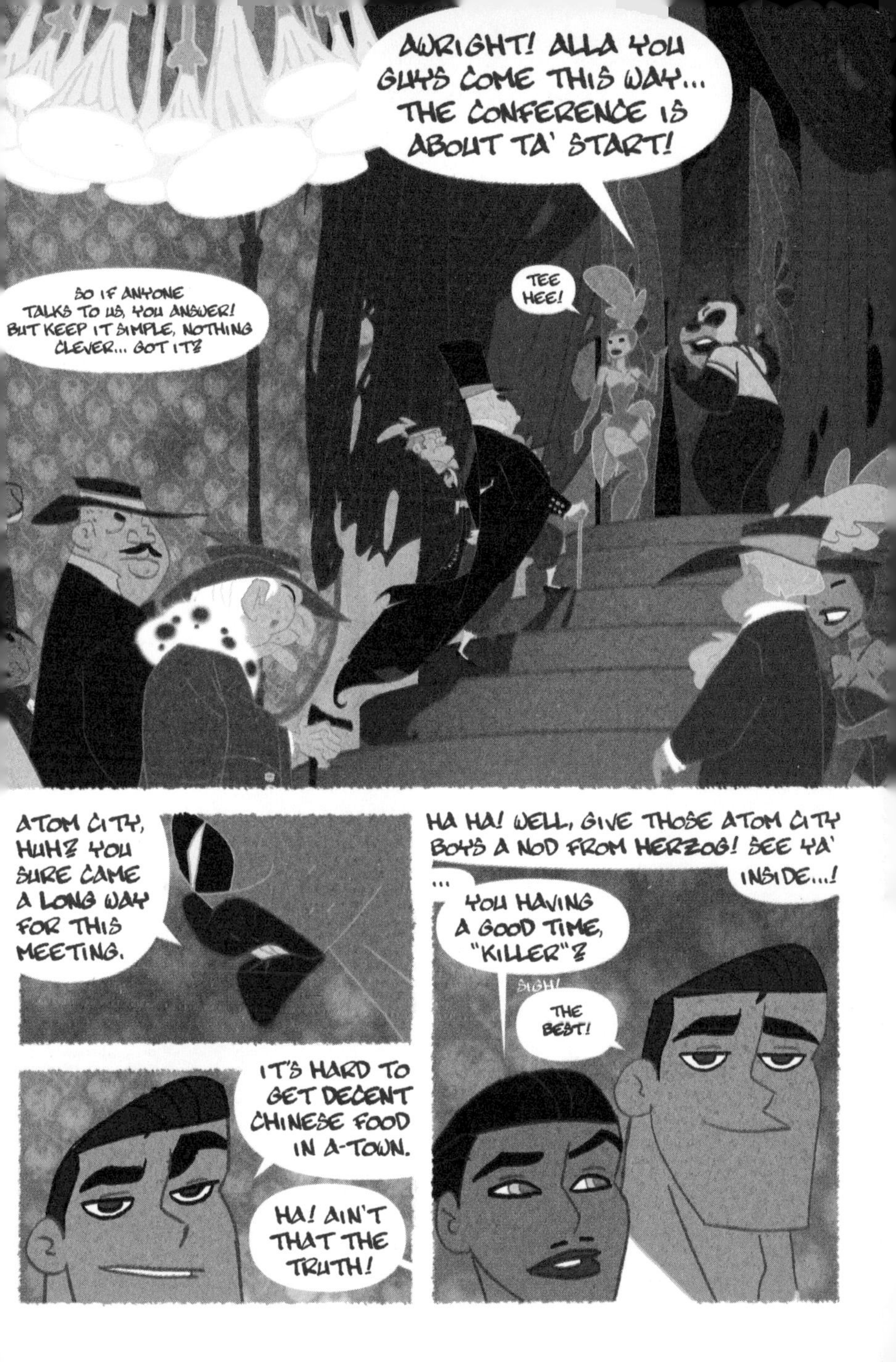
AWRIGHT! ALLA YOU GUYS COME THIS WAY... THE CONFERENCE IS ABOUT TA' START!
SO IF ANYONE TALKS TO US, YOU ANSWER! BUT KEEP IT SIMPLE, NOTHING CLEVER... GOT IT?
TEE HEE!
ATOM CITY, HUH? YOU SURE CAME A LONG WAY FOR THIS MEETING.
IT'S HARD TO GET DECENT CHINESE FOOD IN A-TOWN.
HA! AIN'T THAT THE TRUTH!
HA HA! WELL, GIVE THOSE ATOM CITY BOYS A NOD FROM HERZOG! SEE YA' INSIDE...!
...
YOU HAVING A GOOD TIME, "KILLER"?
SIGH!
THE BEST!

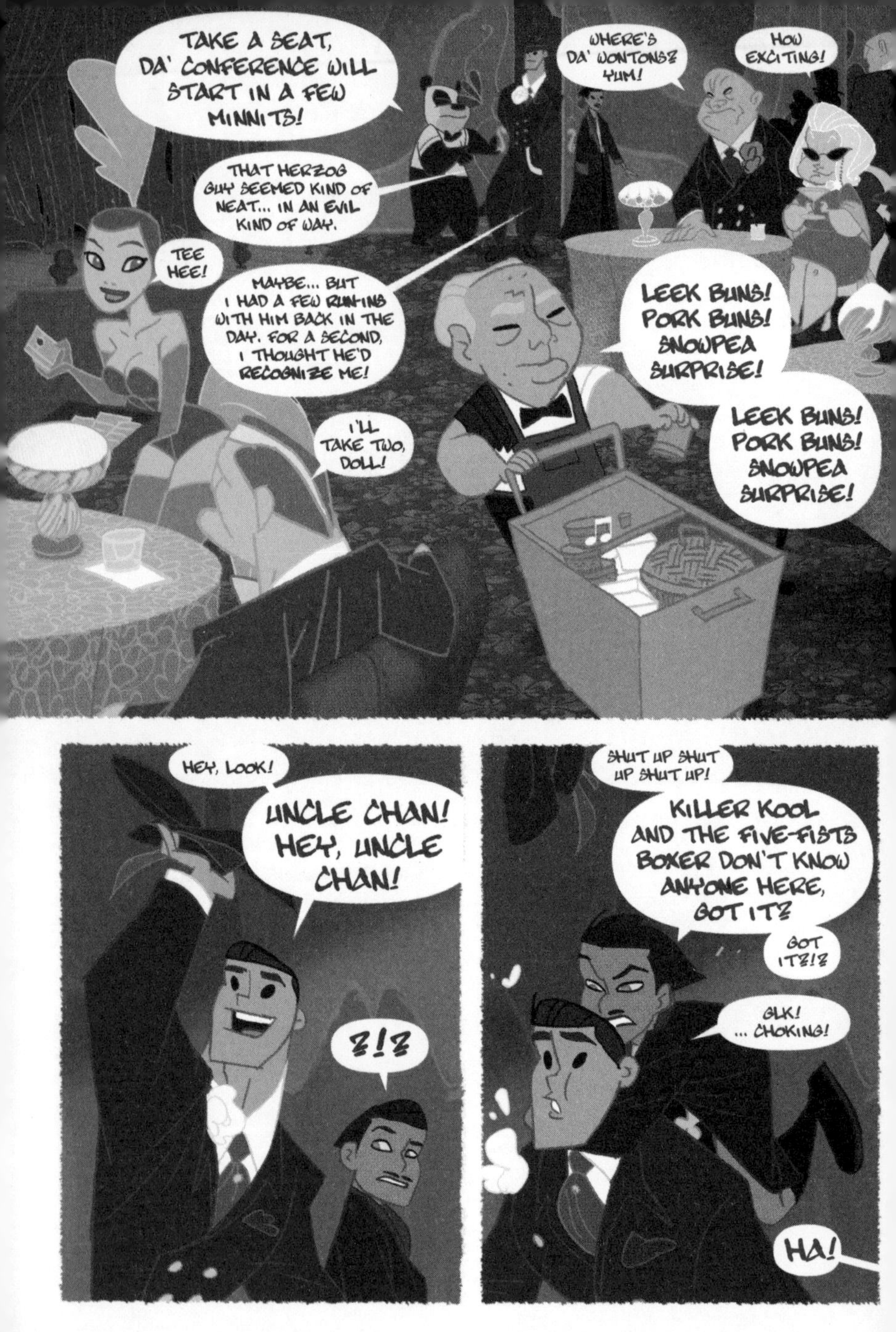
TAKE A SEAT, DA' CONFERENCE WILL START IN A FEW MINNITS!
WHERE'S DA' WONTONS? YUM!
HOW EXCITING!
THAT HERZOG GUY SEEMED KIND OF NEAT... IN AN EVIL KIND OF WAY.
TEE HEE!
MAYBE... BUT I HAD A FEW RUN-INS WITH HIM BACK IN THE DAY. FOR A SECOND, I THOUGHT HE'D RECOGNIZE ME!
LEEK BUNS! PORK BUNS! SNOWPEA SURPRISE!
LEEK BUNS! PORK BUNS! SNOWPEA SURPRISE!
I'LL TAKE TWO, DOLL!
HEY, LOOK!
UNCLE CHAN! HEY, UNCLE CHAN!
?!?
SHUT UP SHUT UP SHUT UP!
KILLER KOOL AND THE FIVE-FISTS BOXER DON'T KNOW ANYONE HERE, GOT IT?
GOT IT?!?
GLK! ... CHOKING!
HA!

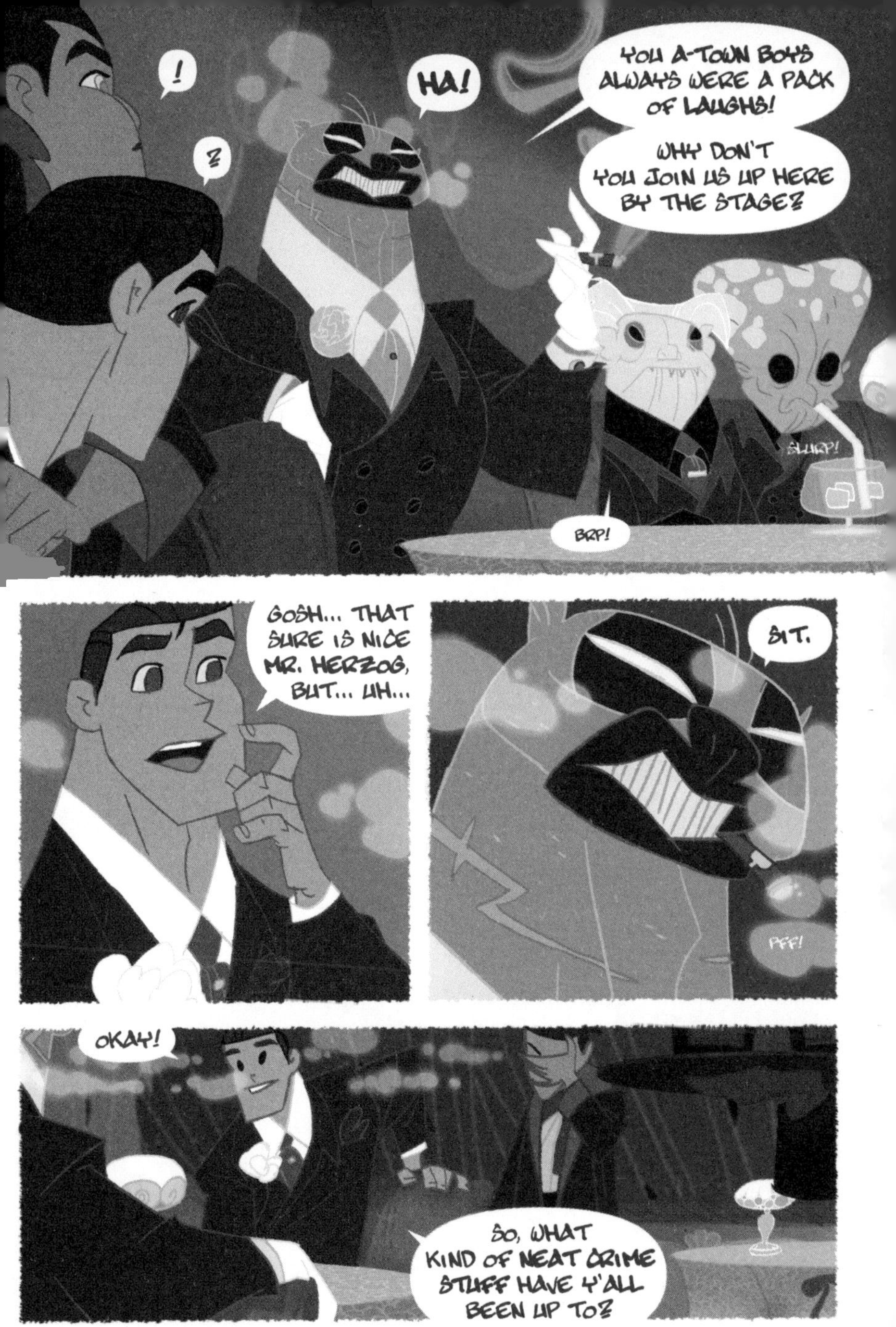
!
?
HA!
YOU A-TOWN BOYS ALWAYS WERE A PACK OF LAUGHS!
WHY DON'T YOU JOIN US UP HERE BY THE STAGE?
SLURP!
BRP!
GOSH... THAT SURE IS NICE MR. HERZOG, BUT... UH...
SIT.
PFF!
OKAY!
SO, WHAT KIND OF NEAT CRIME STUFF HAVE Y'ALL BEEN UP TO?

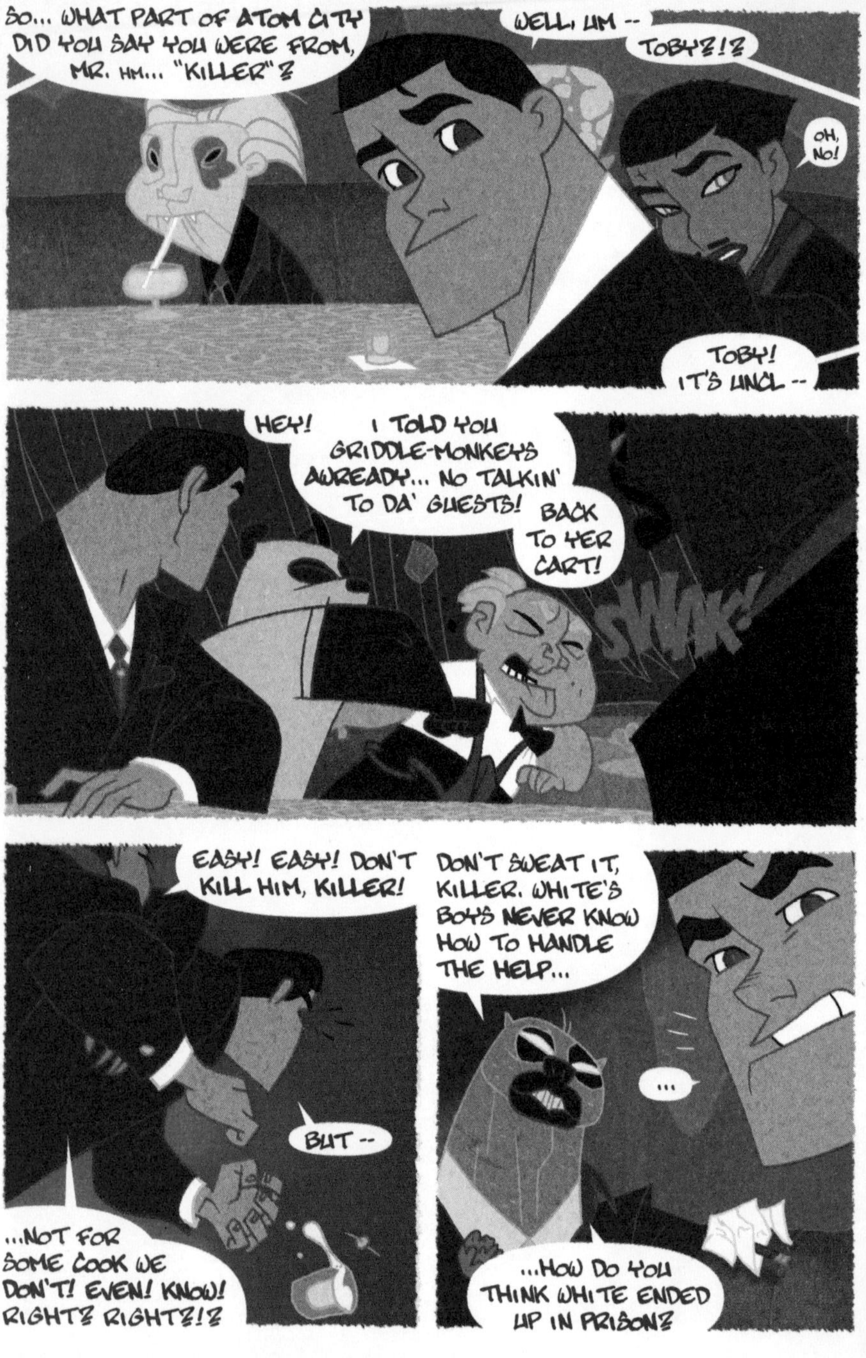
SO... WHAT PART OF ATOM CITY DID YOU SAY YOU WERE FROM, MR. HM... "KILLER"?
WELL, UM --
TOBY?!?
OH, NO!
TOBY! IT'S UNCL --
HEY!
I TOLD YOU GRIDDLE-MONKEYS AWREADY... NO TALKIN' TO DA' GUESTS!
BACK TO YER CART!
SWAK!
EASY! EASY! DON'T KILL HIM, KILLER!
BUT --
...NOT FOR SOME COOK WE DON'T! EVEN! KNOW! RIGHT? RIGHT?!?
DON'T SWEAT IT, KILLER. WHITE'S BOYS NEVER KNOW HOW TO HANDLE THE HELP...
...
...HOW DO YOU THINK WHITE ENDED UP IN PRISON?

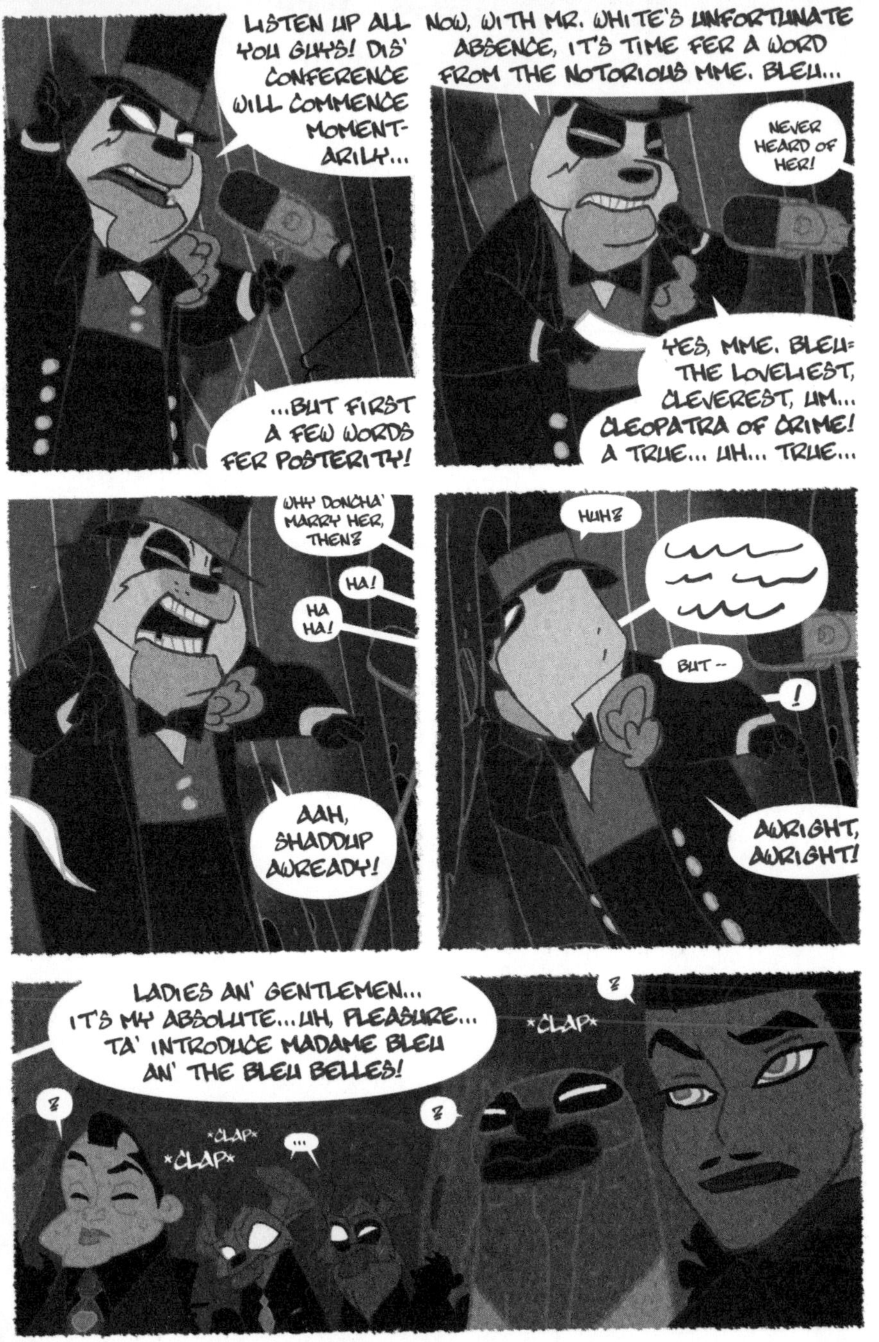
LISTEN UP ALL YOU GUYS! DIS' CONFERENCE WILL COMMENCE MOMENT-ARILY...
...BUT FIRST A FEW WORDS FER POSTERITY!
NOW, WITH MR. WHITE'S UNFORTUNATE ABSENCE, IT'S TIME FER A WORD FROM THE NOTORIOUS MME. BLEU...
NEVER HEARD OF HER!
YES, MME. BLEU= THE LOVELIEST, CLEVEREST, UM... CLEOPATRA OF CRIME! A TRUE... UH... TRUE...
WHY DONCHA' MARRY HER, THEN?
HA!
HA HA!
AAH, SHADDUP AWREADY!
HUH?
BUT --
!
AWRIGHT, AWRIGHT!
LADIES AN' GENTLEMEN... IT'S MY ABSOLUTE...UH, PLEASURE... TA' INTRODUCE MADAME BLEU AN' THE BLEU BELLES!
?
CLAP
?
CLAP
CLAP
...
?

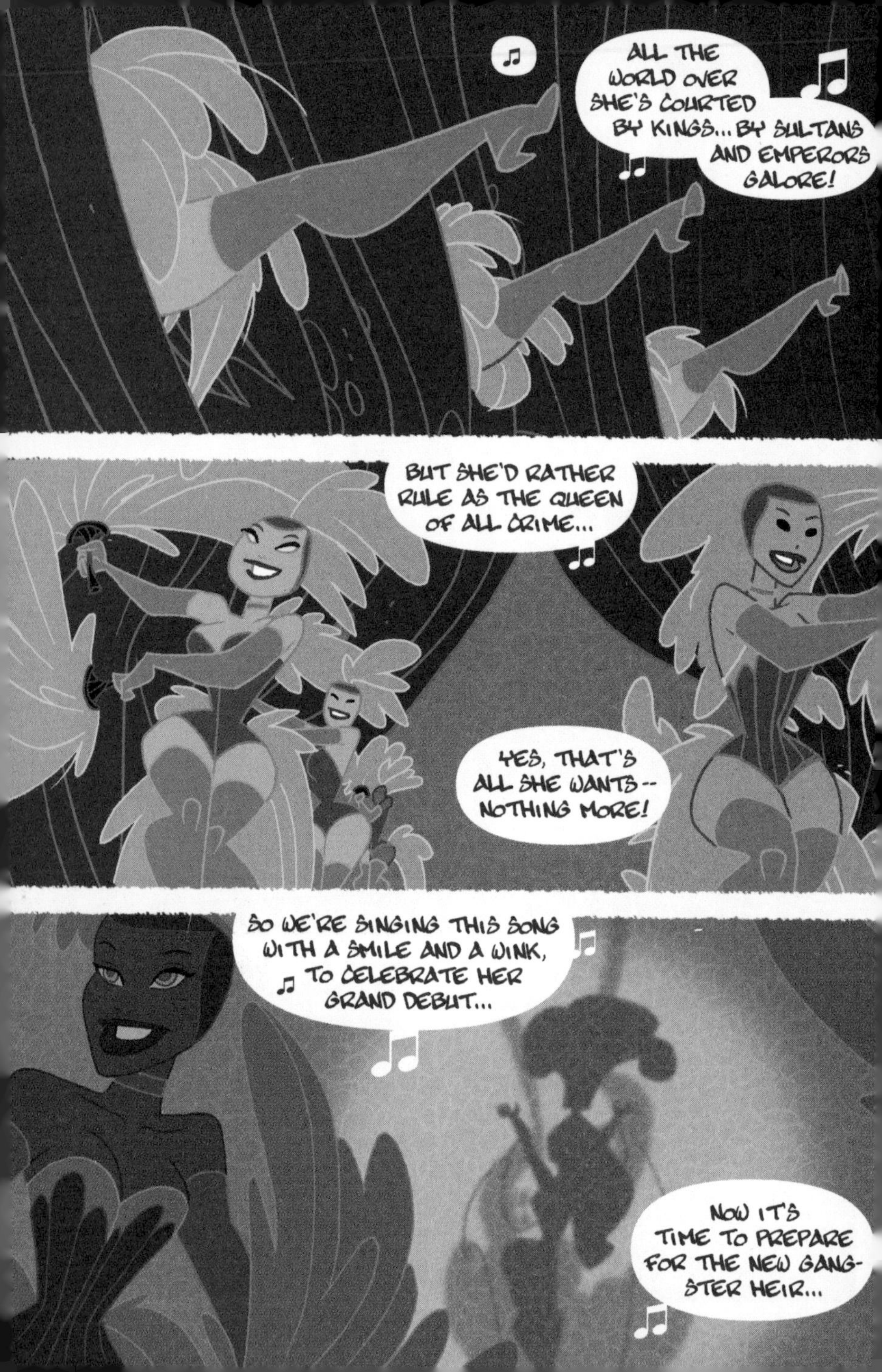

ALL THE WORLD OVER SHE'S COURTED BY KINGS... BY SULTANS AND EMPERORS GALORE!
BUT SHE'D RATHER RULE AS THE QUEEN OF ALL CRIME...
YES, THAT'S ALL SHE WANTS-- NOTHING MORE!
SO WE'RE SINGING THIS SONG WITH A SMILE AND A WINK, TO CELEBRATE HER GRAND DEBUT...
NOW IT'S TIME TO PREPARE FOR THE NEW GANG-STER HEIR...

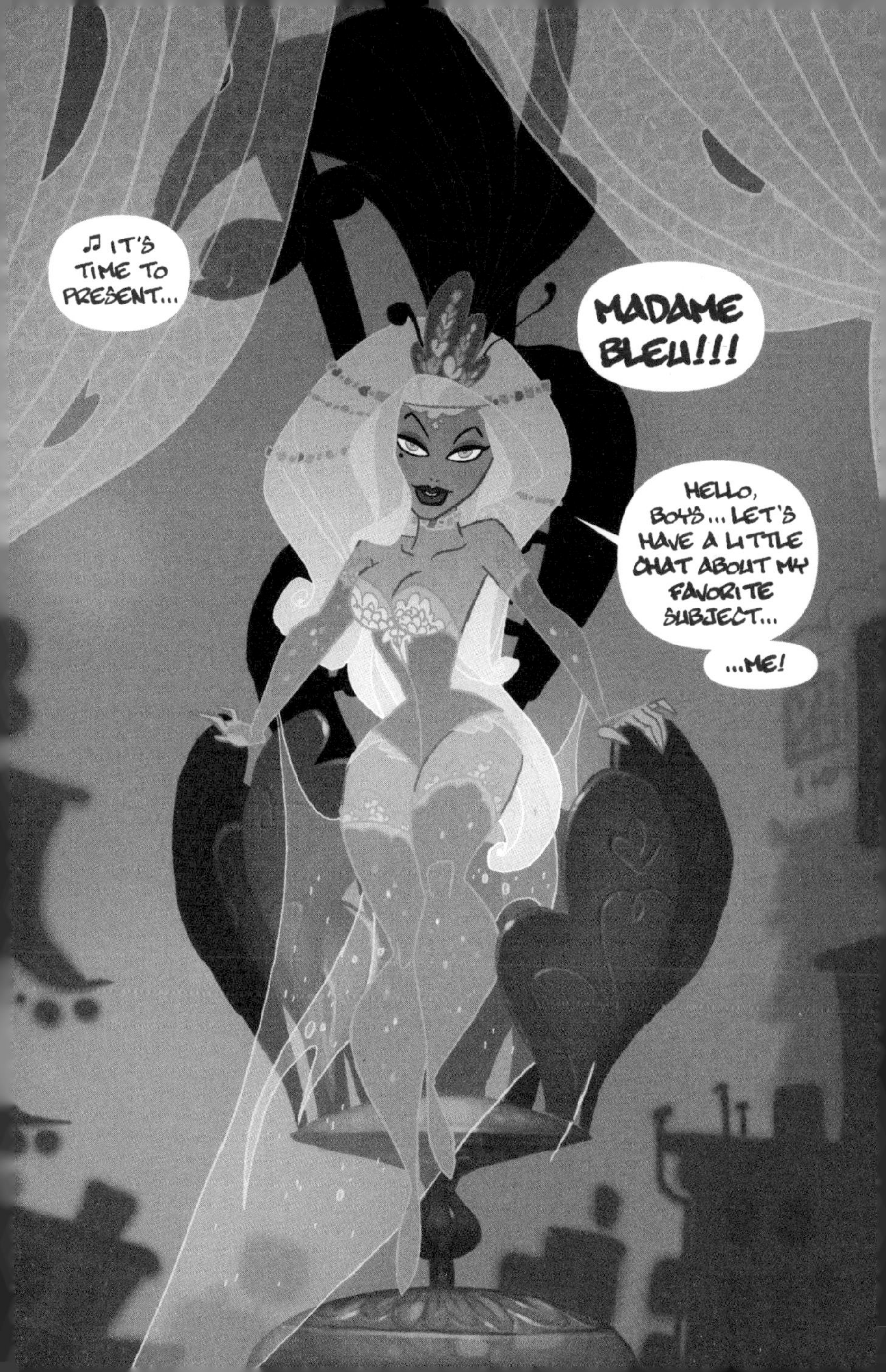
♫ IT'S TIME TO PRESENT...
MADAME BLEU!!!
HELLO, BOYS... LET'S HAVE A LITTLE CHAT ABOUT MY FAVORITE SUBJECT...
...ME!

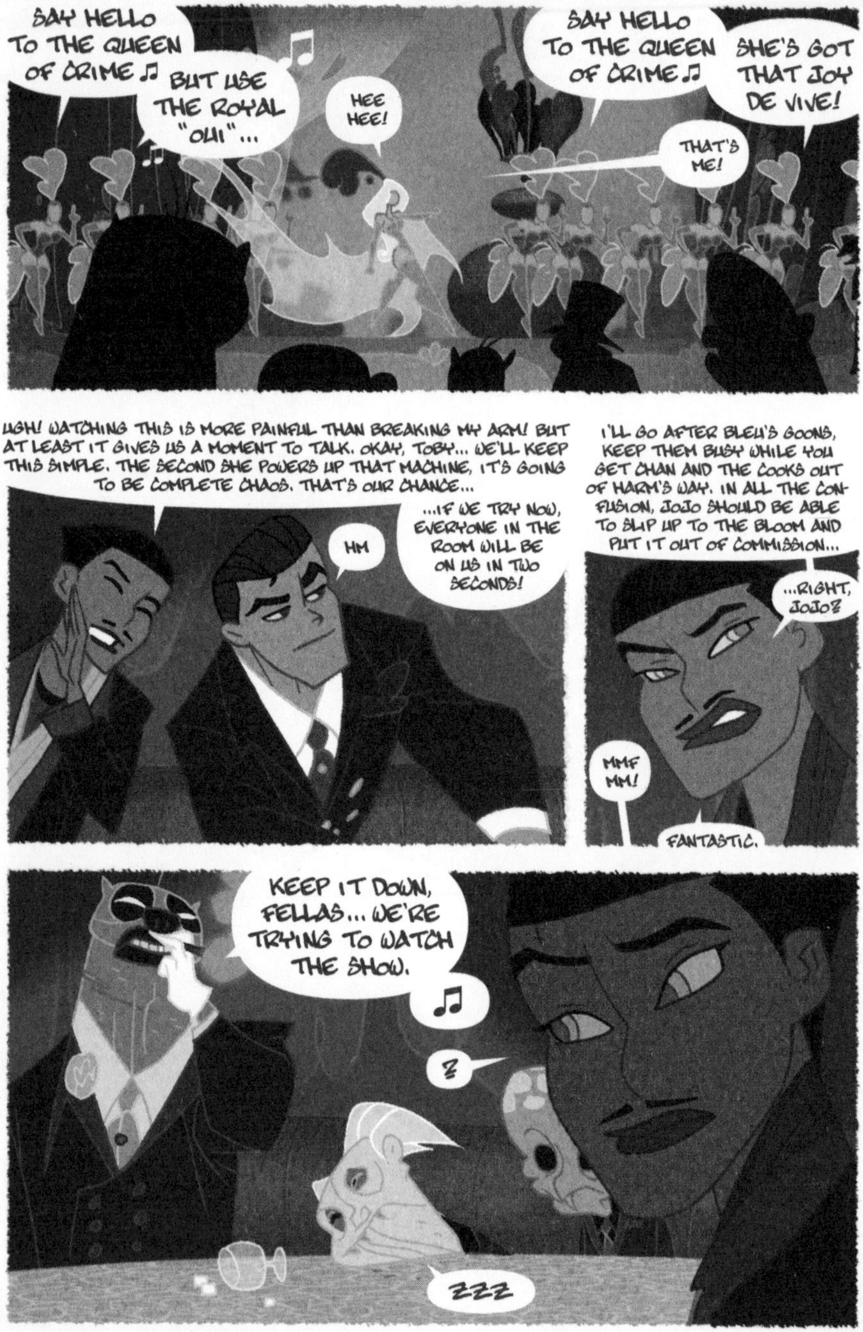
SAY HELLO TO THE QUEEN OF CRIME ♫
BUT USE THE ROYAL "OUI"...
HEE HEE!
SAY HELLO TO THE QUEEN OF CRIME ♫
SHE'S GOT THAT JOY DE VIVE!
THAT'S ME!
UGH! WATCHING THIS IS MORE PAINFUL THAN BREAKING MY ARM! BUT AT LEAST IT GIVES US A MOMENT TO TALK. OKAY, TOBY... WE'LL KEEP THIS SIMPLE. THE SECOND SHE POWERS UP THAT MACHINE, IT'S GOING TO BE COMPLETE CHAOS. THAT'S OUR CHANCE...
HM
...IF WE TRY NOW, EVERYONE IN THE ROOM WILL BE ON US IN TWO SECONDS!
I'LL GO AFTER BLEU'S GOONS, KEEP THEM BUSY WHILE YOU GET CHAN AND THE COOKS OUT OF HARM'S WAY. IN ALL THE CONFUSION, JOJO SHOULD BE ABLE TO SLIP UP TO THE BLOOM AND PUT IT OUT OF COMMISSION...
...RIGHT, JOJO?
MMF MM!
FANTASTIC.
KEEP IT DOWN, FELLAS... WE'RE TRYING TO WATCH THE SHOW.
♫
Z
ZZZ

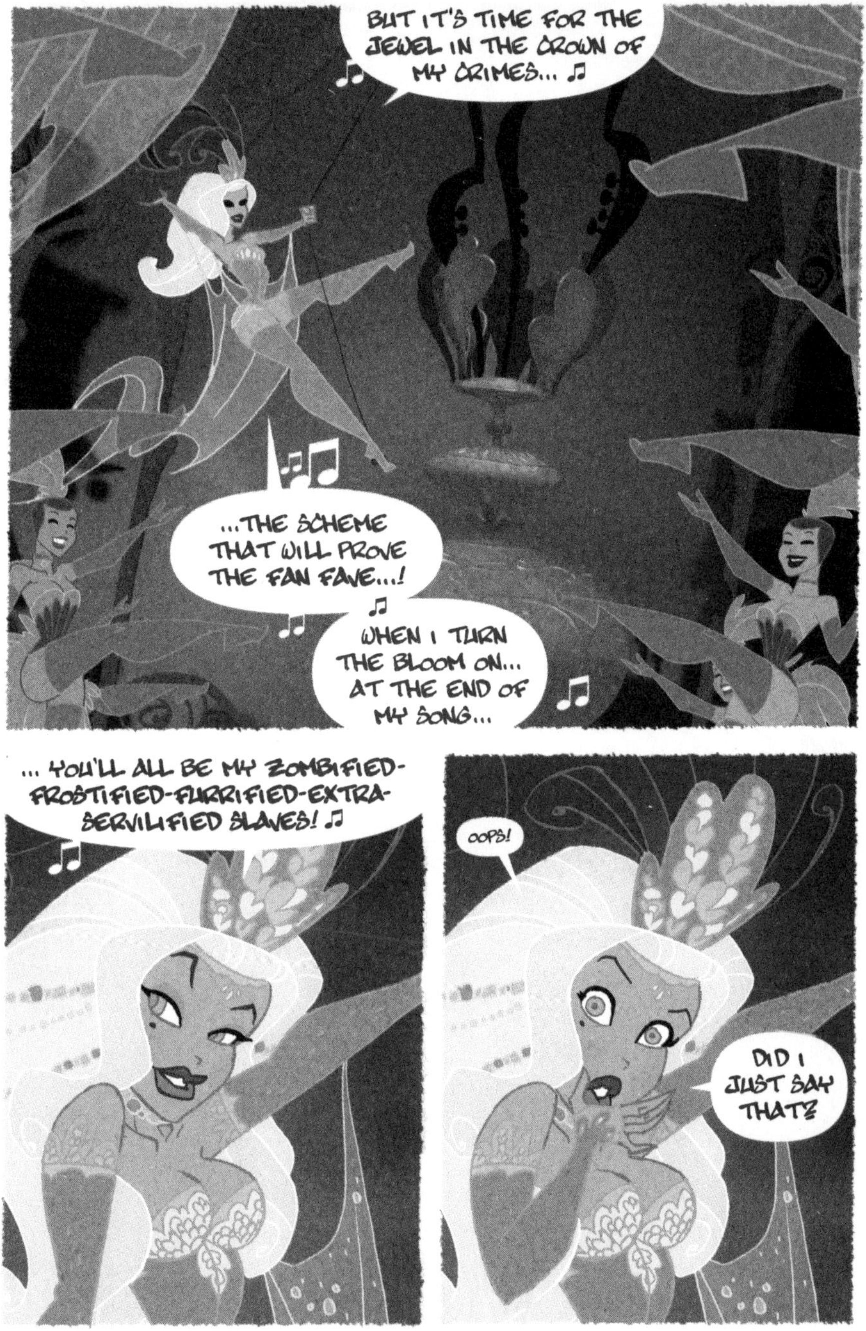
BUT IT'S TIME FOR THE JEWEL IN THE CROWN OF MY CRIMES... ♫
...THE SCHEME THAT WILL PROVE THE FAN FAVE...!
WHEN I TURN THE BLOOM ON... AT THE END OF MY SONG...
... YOU'LL ALL BE MY ZOMBIFIED-FROSTIFIED-FURRIFIED-EXTRA-SERVILIFIED SLAVES! ♫
OOPS!
DID I JUST SAY THAT?

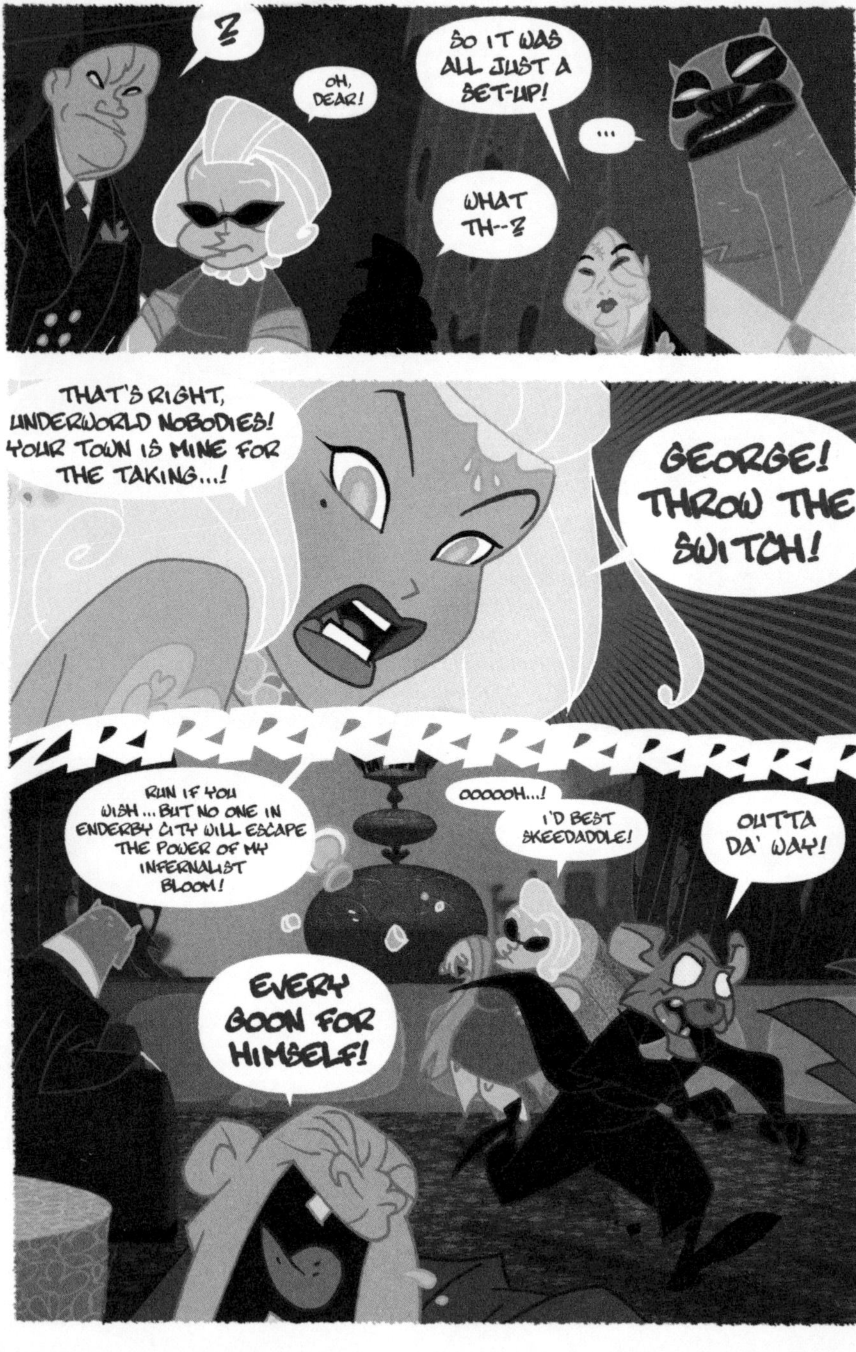
?
OH, DEAR!
SO IT WAS ALL JUST A SET-UP!
...
WHAT TH--?
THAT'S RIGHT, UNDERWORLD NOBODIES! YOUR TOWN IS MINE FOR THE TAKING...!
GEORGE! THROW THE SWITCH!
ZRRRRRRRRRRRRRRR
RUN IF YOU WISH ... BUT NO ONE IN ENDERBY CITY WILL ESCAPE THE POWER OF MY INFERNALIST BLOOM!
OOOOOH...!
I'D BEST SKEEDADDLE!
OUTTA DA' WAY!
EVERY GOON FOR HIMSELF!

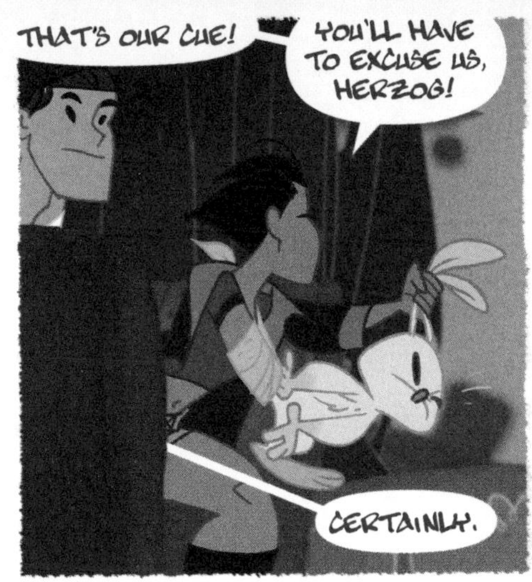
THAT'S OUR CUE!
YOU'LL HAVE TO EXCUSE US, HERZOG!
CERTAINLY.

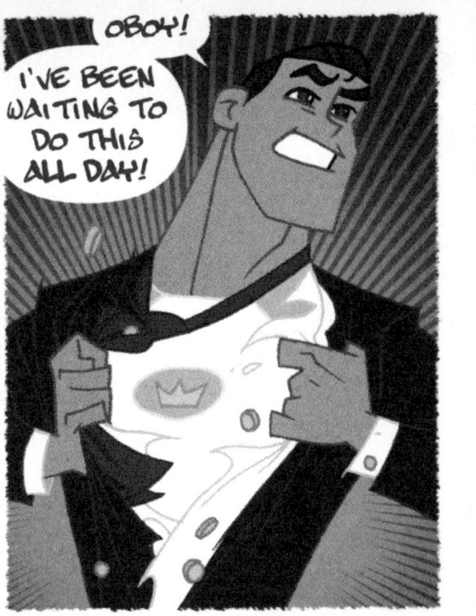
OBOY!
I'VE BEEN WAITING TO DO THIS ALL DAY!

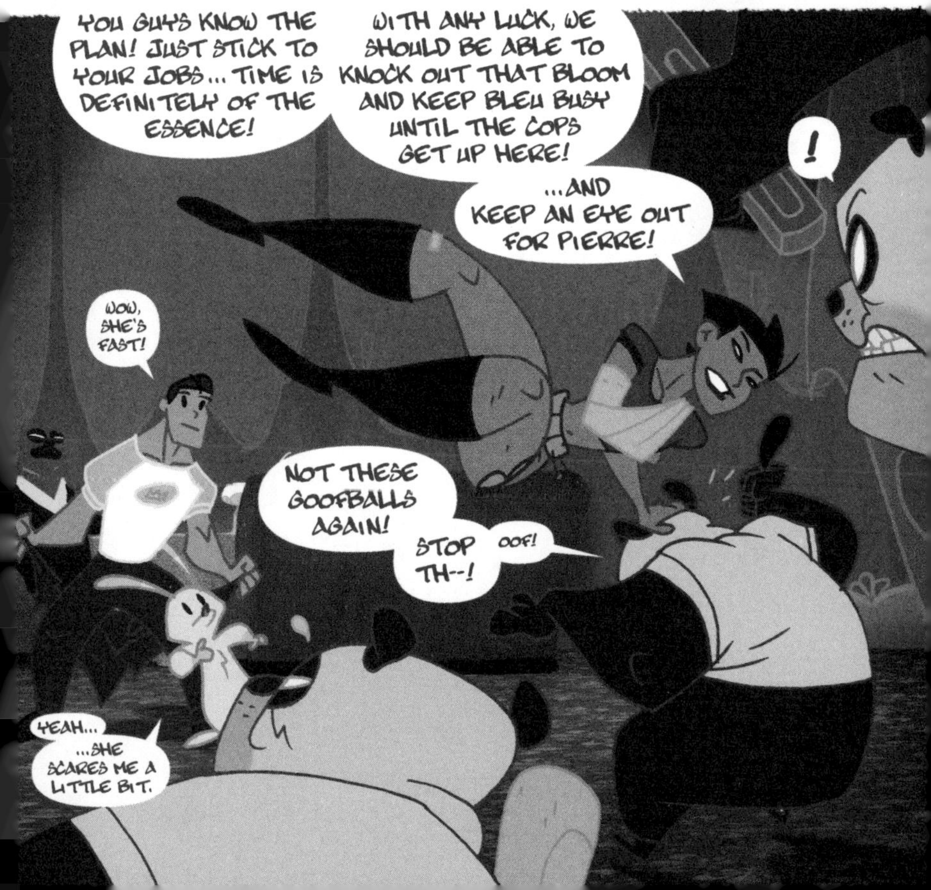
YOU GUYS KNOW THE PLAN! JUST STICK TO YOUR JOBS... TIME IS DEFINITELY OF THE ESSENCE!
WITH ANY LUCK, WE SHOULD BE ABLE TO KNOCK OUT THAT BLOOM AND KEEP BLEU BUSY UNTIL THE COPS GET UP HERE!
...AND KEEP AN EYE OUT FOR PIERRE!
!
WOW, SHE'S FAST!
NOT THESE GOOFBALLS AGAIN!
STOP TH--!
OOF!
YEAH...
...SHE SCARES ME A LITTLE BIT.

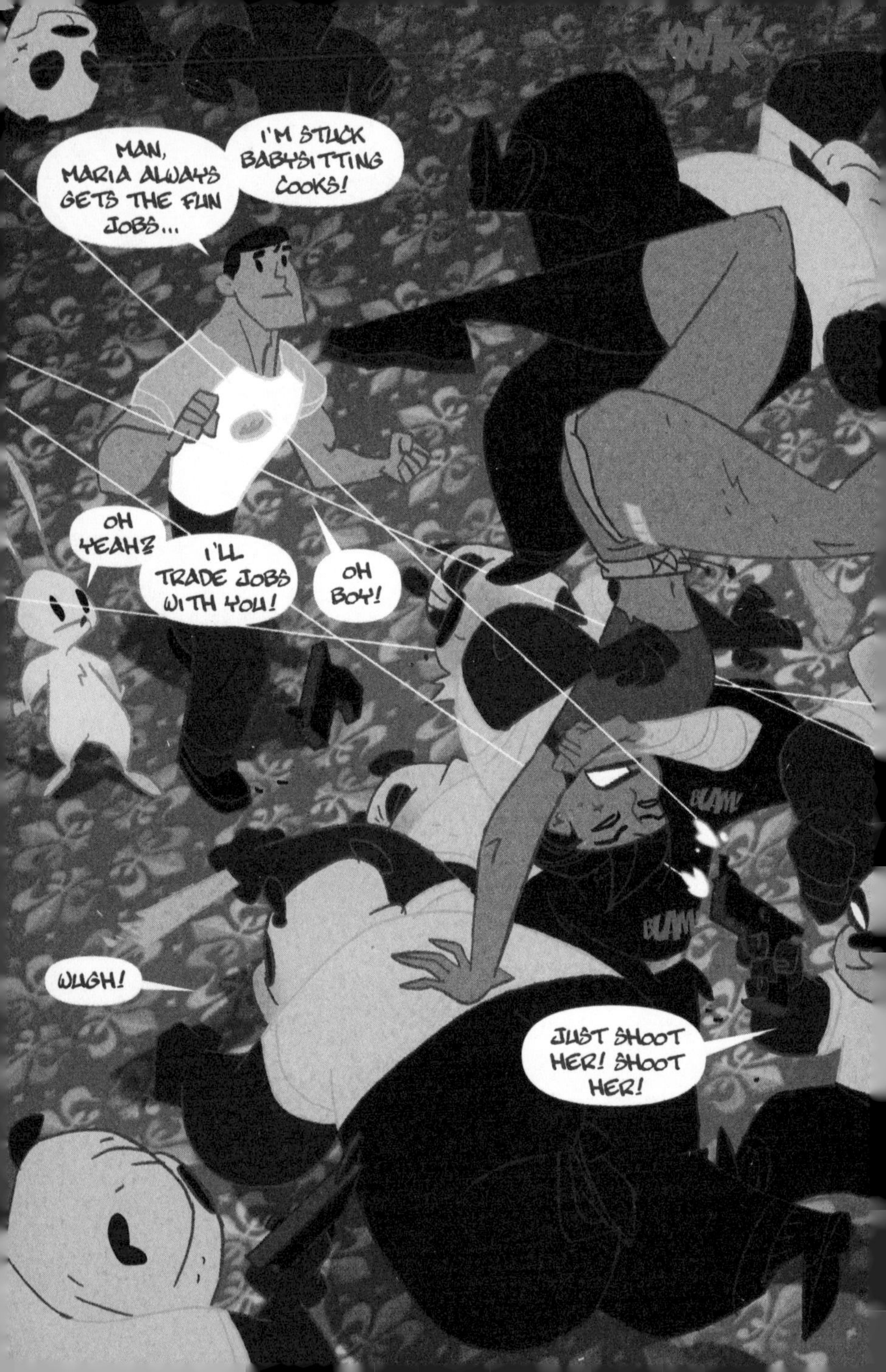
KRAK
MAN, MARIA ALWAYS GETS THE FUN JOBS...
I'M STUCK BABYSITTING COOKS!
OH YEAH?
I'LL TRADE JOBS WITH YOU!
OH BOY!
BLAM!
BLAM!
WUGH!
JUST SHOOT HER! SHOOT HER!

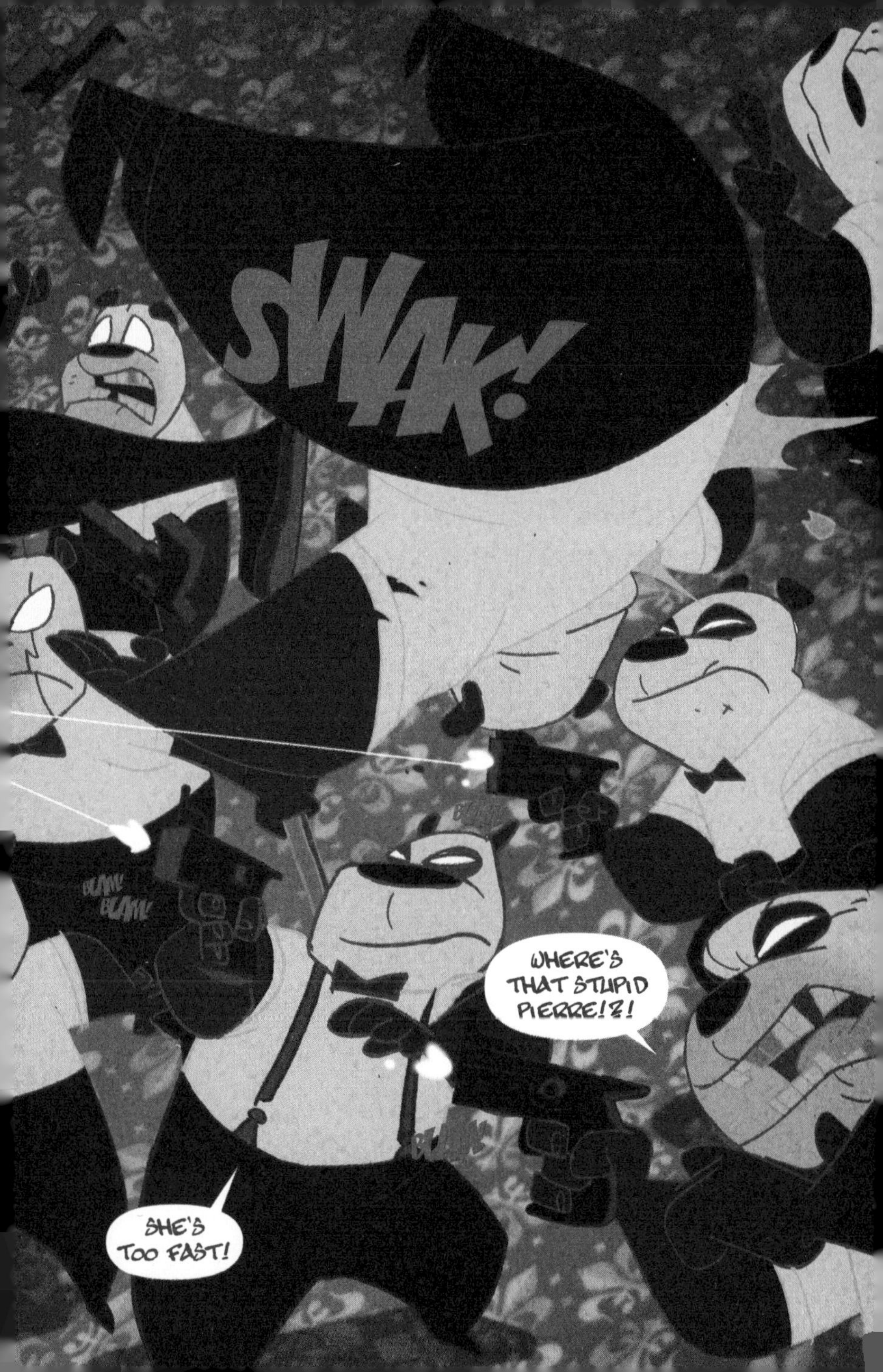
SWAK!
BLAM! BLAM!
WHERE'S THAT STUPID PIERRE!?!
SHE'S TOO FAST!

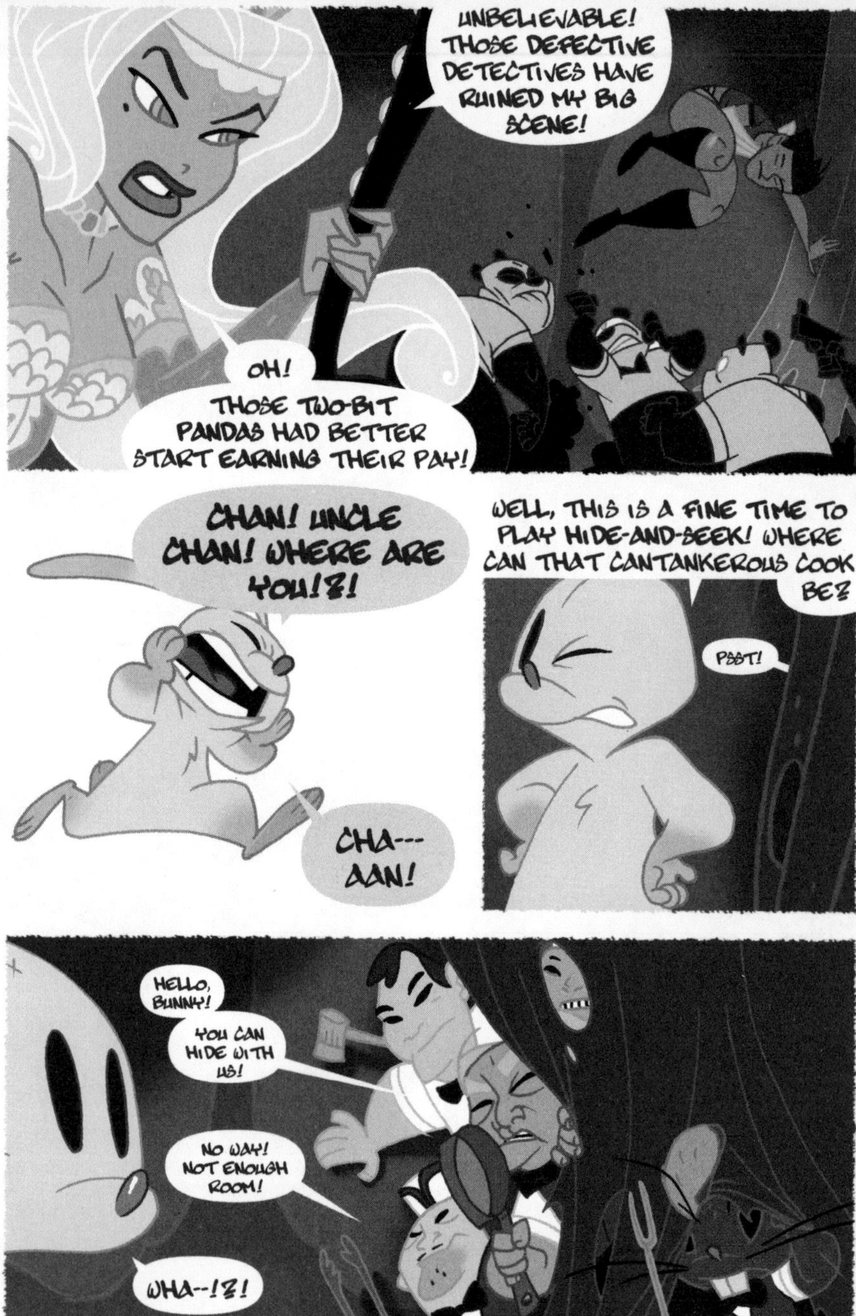
UNBELIEVABLE! THOSE DEFECTIVE DETECTIVES HAVE RUINED MY BIG SCENE!
OH!
THOSE TWO-BIT PANDAS HAD BETTER START EARNING THEIR PAY!
CHAN! UNCLE CHAN! WHERE ARE YOU!?!
CHA--- AAN!
WELL, THIS IS A FINE TIME TO PLAY HIDE-AND-SEEK! WHERE CAN THAT CANTANKEROUS COOK BE?
PSST!
HELLO, BUNNY!
YOU CAN HIDE WITH US!
NO WAY! NOT ENOUGH ROOM!
WHA--!?!

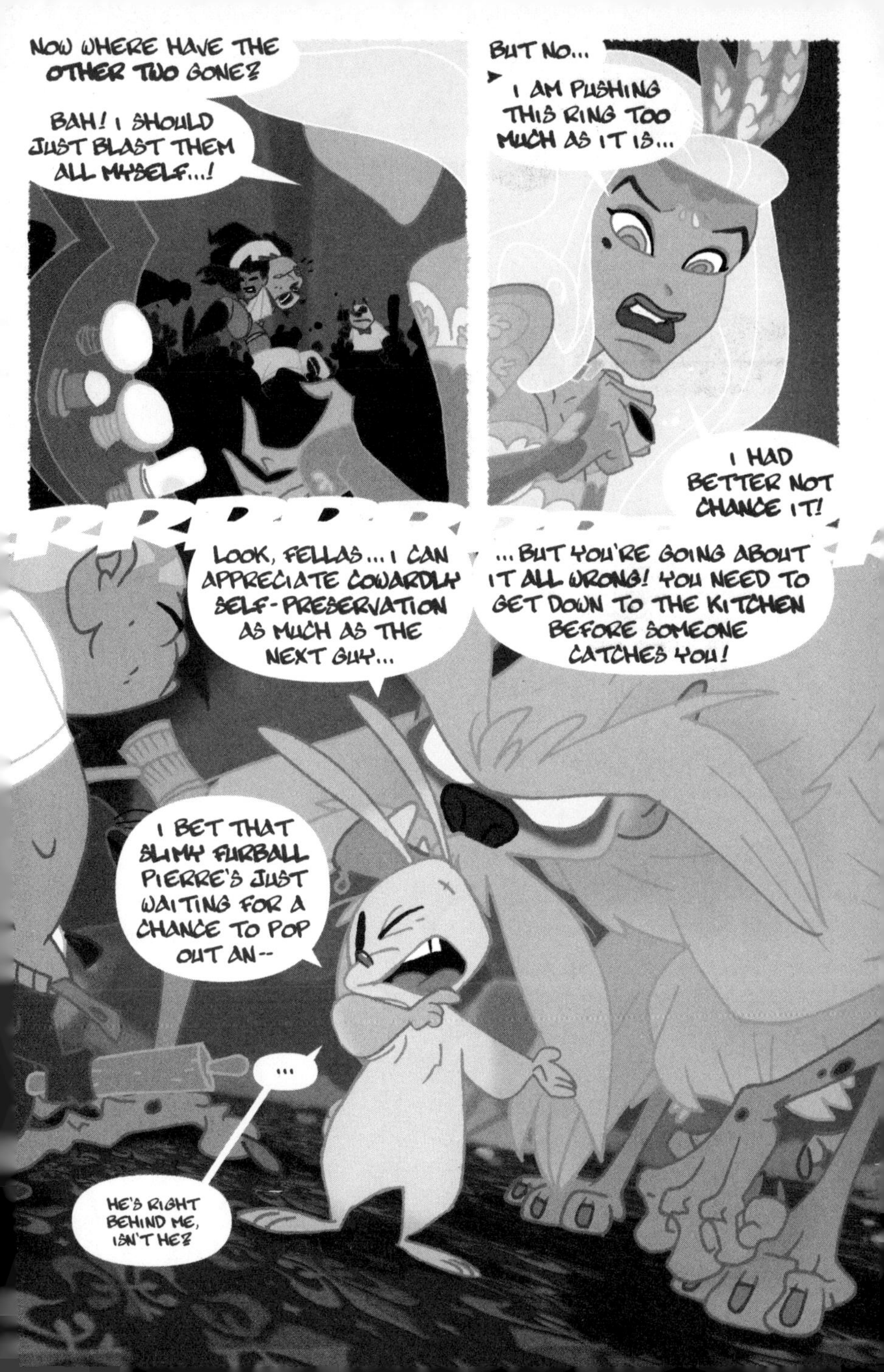

NOW WHERE HAVE THE OTHER TWO GONE?
BAH! I SHOULD JUST BLAST THEM ALL MYSELF...!
BUT NO...
I AM PUSHING THIS RING TOO MUCH AS IT IS...
I HAD BETTER NOT CHANCE IT!
LOOK, FELLAS... I CAN APPRECIATE COWARDLY SELF-PRESERVATION AS MUCH AS THE NEXT GUY...
...BUT YOU'RE GOING ABOUT IT ALL WRONG! YOU NEED TO GET DOWN TO THE KITCHEN BEFORE SOMEONE CATCHES YOU!
I BET THAT SLIMY FURBALL PIERRE'S JUST WAITING FOR A CHANCE TO POP OUT AN--
...
HE'S RIGHT BEHIND ME, ISN'T HE?

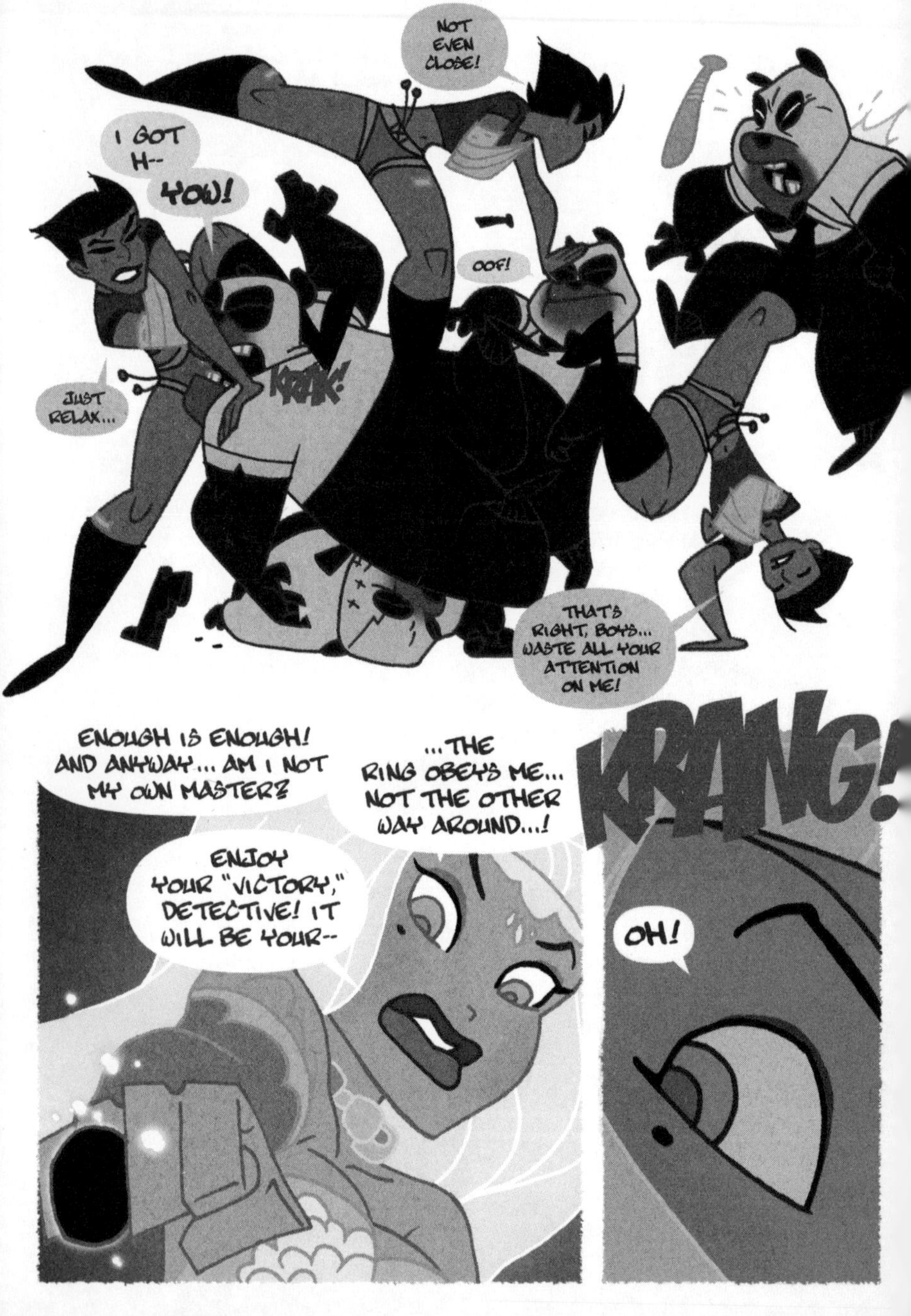
NOT EVEN CLOSE!
I GOT H--
YOW!
OOF!
KRAAK!
JUST RELAX...
THAT'S RIGHT, BOYS... WASTE ALL YOUR ATTENTION ON ME!
ENOUGH IS ENOUGH! AND ANYWAY... AM I NOT MY OWN MASTER?
...THE RING OBEYS ME... NOT THE OTHER WAY AROUND...!
ENJOY YOUR "VICTORY," DETECTIVE! IT WILL BE YOUR--
KRANG!
OH!

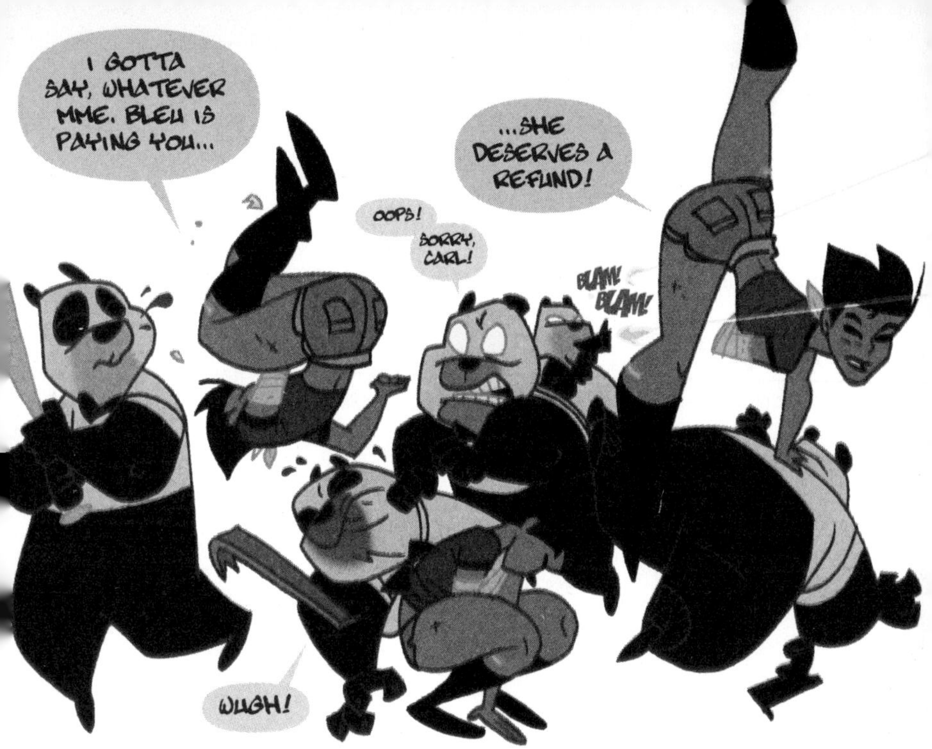
I GOTTA SAY, WHATEVER MME. BLEU IS PAYING YOU...
...SHE DESERVES A REFUND!
OOPS!
SORRY, CARL!
BLAM! BLAM!
WUGH!

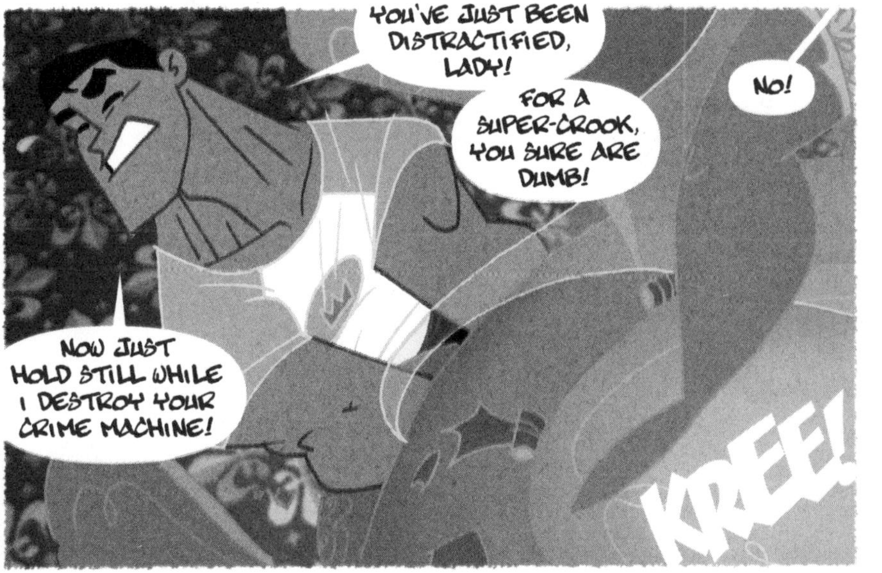
YOU'VE JUST BEEN DISTRACTIFIED, LADY!
FOR A SUPER-CROOK, YOU SURE ARE DUMB!
NO!
NOW JUST HOLD STILL WHILE I DESTROY YOUR CRIME MACHINE!
KREE!

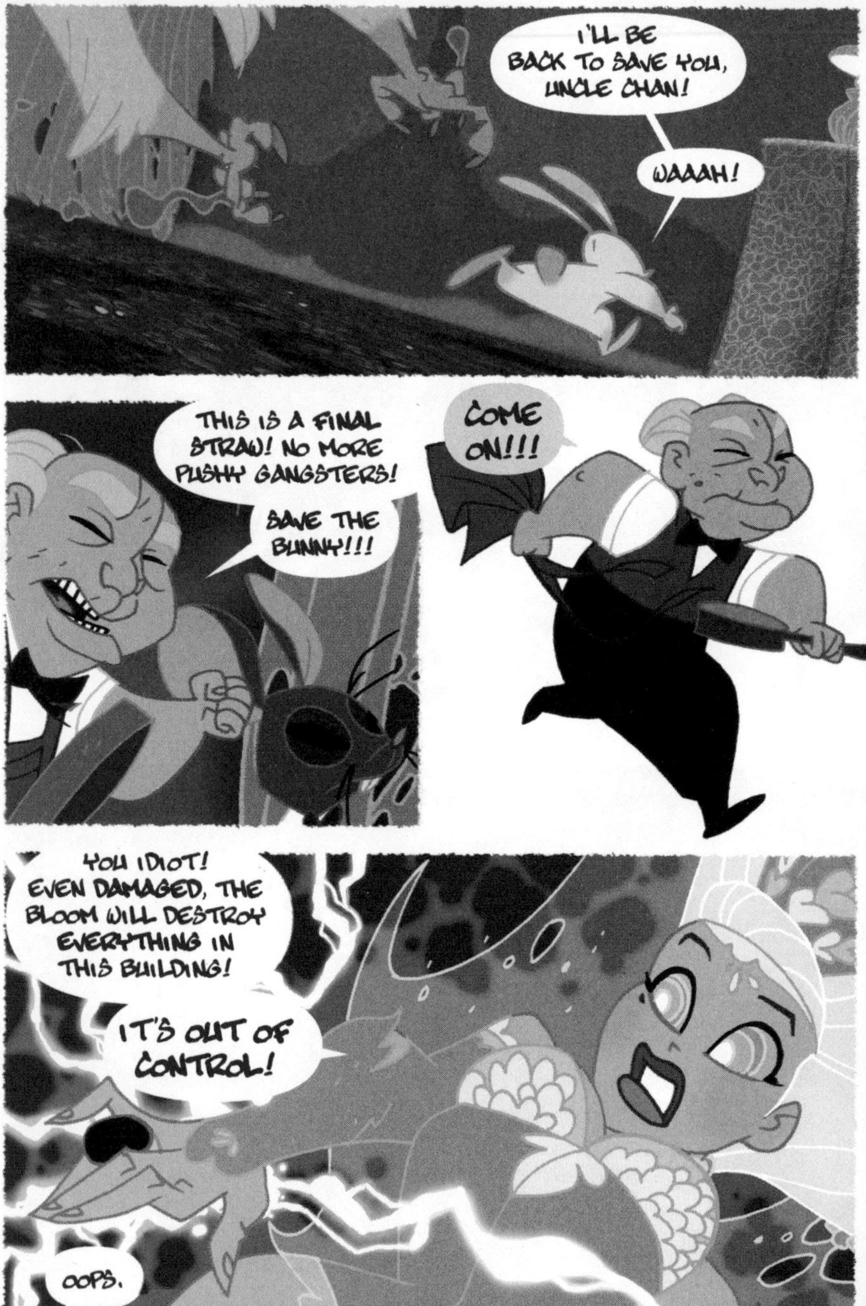
I'LL BE BACK TO SAVE YOU, UNCLE CHAN!
WAAAH!
THIS IS A FINAL STRAW! NO MORE PUSHY GANGSTERS!
SAVE THE BUNNY!!!
COME ON!!!
YOU IDIOT! EVEN DAMAGED, THE BLOOM WILL DESTROY EVERYTHING IN THIS BUILDING!
IT'S OUT OF CONTROL!
OOPS.

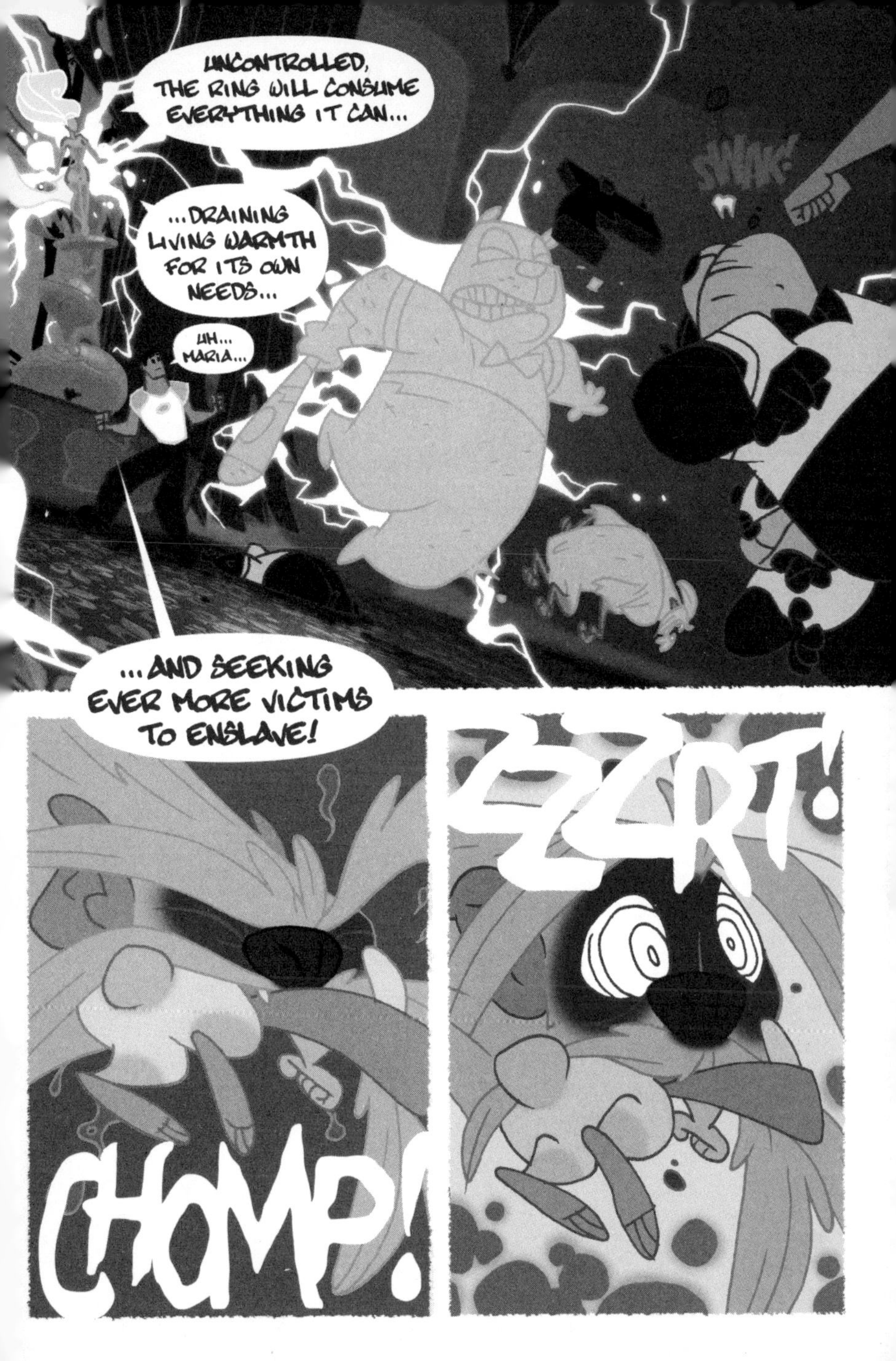
UNCONTROLLED, THE RING WILL CONSUME EVERYTHING IT CAN...
SWAK!
...DRAINING LIVING WARMTH FOR ITS OWN NEEDS...
UH... MARIA...
...AND SEEKING EVER MORE VICTIMS TO ENSLAVE!
CHOMP!
ZZZRT!

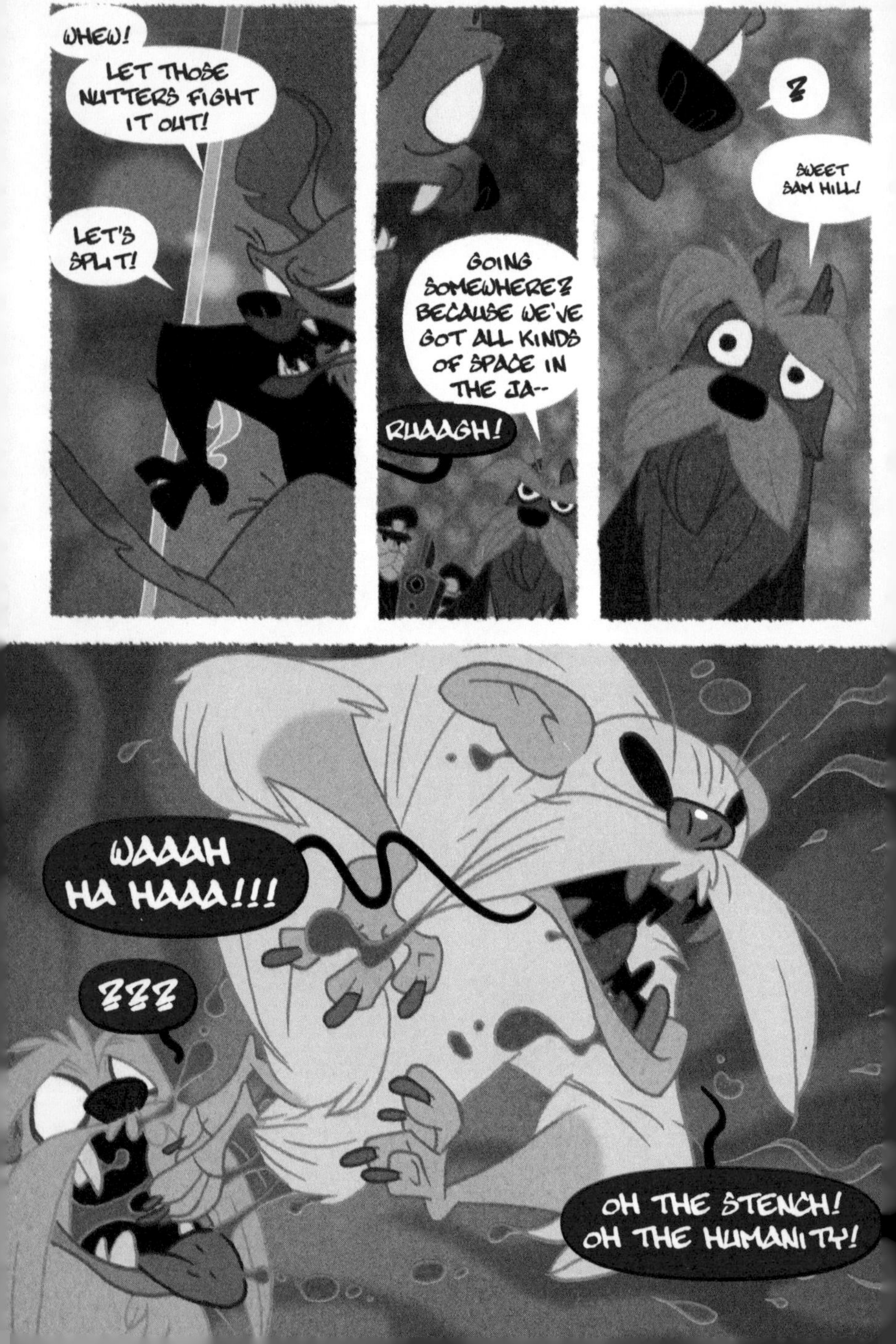
WHEW!
LET THOSE NUTTERS FIGHT IT OUT!
LET'S SPLIT!
GOING SOMEWHERE? BECAUSE WE'VE GOT ALL KINDS OF SPACE IN THE JA--
RUAAGH!
?
SWEET SAM HILL!
WAAAH HA HAAAA!!!
???
OH THE STENCH! OH THE HUMANITY!

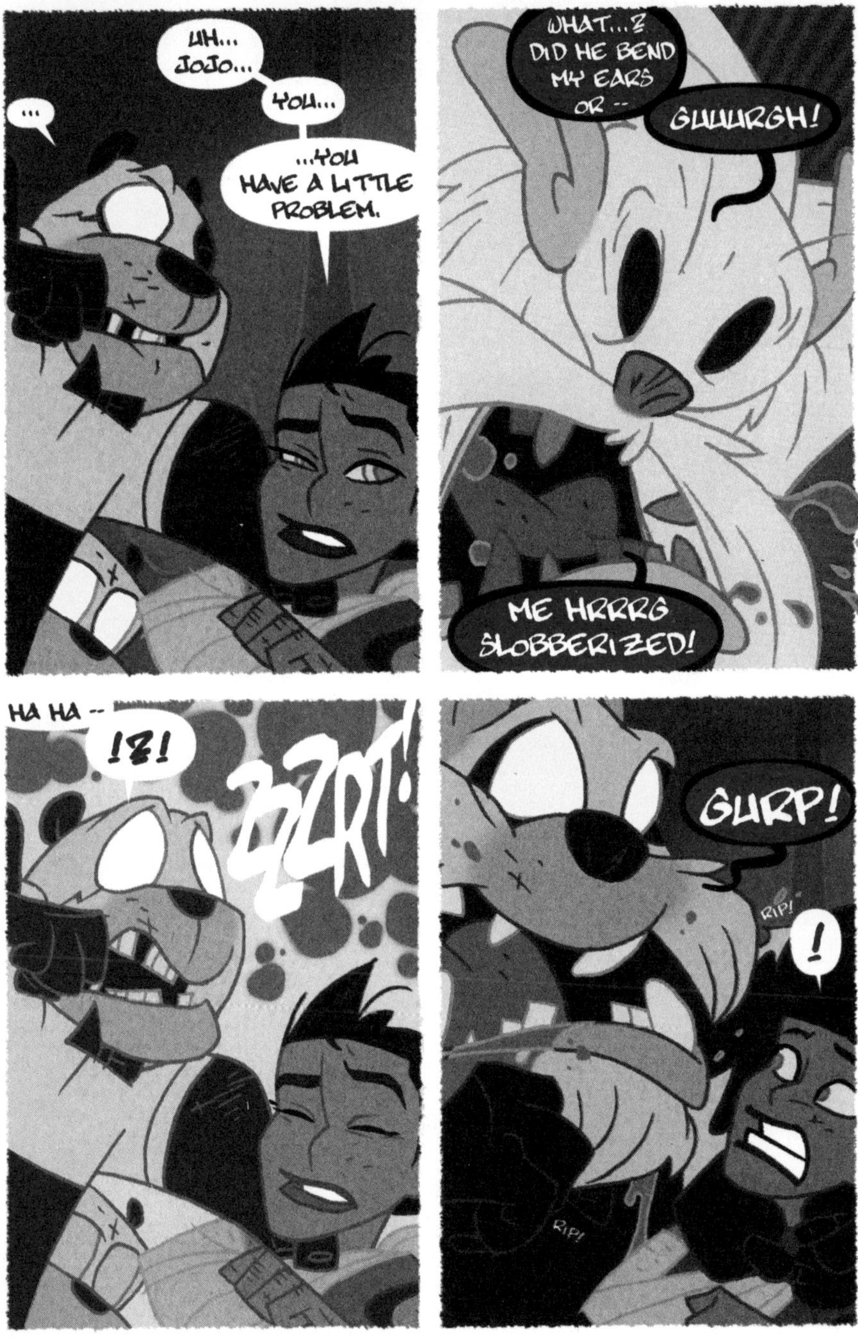
UH... JOJO...
YOU...
...
...YOU HAVE A LITTLE PROBLEM.
WHAT...?! DID HE BEND MY EARS OR --
GUUURGH!
ME HRRRG SLOBBERIZED!
HA HA --
!?!
ZZZRT!
GURP!
RIP!
!
RIP!

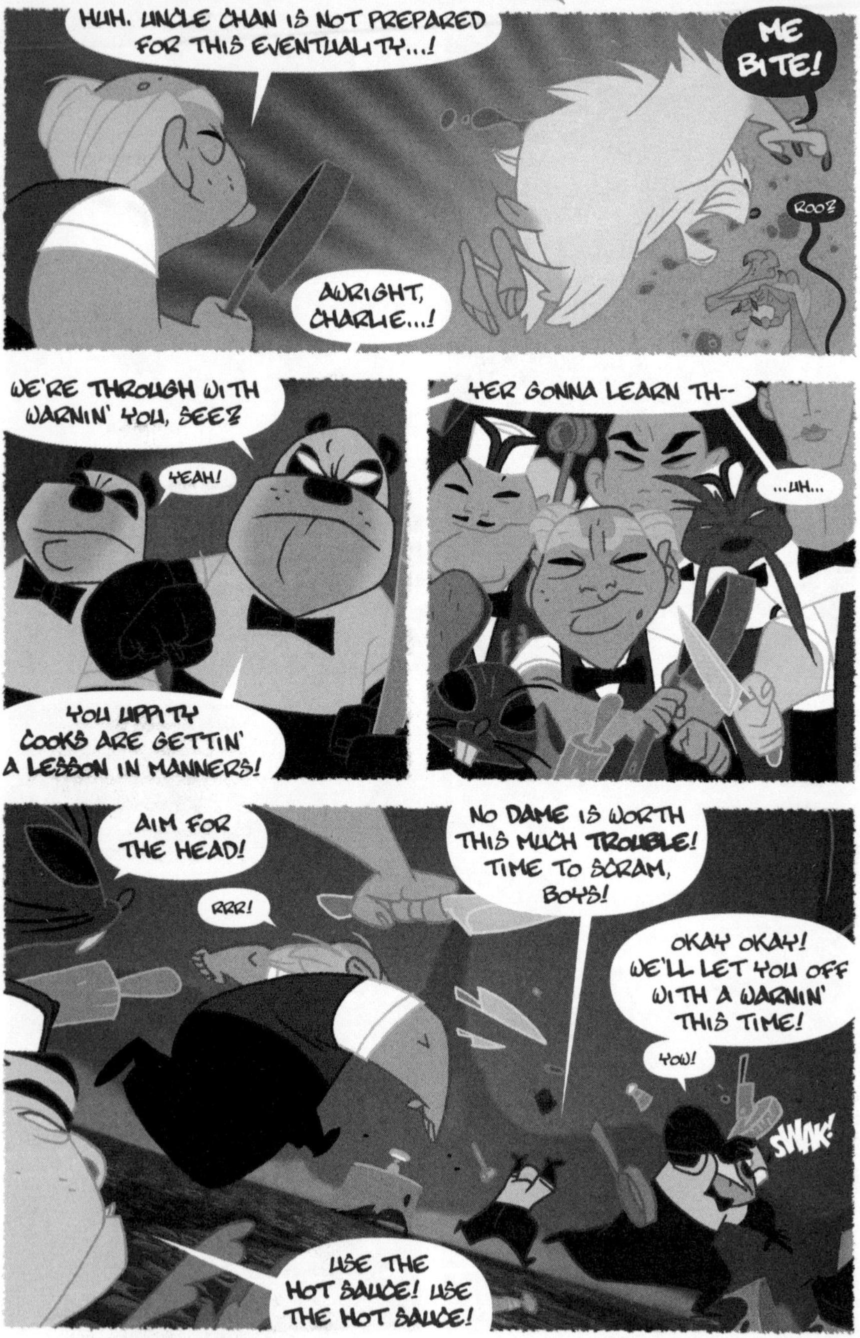
HUH. UNCLE CHAN IS NOT PREPARED FOR THIS EVENTUALITY...!
ME BITE!
ROO?
AWRIGHT, CHARLIE...!
WE'RE THROUGH WITH WARNIN' YOU, SEE?
YEAH!
YOU UPPITY COOKS ARE GETTIN' A LESSON IN MANNERS!
YER GONNA LEARN TH--
...UH...
AIM FOR THE HEAD!
RRR!
NO DAME IS WORTH THIS MUCH TROUBLE! TIME TO SCRAM, BOYS!
OKAY OKAY! WE'LL LET YOU OFF WITH A WARNIN' THIS TIME!
YOW!
SWAK!
USE THE HOT SAUCE! USE THE HOT SAUCE!

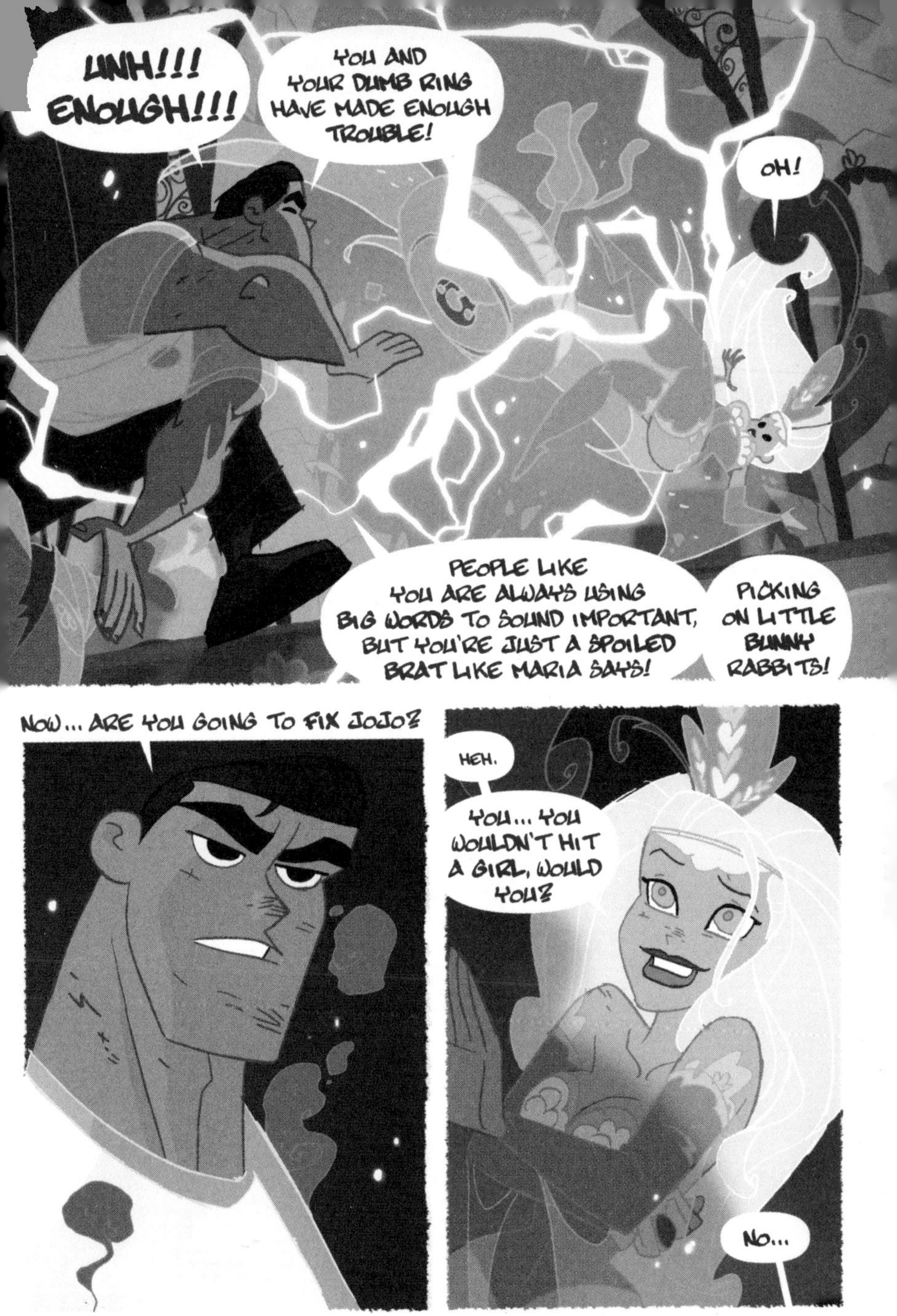
UNH!!!
ENOUGH!!!
YOU AND YOUR DUMB RING HAVE MADE ENOUGH TROUBLE!
OH!
PEOPLE LIKE YOU ARE ALWAYS USING BIG WORDS TO SOUND IMPORTANT, BUT YOU'RE JUST A SPOILED BRAT LIKE MARIA SAYS!
PICKING ON LITTLE BUNNY RABBITS!
NOW... ARE YOU GOING TO FIX JOJO?
HEH.
YOU... YOU WOULDN'T HIT A GIRL, WOULD YOU?
NO...

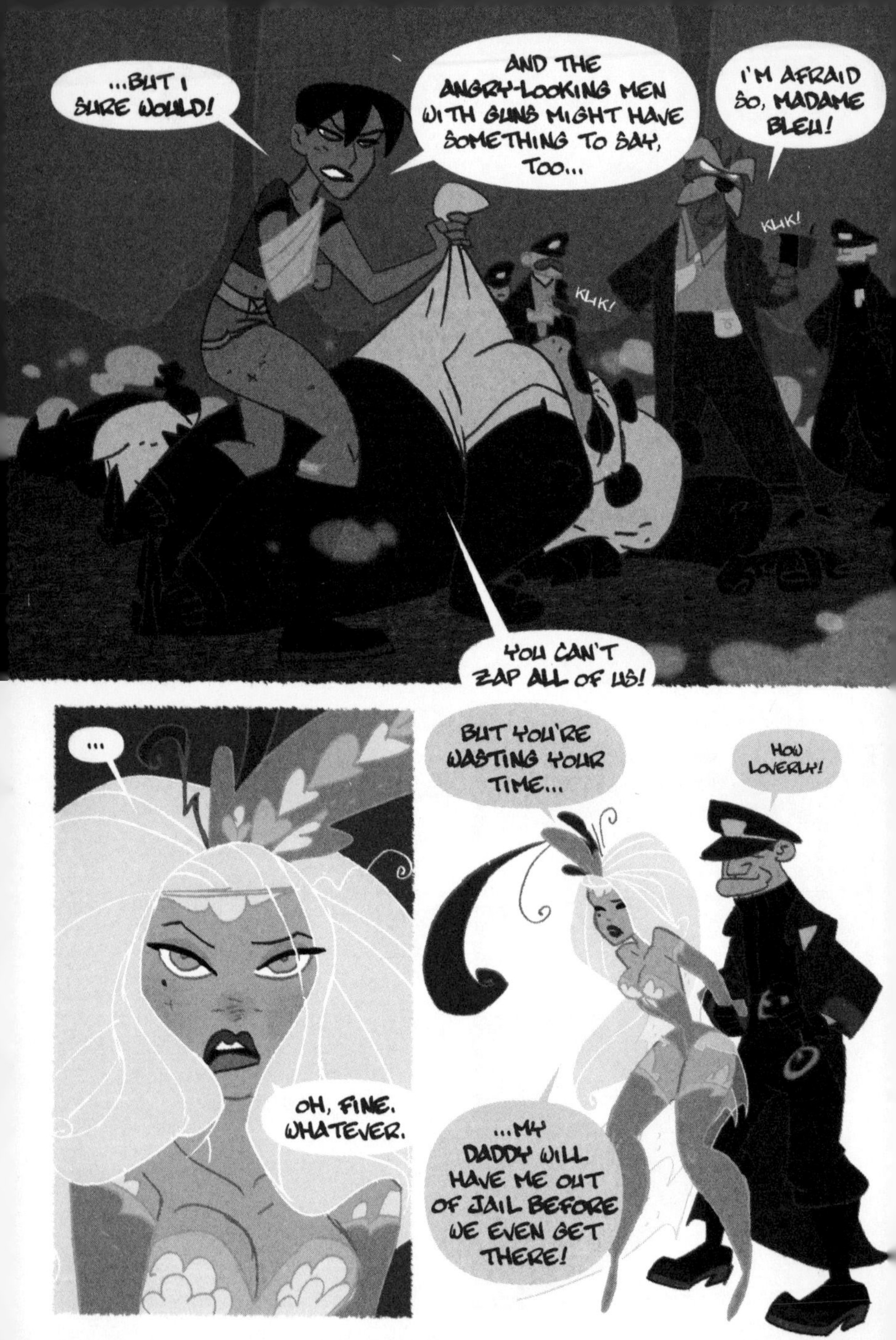
...BUT I SURE WOULD!
AND THE ANGRY-LOOKING MEN WITH GUNS MIGHT HAVE SOMETHING TO SAY, TOO...
I'M AFRAID SO, MADAME BLEU!
KLIK!
KLIK!
YOU CAN'T ZAP ALL OF US!
...
OH, FINE. WHATEVER.
BUT YOU'RE WASTING YOUR TIME...
HOW LOVERLY!
...MY DADDY WILL HAVE ME OUT OF JAIL BEFORE WE EVEN GET THERE!

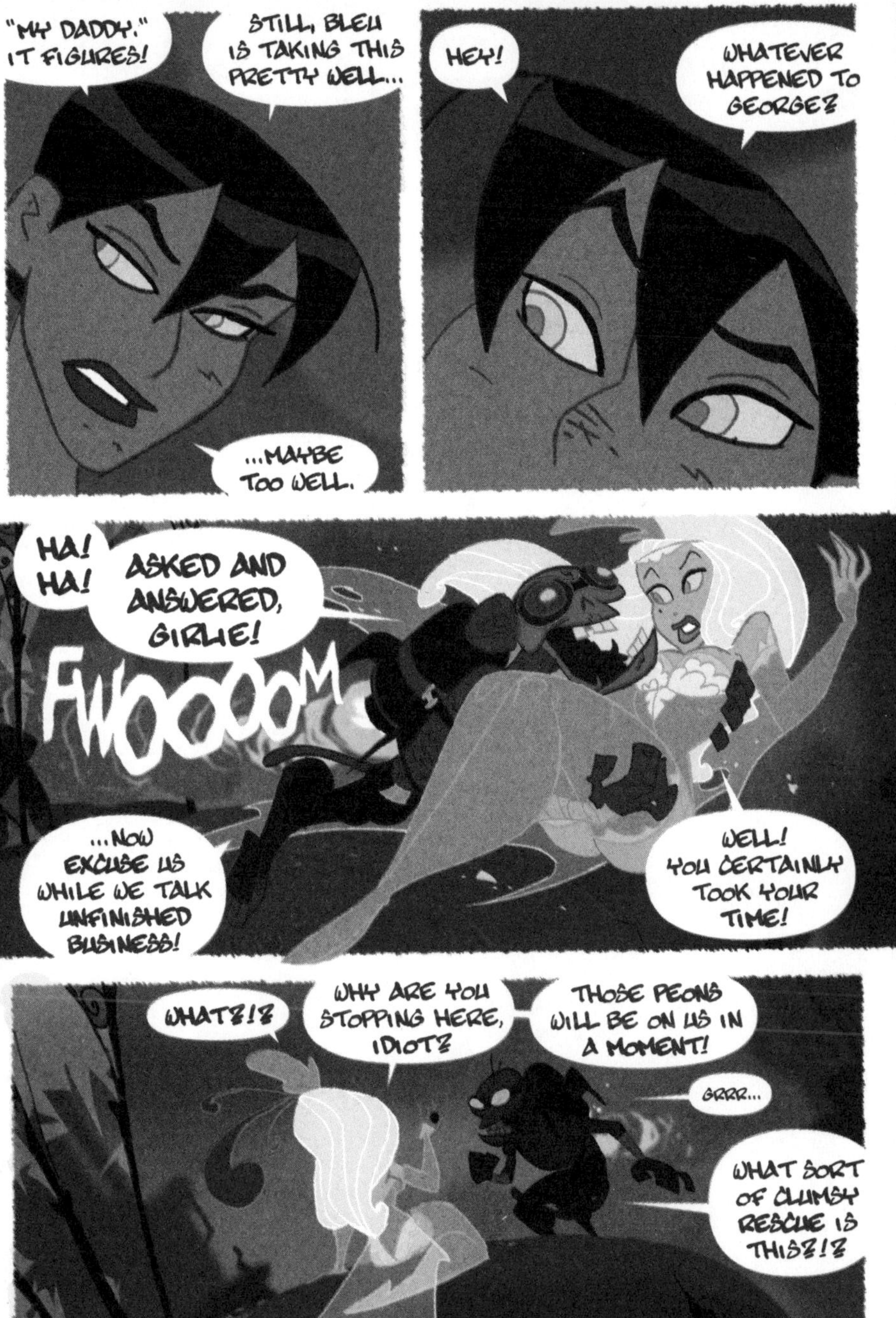
"MY DADDY." IT FIGURES!
STILL, BLEU IS TAKING THIS PRETTY WELL...
...MAYBE TOO WELL.
HEY!
WHATEVER HAPPENED TO GEORGE?
HA! HA!
ASKED AND ANSWERED, GIRLIE!
FWOOOOOM
...NOW EXCUSE US WHILE WE TALK UNFINISHED BUSINESS!
WELL! YOU CERTAINLY TOOK YOUR TIME!
WHAT?!?
WHY ARE YOU STOPPING HERE, IDIOT?
THOSE PEONS WILL BE ON US IN A MOMENT!
GRRR...
WHAT SORT OF CLUMSY RESCUE IS THIS?!?

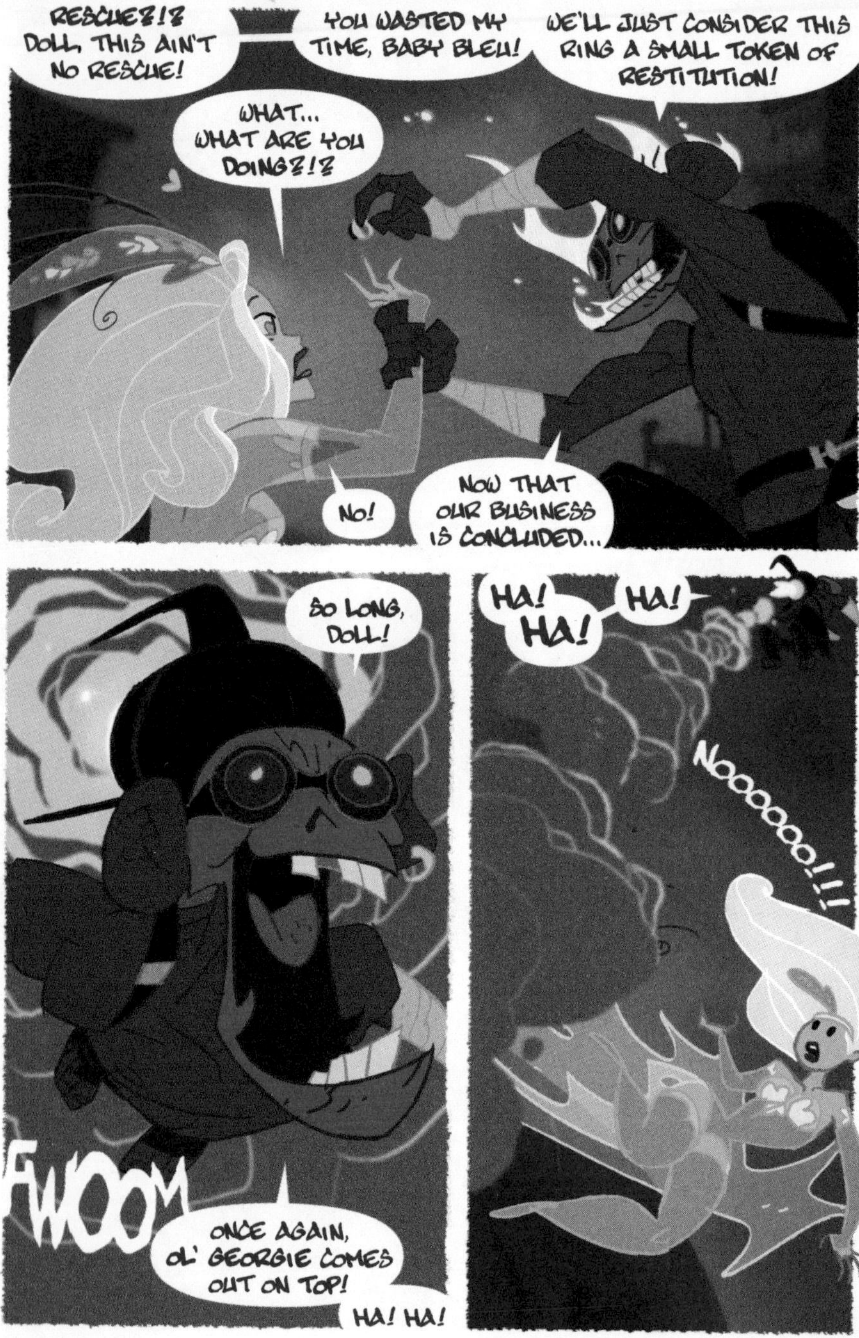
RESCUE?!? DOLL, THIS AIN'T NO RESCUE!
YOU WASTED MY TIME, BABY BLEU!
WE'LL JUST CONSIDER THIS RING A SMALL TOKEN OF RESTITUTION!
WHAT... WHAT ARE YOU DOING?!?
NO!
NOW THAT OUR BUSINESS IS CONCLUDED...
SO LONG, DOLL!
FWOOM
ONCE AGAIN, OL' GEORGIE COMES OUT ON TOP!
HA! HA!
HA! HA!
HA!
NOOOOOOO!!!!

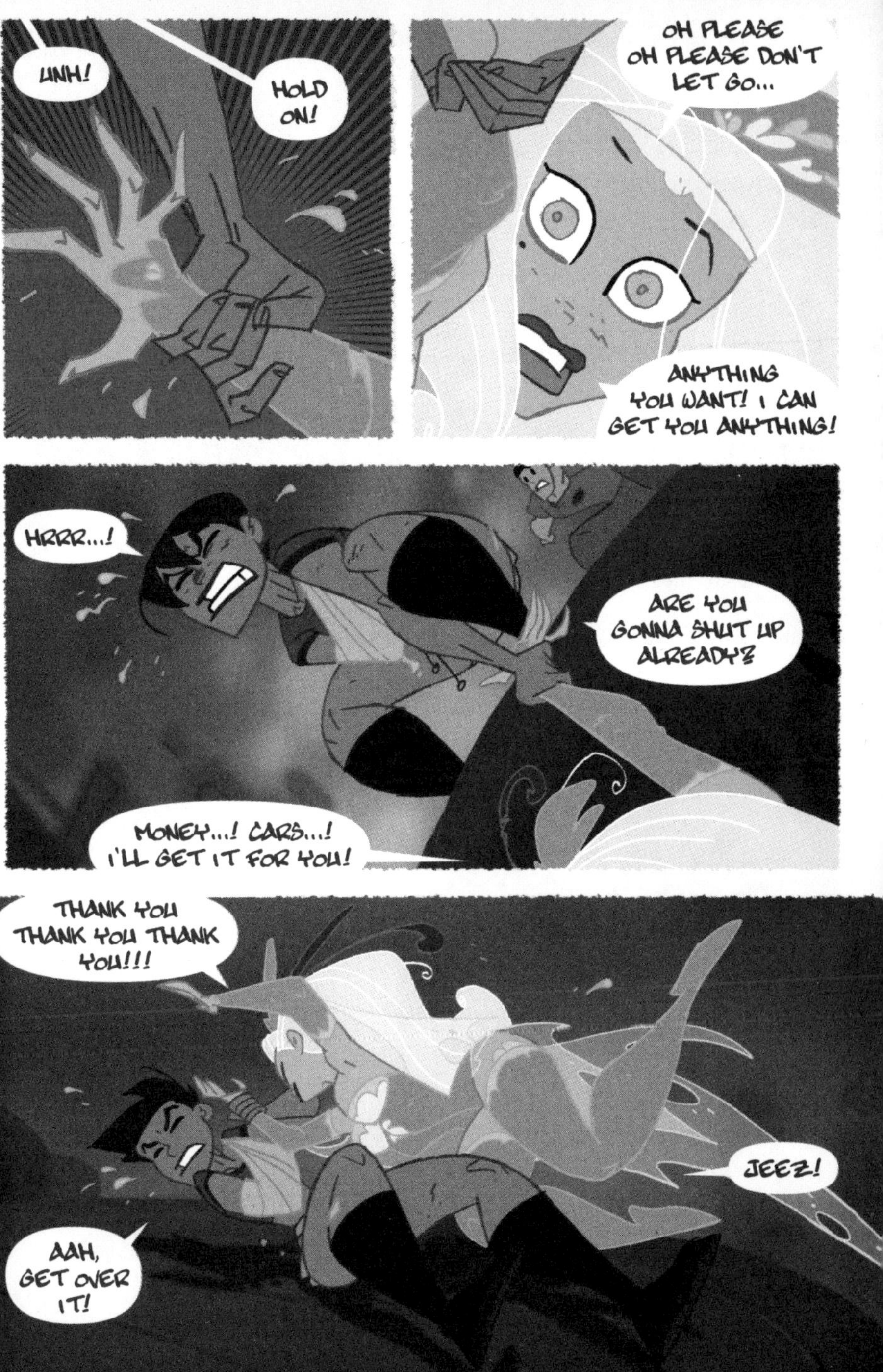
UNH!
HOLD ON!
OH PLEASE OH PLEASE DON'T LET GO...
ANYTHING YOU WANT! I CAN GET YOU ANYTHING!
HRRR...!
ARE YOU GONNA SHUT UP ALREADY?
MONEY...! CARS...! I'LL GET IT FOR YOU!
THANK YOU THANK YOU THANK YOU!!!
JEEZ!
AAH, GET OVER IT!

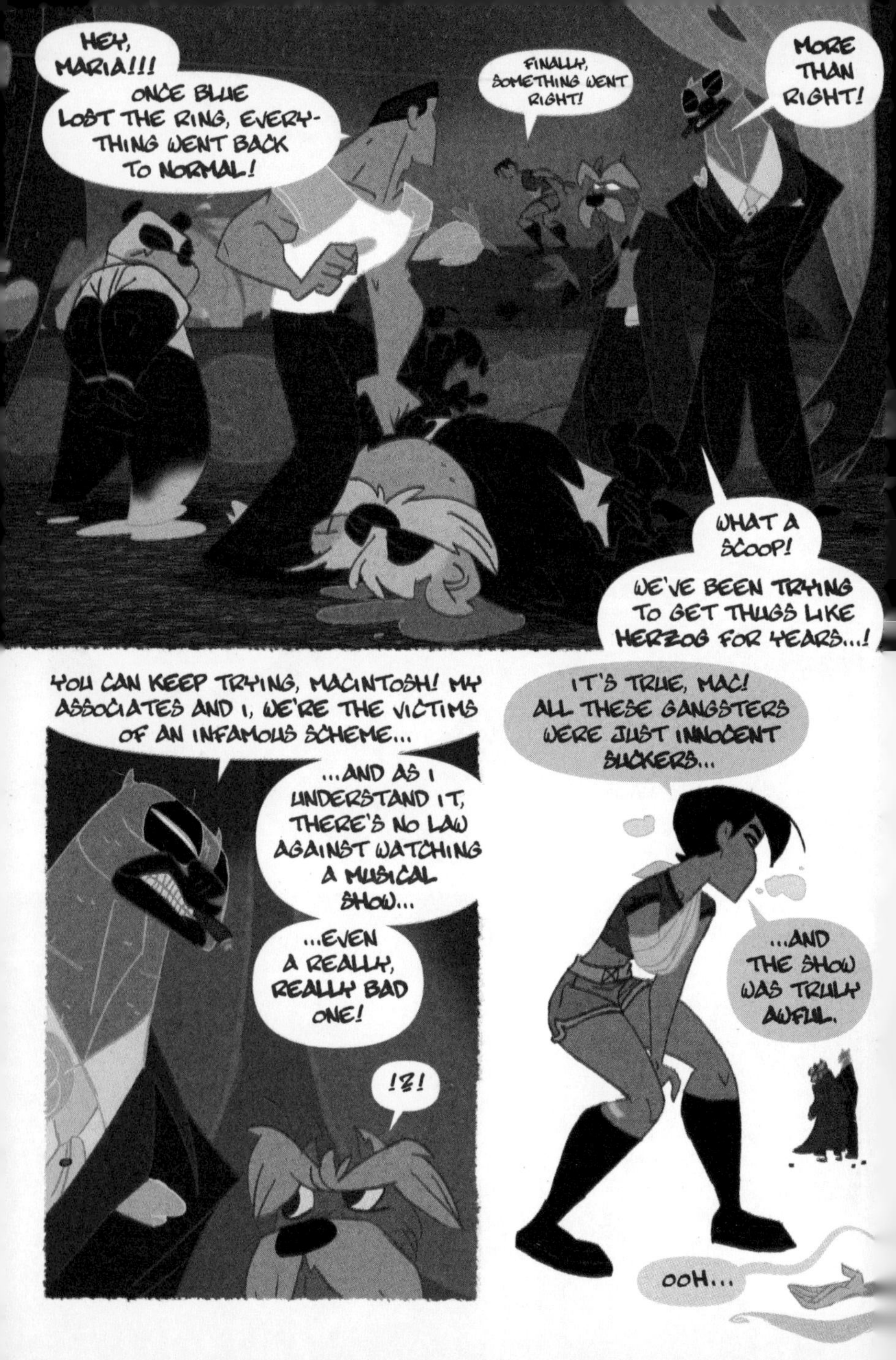
HEY, MARIA!!!
ONCE BLUE LOST THE RING, EVERYTHING WENT BACK TO NORMAL!
FINALLY, SOMETHING WENT RIGHT!
MORE THAN RIGHT!
WHAT A SCOOP!
WE'VE BEEN TRYING TO GET THUGS LIKE HERZOG FOR YEARS...!
YOU CAN KEEP TRYING, MACINTOSH! MY ASSOCIATES AND I, WE'RE THE VICTIMS OF AN INFAMOUS SCHEME...
...AND AS I UNDERSTAND IT, THERE'S NO LAW AGAINST WATCHING A MUSICAL SHOW...
...EVEN A REALLY, REALLY BAD ONE!
!?!
IT'S TRUE, MAC! ALL THESE GANGSTERS WERE JUST INNOCENT SUCKERS...
...AND THE SHOW WAS TRULY AWFUL.
OOH...

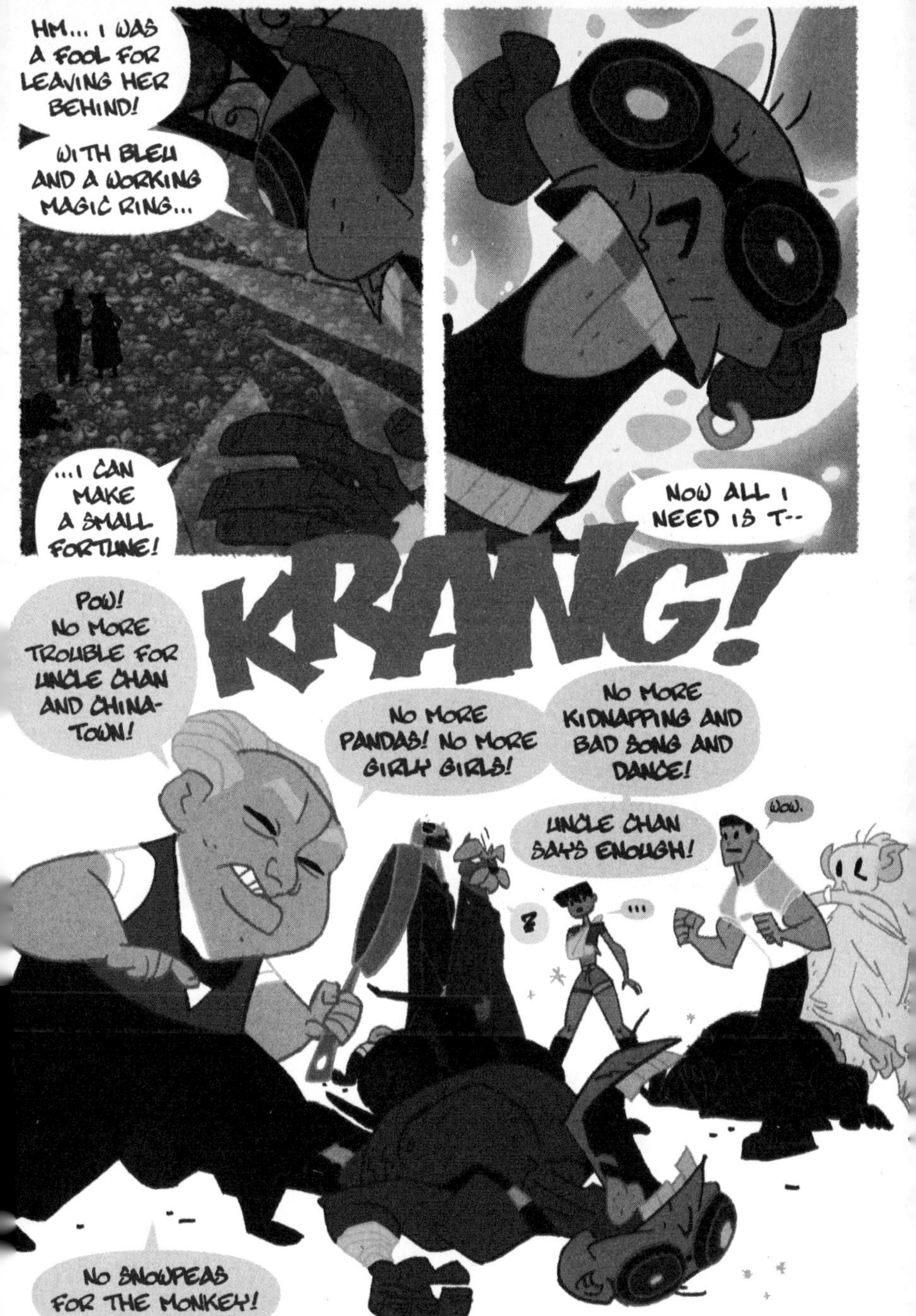
HM... I WAS A FOOL FOR LEAVING HER BEHIND!
WITH BLEU AND A WORKING MAGIC RING...
...I CAN MAKE A SMALL FORTUNE!
NOW ALL I NEED IS T--
KRANG!
POW! NO MORE TROUBLE FOR UNCLE CHAN AND CHINA-TOWN!
NO MORE PANDAS! NO MORE GIRLY GIRLS!
NO MORE KIDNAPPING AND BAD SONG AND DANCE!
UNCLE CHAN SAYS ENOUGH!
WOW.
?
...
NO SNOWPEAS FOR THE MONKEY!

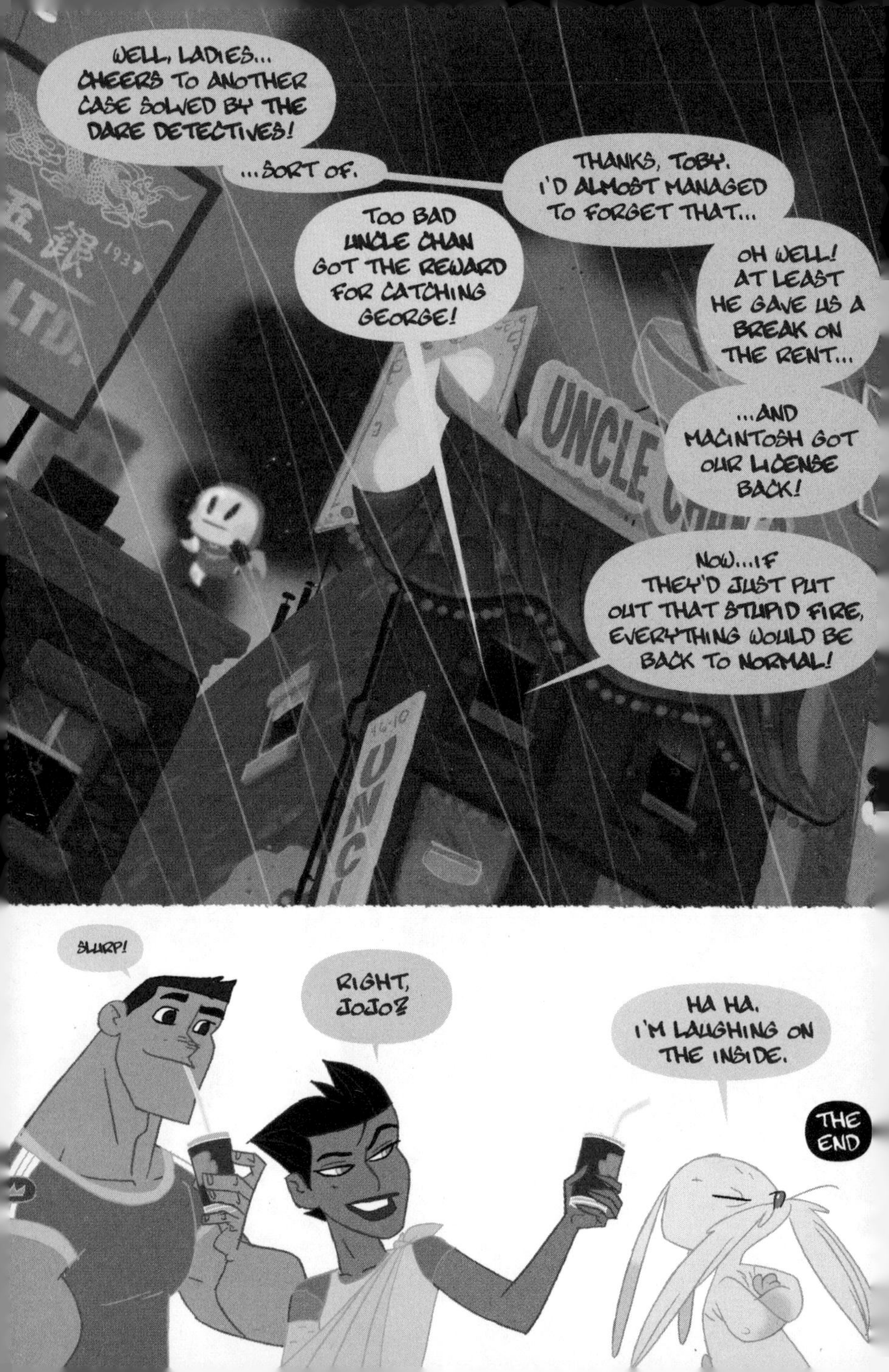
WELL, LADIES... CHEERS TO ANOTHER CASE SOLVED BY THE DARE DETECTIVES!
...SORT OF.
THANKS, TOBY. I'D ALMOST MANAGED TO FORGET THAT...
TOO BAD UNCLE CHAN GOT THE REWARD FOR CATCHING GEORGE!
OH WELL! AT LEAST HE GAVE US A BREAK ON THE RENT...
...AND MACINTOSH GOT OUR LICENSE BACK!
NOW...IF THEY'D JUST PUT OUT THAT STUPID FIRE, EVERYTHING WOULD BE BACK TO NORMAL!
SLURP!
RIGHT, JOJO?
HA HA. I'M LAUGHING ON THE INSIDE.
THE END